D1429903

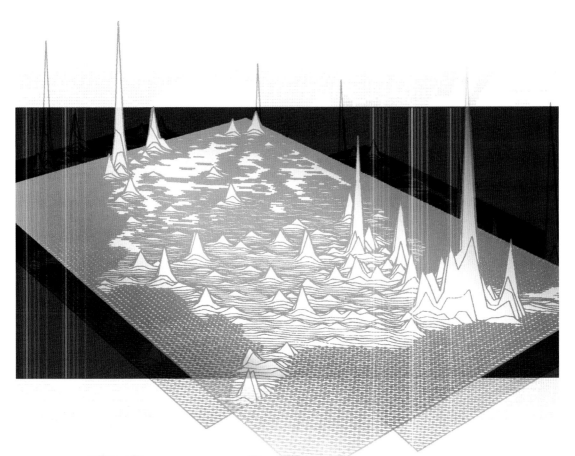

Charting
the Unknown

HOW COMPUTER MAPPING AT HARVARD BECAME GIS

Nick Chrisman

ESRI PRESS
REDLANDS, CALIFORNIA

Cover: *foreground*, population surface of the United States in 1970 (produced by SYMVU; source: LAB-LOG 1977); *background*, Boston nonwhite school enrollment in 1968 by school attendance areas (produced by SYMAP; source: *Red Book* III.41).

ESRI Press, 380 New York Street, Redlands, California 92373-8100

Copyright © 2006 ESRI

All rights reserved. First edition 2006
10 09 08 07 06   1 2 3 4 5 6 7 8 9 10

Printed in the United States of America

Library of Congress Cataloging-in-Publication Data
Charting the unknown : how computer mapping at Harvard became GIS.
        p.   cm.
    Includes bibliographical references and index.
    ISBN 1-58948-118-6 (pbk. : alk. paper)
    1. Geographic information systems.   2. Digital mapping.
    G70.212.C47385 2006
    910.285—dc22   2006017397

ISBN-13: 978-1-58948-118-3
ISBN-10: 1-58948-118-6

Ask for ESRI Press titles at your local bookstore or order by calling 1-800-447-9778. You can also shop online at www.esri.com/esripress. Outside the United States, contact your local ESRI distributor.

ESRI Press titles are distributed to the trade by the following:

In North America, South America, Asia, and Australia:
Independent Publishers Group (IPG)
Telephone (United States): 1-800-888-4741
Telephone (international): 312-337-0747
E-mail: frontdesk@ipgbook.com

In the United Kingdom, Europe, and the Middle East:
Transatlantic Publishers Group Ltd.
Telephone: 44 20 7373 2515
Fax: 44 20 7244 1018
E-mail: richard@tpgltd.co.uk

Cover design, book design, and production by Jennifer Galloway

Contents

Contents of the CD

Movies

Three short films illustrate early attempts at 3D cartographic visualization of geographic change and movement over time. The first film was produced by one of the Harvard Laboratory's most prominent figures; the second two were produced at the Lab by one of its most prolific researchers.

- *Lansing Urban Growth Dynamics 1850–1965: A pictorial history of the expansion of the metropolitan area* (Allan Schmidt); produced at Michigan State University, 1967.

- *American Graph Fleeting: The Movie* (Geoffrey Dutton); produced at the Harvard Laboratory for Computer Graphics and Spatial Analysis, 1978.

- *AIR (Animated Information Retrieval)* (Geoffrey Dutton); produced at the Harvard Laboratory for Computer Graphics and Spatial Analysis, 1981.

Interviews

The videotaped interviews reassemble some key members of the Laboratory's staff. The interviewees discuss important concepts and difficulties of the early technology. Most importantly, despite the decades-long passage of time, the interviews capture the fascination of being present for the creation of a new technology—a true "charting the unknown."

- **Eric Teicholz,** former associate director of the Lab (at Lab 1966–1981); now president of Graphic Systems.

- **Allan Schmidt,** former executive director of the Laboratory (at Lab 1967–1981); now retired.

- **Tom Poiker** (formerly Peucker), former visiting scholar at the Lab (1968; also 1973–1974) while he was professor of geography at Simon Fraser University; now professor emeritus at SFU.

- **Jack Dangermond,** former student at the Harvard Graduate School of Design and research assistant at the Lab (at Lab 1968–1969); now president of ESRI.

- **Nicholas Chrisman,** former research associate at the Lab (at Lab 1972–1982); now professor of geomatic sciences at Université Laval, Quebec, Canada, and scientific director of the GEOIDE (Geomatics for Informed Decisions) Network.

- **Bruce Rowland,** former student at the Harvard Graduate School of Design (1973–1975); now business manager, Implementation Services Department at ESRI.

- **R. Denis White,** former associate director of the Lab (at Lab 1975–1986); now a geographer at the Environmental Protection Agency's Western Ecology Division Laboratory in Corvallis, Oregon.
- **Scott Morehouse,** former lead programmer at the Lab (at Lab 1976–1981); now director of software development at ESRI.
- **Duane Niemeyer,** former research assistant at the Lab (at Lab 1980–1982); now manager of the Defense Services Department at ESRI.
- **Hugh Keegan,** former research assistant at the Lab (at Lab 1980–1982); now manager of the Applications Prototype Lab at ESRI.

Context *newsletters*

Context was a sporadic publication of the Laboratory that described the Lab's projects and kept software users informed of new versions and new products. Included are scanned images of each of the total 11 *Context* newsletters produced from the late 1960s through the early 1980s.

Context 1 February 1968

Context 2 September 1972

Context 3 December 1972

Context 4 June 1973

Context 5 November 1973

Context 6 April 1974

Context 7 November 1974

Context 8 May 1976

Context 9 January 1978

Context 10 Spring 1979

Context 1982·83

Lists

- *Harvard Papers in Theoretical Geography.*

- Attendees at the First International Advanced Study Symposium on Topological Data Structures for Geographic Information Systems, Endicott House, October 16–21, 1977.

- Bibliographic citations to publications of the later period of the Laboratory.

There are many stories about the origins of geographic information systems (GIS) technology, and a few of them are true. No matter which story you hear, if you probe a little bit, you will find a connection to the Harvard Laboratory for Computer Graphics and Spatial Analysis. At this center of innovation, beginning in 1965, a varied collection of planners, geographers, cartographers, mathematicians, computer scientists, artists, and others from many other fields converged to rethink thematic mapping, spatial analysis, and what we would now call geographic information systems.

This book explores some of the themes addressed by this fertile interdisciplinary collaboration. It describes some of the early computer mapping software and experimentation in cartography, as well as some of the spatial analysis and applications to environmental planning conducted at the Laboratory. It charts the cycles of expansion and decline as the creativity confronted challenges on many fronts. Around the edges are glimpses of some of the key figures involved in this exploration.

This is a book about a place. Viewed from Massachusetts Hall, where the President and Fellows of Harvard College preside over the many units of Harvard University, the Laboratory for Computer Graphics and Spatial Analysis was a component of the Graduate School of Design between 1965 and 1991. "Laboratory" is one of the possible nouns that can be applied to a unit in a university, but it is a somewhat curious choice for a component of a school of architects, designers, and planners. The word was certainly chosen to evoke an image of work being done, rather than what the more staidly academic "center" might suggest. It was an age—the 1960s—when computers were precious, rare beasts associated with science, requiring special conditions to operate.

An administrative view of the Laboratory would recognize the people at the Laboratory in their various bureaucratically created roles—some people appointed quite formally with academic titles; others considered staff; and then the students, at once the lifeblood of an academic institution, yet at the bottom of the chain of command. But this formal viewpoint misses the key interplay that occurs in a creative institution. Many exchanges and interactions are simply lost in the formal hierarchical scheme. Some of the lowest in the hierarchy made the most important contributions. This book will attempt to chart the connections between people, recognizing that the results of the Laboratory came from the spirit of the place, not just the formal hierarchy.

The Laboratory began while the Graduate School of Design was still in Robinson Hall, and it was quickly assigned to the basement of Memorial Hall. This monumental building, with a highly ecclesiastical air, was constructed to serve as the dining hall for Harvard College as a memorial to the Civil War dead. The plaques on the walls record a period when Harvard graduates were expected to volunteer to serve as lieutenants with swords, leading straight lines of blue-uniformed soldiers into battle. Of course, some of those graduates were wearing gray, too, though those plaques are less prominent. This nineteenth-century monument set the tone for a Harvard that still exists in some modified way, though it contributes a much lower proportion of military officers.

The east end of Memorial Hall held the remarkable wooden Sanders Theatre, and the west end held the dining hall, still in use in the 1960s. By the 1960s, the basement had become a collection of offices for a miscellaneous residue of players in campus politics who might have deserved space, but did not have the power to acquire more prestigious locations (with such amenities as windows). Under Sanders Theatre, some student organizations were granted little offices. One of these organizations, Students for a Democratic Society (SDS), was about to burst from its anodyne name into political prominence. The president of the university would know that he had an SDS chapter on campus by the end of 1968; after all, they occupied his office until he mobilized the police to eject them. Campus politics at almost any institution has always concerned space, the most valued of possessions.

The Laboratory occupied a block of rooms in the middle of the west wing. On the south side were small windows, high up, that let in a bit of sunlight, while many rooms in the center of the building were cut into odd shapes with no window. The space was cluttered with overhead pipes. One office had four desks in a row; to let the person in the last desk get in, the other three people had to stand and push their chairs under their desks. This physical environment led to research conversations conducted as one person did chin-ups on the pipes.

A modern visitor would look in vain for a computer, even a screen or a mouse. All the Laboratory had for equipment was a keypunch, an infernal keyboard to inscribe commands and data onto 80-column cards, and a digitizer table. Harvard had a single computer to handle all its academic users, housed in a Computing Center with a league of minions to ensure its smooth operation. There was a continuous pilgrimage from the Laboratory to deposit decks of cards and pick up stacks of printed output.

◀ **Memorial Hall, Harvard University.** *(Photo: Nick Chrisman)*

Memorial Hall has changed so that the environment of the early Laboratory is no longer recognizable. The dining services left the upstairs decades ago as meal service was decentralized, privatized, and reorganized many times. The basement is now a food court, featuring brand-name establishments from the malls of suburban America. The walls of the Laboratory offices have all been removed. In place of the dark narrow passages is an open space with overhead track lighting. There are plasma screen computers for e-mail access scattered about. Each of these computers, left casually for individual student convenience, exceeds the capacity and capability of the single Harvard mainframe of the 1960s by factors of millions or billions.

This book will attempt to reconstruct the time before these changes, to recapture what it was like to be a part of that collection of researchers, programmers, secretaries, students, artists, and passersby who happened to play a part in creating what we now call GIS.

Chapter 1 follows Howard Fisher as he assembled the coalition of alliances that brought the Laboratory into being in 1965. It will also provide some context for other centers of innovation where computer mapping and geographic information systems were under construction in roughly the same period. Chapter 2 digs into SYMAP, the software that served as the primary focus for Fisher's efforts. Chapter 3 examines the efforts of some Laboratory staff to use computer tools for environmental planning, leading away from SYMAP toward a set of grid-based analytical software. Chapter 4 covers the more theoretical realms of spatial analysis developed under the leadership of William Warntz. Chapter 5 explores the developments made possible by expanding computer display beyond the line printer.

The early Laboratory rose to around 40 staff of various descriptions around 1970, but it declined to only six by 1972 for a number of reasons. Chapter 6 covers this period of transition, decline, and rebuilding. Chapter 7 deals with the emergence of a topological approach to cartographic data structures, a development that launched the next period for the Laboratory. Chapter 8 dives into the ODYSSEY system of software produced in the late 1970s. Chapter 9 covers the diverse collection of projects and products that occurred alongside the ODYSSEY project. By 1980, the Laboratory was once again at a point of great accomplishment and unknown potential, a second higher peak than in 1970. Chapter 10 exposes the conflicts over the direction of this work and the decline that followed. Chapter 11 continues the final period of the Laboratory to its quiet disappearance in 1991. Chapter 12 reflects on the enduring traces of the Laboratory and why this curious place still matters to the science and practice of GIS. Each chapter ends with notes on the materials cited in that chapter. A complete bibliography is at the end of the book. An accompanying compact disc contains movies produced by Laboratory staff and recent interviews with some who passed through the Laboratory.

The standard advice to authors is to "write about what you know." At one point in the unfolding of the Laboratory (after 1972), I appear in the story. So, in writing the book I have had to confront myself as I was 30 years ago. The act of writing is a personal one, and it would be counterproductive to hide my perspective as observer, participant, and now author. Understanding the risks of overdramatizing my personal role in a complex sequence of events, I have decided to use the first person to report on those events in which I was a direct participant. I hope this brings the reader closer to the excitement of the times without making me cast a disproportionate shadow. I have relied on written evidence, even for my own participation, over recollections. I hope that the result captures the spirit of the Lab as we lived it.

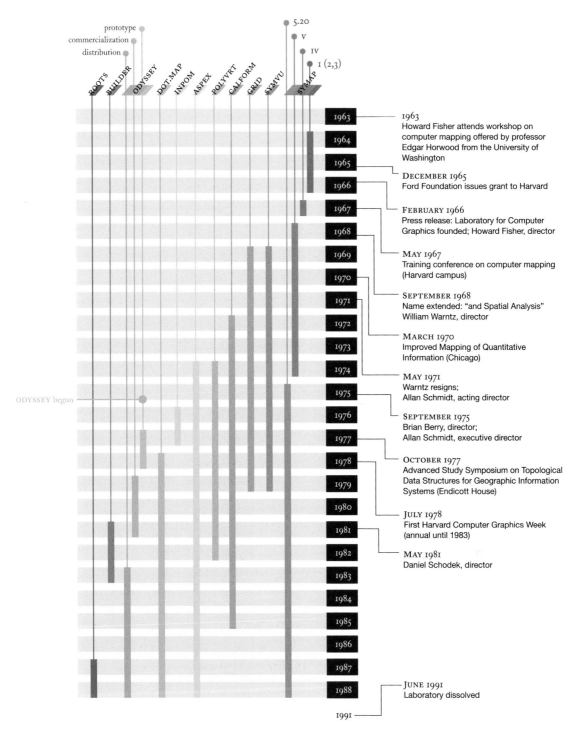

prototype
commercialization
distribution

5.20
V
IV
I (2,3)

ROOTS
BUILDER
ODYSSEY
DOT.MAP
INPOM
ASPEX
POLYVRT
CALFORM
GRID
SYMVU
SYMAP

ODYSSEY begun

1963
1964
1965
1966
1967
1968
1969
1970
1971
1972
1973
1974
1975
1976
1977
1978
1979
1980
1981
1982
1983
1984
1985
1986
1987
1988
1991

1963
Howard Fisher attends workshop on
computer mapping offered by professor
Edgar Horwood from the University of
Washington

DECEMBER 1965
Ford Foundation issues grant to Harvard

FEBRUARY 1966
Press release: Laboratory for Computer
Graphics founded; Howard Fisher, director

MAY 1967
Training conference on computer mapping
(Harvard campus)

SEPTEMBER 1968
Name extended: "and Spatial Analysis"
William Warntz, director

MARCH 1970
Improved Mapping of Quantitative
Information (Chicago)

MAY 1971
Warntz resigns;
Allan Schmidt, acting director

SEPTEMBER 1975
Brian Berry, director;
Allan Schmidt, executive director

OCTOBER 1977
Advanced Study Symposium on Topological
Data Structures for Geographic Information
Systems (Endicott House)

JULY 1978
First Harvard Computer Graphics Week
(annual until 1983)

MAY 1981
Daniel Schodek, director

JUNE 1991
Laboratory dissolved

▲   A timeline of significant events at the Harvard Laboratory for Computer
Graphics and Spatial Analysis, 1963 to 1991.

ONE

Founding the Laboratory for Computer Graphics

Over and over again, publications from the Laboratory used this sentence to announce the origins of the unit: "Howard Fisher founded the Laboratory with a grant from the Ford Foundation." It is a sentence that hides as much as it reveals. These events did occur: Harvard University created a Laboratory for Computer Graphics; Howard Fisher was appointed director; and the Ford Foundation gave money to support this operation. But in telling this story, it will be important to reach back before this linear plot line occurred. How did Fisher get all these diverse interests aligned to make these events occur? Why did this process happen at Harvard? Why Howard Fisher?

An architect redesigns computer mapping

In 1957, after 30 years of commercial architecture in Chicago, Howard Fisher[1] closed his practice and started to teach at the Technological Institute, part of Northwestern University. He covered planning, problem solving, and design. In 1963, he attended a short course at Northwestern given by Edgar Horwood from the University of Washington, in which Horwood demonstrated that a computer could be used to make maps.[2] As soon as he saw Horwood's maps, Fisher realized he could make better ones. Rather than printing data values at approximate centers of census tracts or using a single character to represent each area, such as a census block, Fisher wanted the whole object to get filled in. Better yet, he wanted to interpolate the phenomenon and generate contours of a continuous surface. Fisher lost no time. He engaged a professional programmer, Betty Benson, and in less than a year had a functional prototype.[3] Even at this early exploratory stage, this effort required alliances and cooperation with different units; the computing budget for this effort came from a variety of sources, some at Northwestern, some from the University of Chicago's Urban Studies Center.[4]

Fisher conceived of a program that would generate the whole map on the computer, not relying on separate graphic overlays and other processing as Horwood's programs did. More importantly, his program, referred to as SYMAP, could handle different forms of maps, including choropleth and contour maps (with a rudimentary interpolation system that required a lot of user input). Because SYMAP is so important to the Laboratory, the next chapter will go into the capabilities of the program and how they developed from the prototype at Northwestern in 1964 to the versions distributed by Harvard.

Instead of stopping once he had a working program, Fisher wanted to get this innovation into the hands of practicing planners. Fisher started running his own training courses,[5] the first in December 1964, the next in September 1965. (Kenneth Dueker attended the first and Waldo Tobler attended the second session, connections whose significance will be explained later on in this chapter.) Fisher's proposal to the Ford Foundation reflected this desire to reach the world of practice in larger numbers than these initial training courses. As a more conceptual goal, Fisher also wanted to reform thematic cartography. Just as he thought that he could do better than Horwood's mapping programs, Fisher thought that he could provide a more logical framework for the graphic display of geographic facts. His vision required a new set of terms, a move that did not attract him many followers among academic cartographers.[6] He started writing a book with his revised taxonomy of mapping problems. The manuscript he worked on for the rest of his life was eventually published three years after his death.[7]

Howard Fisher, when director of the ▶
Harvard Laboratory. *(Photo courtesy of the Harvard News Office.)*

APPLYING TO THE FORD FOUNDATION

While Horwood had built his programs under grants and contracts from various public institutions (particularly the National Science Foundation and the federal Housing and Home Finance Agency), Fisher opened connections to the Ford Foundation, then one of the largest private granting organizations. Some time in 1964, he showed his work to Louis Winnick, who dealt with planning issues in the foundation's Public Affairs Program. Winnick encouraged Fisher to apply for a grant, probably in a conversation. In Fisher's papers there is no explicit note on the expectations of the foundation, but it appears that Fisher had some idea how big a grant might be entertained, and that he needed certain elements, such as a small unrestricted private matching grant and a university sponsor to make the package successful.

When Fisher wrote a letter reporting on his progress toward a grant application in early 1965, Winnick's response said that since other institutions were moving ahead doing this kind of mapping, "the bloom might be off the rose."[8] Foundations do not like to follow others, and Winnick was probably influenced by reports of the successful training courses run by Horwood and other developments described later in this chapter. Despite these somewhat negative portents, Fisher persisted. Fisher first had to attach himself to an institution to support the Laboratory that he envisioned.

WHY HARVARD?

Because Fisher worked at Northwestern University, it would have been most straightforward for him to have simply submitted his proposal from there. Here is where some of the nuances of academic life enter the picture. Fisher had come into the Technological Institute from professional practice. Professionals were welcomed as teachers, but they did not acquire full-fledged academic jobs, particularly if they had no graduate degrees. Through some process not entirely documented, Fisher got the message that he had to look elsewhere.

He took his ideas to Brian Berry at the Urban Studies Center of the University of Chicago. (Berry will appear in various roles dealing with quantitative geography and the Harvard Laboratory later on.) When Fisher first started his work, Berry took interest in early versions of SYMAP and had provided some of the funding for the programming efforts of Betty Benson. In December 1964, Fisher worked with Berry and others at Chicago on a proposal to the Ford Foundation, but the negotiations did not go through. One of the sticking points was Fisher's insistence on an academic appointment as professor despite his lack of advanced degrees.[9]

Fisher then took his ideas to Harvard University, where he had graduated from Harvard College in 1926 and had studied architecture from 1926 to 1928. There is no documentation on why he did not receive a master's degree in architecture following this period of study. As an alumnus (and the brother of a prominent professor of the law school), Fisher was given a chance to write his proposal to the Ford Foundation through the Department of City and Regional Planning. The Harvard Graduate School of Design hired practicing design professionals and did not insist on an advanced degree in that period. Fisher was appointed lecturer and given some teaching responsibilities in the freshman seminars of Harvard College until the grant was confirmed in December 1965. The budget submitted with the proposal projected expenditures of $650,817 over a five-year period, much of it from anticipated, unconfirmed sources.[10] The Ford Foundation agreed to provide $294,000 for the first three and a half years. With the initial funds in hand, Harvard was willing to announce the Laboratory for Computer Graphics, and Fisher was appointed director and professor.[11] The story of the Laboratory began.

Before the beginning

Howard Fisher and the Laboratory have consistently and openly acknowledged an intellectual debt to Edgar Horwood,[12] whose training workshop in 1963 at Northwestern University inspired Fisher to create SYMAP. It makes sense to examine who Horwood was and what his computer programs could (and couldn't) do. Horwood was not the sole influence on Fisher; a community of quantitative geographers also played a significant role in the intellectual development of the Laboratory.

HORWOOD'S MAPPING PROGRAMS

The 1963 workshops had presented two cartographic programs called by their device-oriented names: Card Mapping Program and Tape Mapping Program.[13] Both of them displayed thematic data associated with geographic objects called geographic mapping units (GMU), typically statistical or administrative zones such as census tracts, school districts, or city blocks, but all represented as points, not polygons. The basic distinction between the two programs concerned the amount of data accommodated in an era of very limited computer memories. Written first, the Card Mapping Program supported detailed studies restricted to small numbers of GMU (about one hundred). It was limited by the small amount of memory available for sorting the points as well as the slow rate of reading cards. These computers had such minimal operating systems that the card readers and printers ran directly under the control of the program, without spooling. The Card Mapping Program did not use symbolism; it printed the numerical values of the thematic data in five characters beginning at the specified point for the GMU. Additional thematic values could appear in a line below the first. Because it used so many more characters per GMU, the Card Mapping Program was intended for more detailed studies of constrained areas.

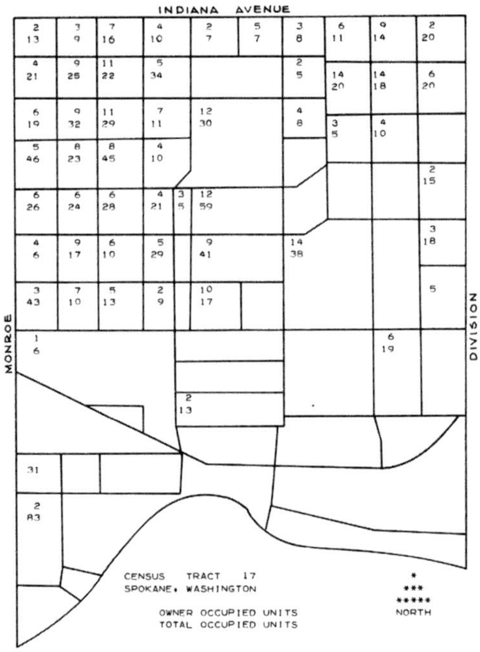

FIGURE 1-0
SAMPLE OF CARD MAPPING OUTPUT

Sample output from the Card Mapping Program—census tract 17, Spokane, Washington. Figures for each block show the total number of houses and the number of houses occupied by their owners. The streets and text labels for the streets are not produced by the computer, but are overlaid onto a composite graphic. *(Source: Horwood 1963, figure 1-0)*

Edgar Horwood

Edgar Horwood was a professor of Urban Planning and Civil Engineering at the University of Washington from the 1950s to his death in 1985.[14] The Urban Data Center that he founded remained a center of innovation for decades. He and his graduate students ran a series of meetings in the early 1960s that would turn into the Urban and Regional Information Systems Association (URISA). What was later called the first URISA meeting was a reunion in 1963 of attendees of the first training session in computer mapping in 1962 at the University of Southern California. Horwood's group had continuous support from a wide range of federal agencies, particularly those involved in housing and transportation planning. In the era of Presidents Kennedy and Johnson, many new programs generated demand for planning and information gathering.

At the Seattle URISA meeting in 1984, the poster distributed to all attendees in honor of Ed Horwood proclaimed a set of principles for a database project that combined the wisdom of years of experience with a sense of humor.[15] To this day, copies of the poster adorn the offices of long-term members of the GIS profession. Listed are "Horwood's Short Laws of Data Processing and Information Systems":

1. Good data is the data you already have.

2. Bad data drives out good.

3. The data you have for the present crisis was collected to relate to the previous one.

4. The respectability of existing data grows with elapsed time and distance from the data source to the investigator.

5. Data can be moved from one office to another but it cannot be created or destroyed.

6. If you have the right data, you have the wrong problem and vice versa.

7. The important thing is not what you do but how you measure it.

8. In complex systems there is no relationship between information gathered and the decision made.

9. Acquisition of knowledge from experience is an exception.

10. Knowledge grows at half the rate at which academic courses proliferate.

Edgar Horwood, as portrayed on a 1984 ▶ commemorative poster. *(Source: URISA Journal, used with permission)*

A tape device was necessary to process larger numbers of units (thousands were contemplated), using a tape-based sort–merge utility. Tapes were significantly faster as well. The Tape Mapping Program required a completely rewritten program and a reduced, more symbolic output to fit all the data on the page. It produced maps that were graphically very simple—just one character to represent a GMU, no matter how big or small. In contrast to this graphic simplicity, the program had some rather elaborate abilities to manipulate attribute values algebraically. Curiously, the formulae supported addition, subtraction, multiplication, and exponentiation, but not division. This was because some of the computers available (like the IBM 1401 processor) could not do division. Exponentiation by minus one was used to obtain a divisor. In the original form of the program, the display used a test for negative, zero, or positive values, thus only three different classes were possible. A particular character was printed at the chosen spot on the paper to symbolize each GMU. In later versions, class limits were implemented, providing somewhat more information about the thematic distribution.

The design of this display program conformed to a method of planning analysis called "multiphasic screening." Appendix B of the program manual described a technique to identify the "worst of the worst" or "best of the best" by accumulating the instances of "deviant" values. This procedure relied on a series of thresholds for different measures and identified objects that were consistently low (or high). The motivating question at the time was "urban blight," a phenomenon that was supposed to relate physical characteristics of housing stock, population characteristics, and economic measures. Horwood's research direction had a particular view of how to combine multiple attributes. As chapter 3 will demonstrate, other groups of planners used different techniques of combination for environmental problems with more reliance on weighted addition, not thresholds. Each program in this early period reflects the theoretical perspectives and methodological orientations of the authors.

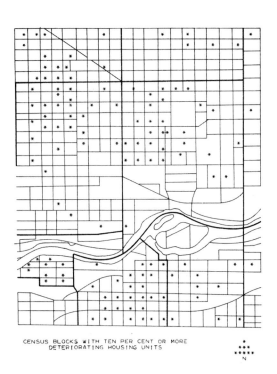

CENSUS BLOCKS WITH TEN PER CENT OR MORE
DETERIORATING HOUSING UNITS

FIGURE 5-0
SAMPLE OF TAPE MAPPING OUTPUT
(PORTION OF LARGER MAP)

▲ Portion of a map produced by the Tape Mapping Program. A single character indicates a block with over 10 percent of housing "deteriorating." The streets are overlaid with the computer output optically.

(Source: Horwood 1963, figure 5-0)

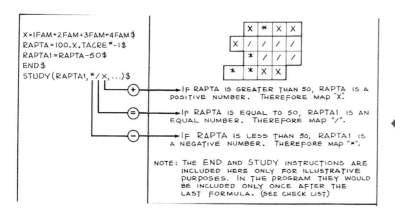

Sample instructions to the Tape Mapping Program. The program calculates a density of housing units, then maps "x" for density over 50, "*" for under 50. The "/" indicates equal to 50. *(Source: Horwood 1963, figure 5-5)*

While there were substantial capabilities in both programs to manipulate attribute values, there was no way to manipulate the geometric data—the spatial positions of the GMUs. The coordinates of each object were specified by locations on the printed output in rows and columns as integers—whole numbers. There was no provision to change the scale, the map window, or anything related to the map geometry. It was all tied to the printed page; the down axis was called "x", across was "y" in the same inversion of the Cartesian convention as SYMAP made. No doubt these coordinates made sense to the programmer dealing with the line printer. The processing of these points was done with a sorting procedure. Points were ordered down the page. The program had to read in only the points on that row, decide on their symbolism, print the result, then move on to the next row. The amount of memory required was primarily for the attribute values, not the geometric representation. It must be remembered that these computers had less memory than a current hand calculator.

To produce these maps, the user was expected to digitize the point locations for the specific map page using a rudimentary procedure. There was no concept of a shareable geographic base file to be reused for maps of different scales. The procedure worked as follows: a field of plus characters would be printed and slid under a transparency of the geographic objects (census tracts or census blocks); each object (GMU) would be given a character location more or less adjacent to its center. Some generalization was required for small or thin objects; the Card Mapping Program also required attention to potential overlap of the five-character blocks in which the attribute values would appear. These programs were not designed to produce a complete cartographic display. The designers expected to produce a final output by running a diazo copy of the printed output with the transparency on top (to provide the labeling and the geographic context). In addition, the program provided for "registration points"—locations marked on the printout to align them with the transparency. Thus, the computer output was combined with the existing, and well-established, optical creation of maps from transparent overlays.

Horwood's programs had some features far in advance of SYMAP (particularly in creating algebraic combinations of attributes), but overall these programs were less flexible about geometry and much less polished as graphic products. The programs were developed for a specific client, the city of Spokane, with substantial funding from the U.S. Urban Renewal Administration. Horwood gained great attention by running training programs and inspiring potential users. His manuals provided a flowchart of the programs, but he was hesitant to distribute source code. Rather than distributing the programs, Horwood envisioned a centralized computing service bureau that would receive decks of cards and mail the results back to users. These decisions opened opportunities for Fisher's SYMAP.

QUANTITATIVE REVOLUTIONARIES

Horwood was not the only influence on Fisher and the Laboratory from the University of Washington. Prior to his mapping programs, students and faculty in Washington's Department of Geography had engaged in a flurry of activity later given the portentous title of "Quantitative Revolution." Inside the field of academic geography this story has been told from a number of perspectives,[16] and it is not the intent here to recreate the whole process. However, there are a remarkable number of connections between key members of the quantitative movement and the Harvard Lab.

In 1955, the Geography Department at the University of Washington was ruled by Donald Hudson, a geographer and student of Charles Colby at the University of Chicago. Colby had advocated the use of quantitative measures back in the 1930s and had directed Hudson to work at the Tennessee Valley Authority on projects that involved innovation in photogrammetry and land-use mapping. Hudson, in the role of department chair, left nothing to chance, exercising control over everything from the curriculum to which advisor each graduate student would get—assignments he would make while escorting each incoming student down the corridor to their allotted desk. Only the most determined students could resist. Nothing that Hudson did, however, could have foreshadowed how central the fall 1955 incoming class of graduate students would become to the development of geography. In part, instructors like Edward Ullman and William Garrison (also connected to Colby) inspired the students to explore beyond the mechanics of statistics. But also the incoming class of '55 included several of the names that reappear in this story—Brian Berry, later director of the Laboratory; Richard Morrill, who applied statistical methods to the analysis of urban demographics and economics; and Duane Marble, who did similar work directed at transportation issues. The next year's class included Michael Dacey, who took an abstract mathematical approach, and Waldo Tobler, who studied with cartographer John Sherman and launched a career in analytical cartography, including early digital experiments. Each of these students worked with the early electronic calculators and primitive computing. They also took courses from Horwood on the mechanics of urban analysis with computing equipment (though not yet with a mapping component). As is often the case, it is not clear whether the students or the professor were the more advanced. Tobler and his colleagues were certainly making maps with computers before Horwood's contract work for Spokane.[17] Yet, interestingly, the immediate product of this ferment was not packaged software for others to use. Instead, there was a flurry of ardent debate at conferences, foundational articles hard-fought through the peer-review process, and collaborative books. Theirs was a revolution of academics for academics by academics.

How did all of this influence Fisher and the founding of the Laboratory? Berry moved to the University of Chicago in 1958.[18] Garrison left the University of Washington in 1960 to move to Northwestern University in Evanston, Illinois. Marble and Dacey joined him working at Northwestern's Transportation Research Center. Garrison teamed with William Krumbein on a grant to treat geological surfaces and display them with computers. Morrill spent a year at Northwestern before moving back to the University of Washington, which was presenting short courses like Horwood's training session in computer mapping. The assistants for Horwood's whirlwind tour of training courses in 1962 and 1963 were Kenneth Dueker, a UW PhD student in civil engineering, and William Beyers, a UW graduate student in Geography. In 1964, Dueker was hired by Garrison to replace Fisher to teach planning at Northwestern while Fisher wrote his Ford Foundation proposal. Dueker stayed for two years, working on Garrison's research projects as well as teaching. Dueker returned to Horwood's program at UW to finish his PhD, tightening the linkage between these programs at Northwestern and the University of Washington. In this same period, Berry helped found the Urban Studies Center at the University of Chicago, and collaborated on joint projects with the Northwestern group. This coalition operated two-week-long training sessions on quantitative geography at Northwestern in 1961, 1962, and 1963 (as well as a course in regional science at the University of California, Berkeley, also running for three years). Horwood's course connected to these events. The hotbed of the revolutionaries had migrated to Chicago, and Fisher happened to be working nearby.

While Fisher was looking for a place to found his planned Laboratory, there were many signs of change. As Winnick had observed from the Ford Foundation, multiple groups were sprouting up to develop geographic information technology. Computer mapping was in the air. Garrison, with Marble, Dacey, and others, had a grant from the Office of Naval Research to study small-area data and the potentials of remote sensing.[19] The possibility of a civilian (and unclassified) remote sensing capability was dangled tantalizingly out of reach of geographers by the National Aeronautical and Space Administration (NASA) with its treasure chest of limitless funding.[20] On another front, the U.S. Census Bureau had begun its laborious decennial process of reinventing itself. Morrill, Berry, and Tobler, acting as a subcommittee of the Association of American Geographers, had recommended coordinate measurements of tract centroids in 1963 with the clear intent to promote computer processing and mapping.[21] In 1964, the Census Bureau convened an "Advisory Committee on Small Area Data," with Garrison as chairman. Not too surprisingly, the mandate given to the Census Use Study for the test census in New Haven, Connecticut, (in 1967) included address matching and computer mapping. At this point, Fisher was not the only person to promote a vision of computer handling for spatial data, nor was his proposal seen by the community as the most promising.

Making the Laboratory a center of activity

Fisher understood that this Laboratory had to assemble a collection of researchers from different disciplines and also make connections to a wide range of supporters. He threw himself into the process with great energy, first making allies among academics and hiring some of them, then reaching out to a broader professional world.

REACHING OUT TO ACADEMICS
Fisher's first audience was the Harvard faculty and the nearby academic community (from MIT, Boston University, and Brandeis University). He set up a speaker series with weekly events during 1966 and 1968. There appear to have been about 24 of these events, with an invited speaker usually from out of town, organized discussants, and a regular list of participants (called "Computer Graphics Aficionados" by Fisher). These events were held at the Faculty Club and clearly linked to lunch, but the speakers were warned that the sessions were intended to continue until 4 PM.

HOWARD FISHER'S "COMPUTER GRAPHICS AFICIONADOS" SESSIONS

April 13, 1966

Lynn Yarbrough, Harvard Computing Center · *Current research on equipment and program for computer graphics*

April 20, 1966

Robert Williams, Map Library, Yale University · *Problems in statistical mapping*

An informal seminar following Mr. Williams's talk included:

Walter Isard, Professor of Regional Science, University of Pennsylvania

George Lewis, Professor of Geography, Boston University

David Drew, Staff Analyst, Harvard Computing Center

David Heer, Assistant Professor of Biostatistics and Demography, Harvard School of Public Health

April 27, 1966

William Warntz, · *Statistical and other surfaces: Watersheds and divides*
American Geographical Society

An informal seminar following Dr. Warntz's talk included:

Howard Hirt, Professor of Geography, Boston University

Peter Nash, Professor of Geography and Regional Planning, University of Rhode Island

William Alonso, Associate Professor of Regional Planning, Harvard Graduate School of Design

Eliahu Romanoff, Assistant Professor of Regional Science, Harvard Graduate School of Design

May 4, 1966

Waldo Tobler, University of Michigan · *Surface smoothing as a form of map generalization*

An informal seminar following Dr. Tobler's talk included:

Robert Batchelder, Associate Professor of Geography, Boston University

Robert Kates, Associate Professor, Graduate School of Geography, Clark University

Joseph Harrington, Professor of Environmental Health Engineering, Harvard School of Public Health

Dean Whitla, Director of Tests, Harvard University

May 11, 1966

Donald Shepard, Harvard College · *Contour interpolation: Problems and methods*

An informal seminar following Mr. Shepard's talk included:

Robert Aangeenbrug, Assistant Professor of Geography, Boston University

William Warntz, Research Associate, American Geographical Society

Pearn Niiler, Research Fellow in Geophysical Fluid Dynamics, Division of Engineering and Applied Physics, Harvard University

Norman Zachary, Manager, Harvard Computing Center,

plus the members of the seminar upon whose efforts Mr. Shepard has been building

May 18, 1966

Howard Fisher, LCG · *Issues in map interpretation*

An informal seminar following Mr. Fisher's talk included:

Charles Harsh, Westinghouse Advanced Study Group

Richard Held, Professor of Psychology, Massachusetts Institute of Technology

Daniel Forsyth, Research Fellow, Center for Cognitive Studies, Harvard University

George Gibson, Director of the Division of Audio-visual Education, Harvard Graduate School of Business Administration

October 6, 1966

W. Newman, Imperial College · *A computer-aided building design film*
and
IBM · *By the numbers: Film on conversion of aerial photography into detailed maps*

October 13, 1966

George Cowgill, Anthropology, · *Computer techniques in anthropology*
Brandeis University

October 20, 1966

Lynn Yarbrough, Harvard Computing Center

The use of the SC4020 high-speed scope plotter: Current research on equipment and program for computer graphics

October 27, 1966

David Packard, PhD student in Classics, Harvard University

The new freedom in graphic symbolism

November 3, 1966

W. Newman, Imperial College

Graphic techniques for computer-aided architectural design

An informal seminar following Mr Newman's talk included:

Lawrence Anderson, Dean of the School of Architecture and Planning, Massachusetts Institute of Technology

Arcangelo Casieri, Dean of the Boston Architectural Center

José Luis Sert, Dean, Harvard Graduate School of Design

Benjamin Thompson, Chairman of the Department of Architecture, Harvard Graduate School of Design

IBM

By the numbers: Film on conversion of aerial photography into detailed maps

November 10, 1966

Allan Schmidt, Michigan State University

The role of computer mapping in the planning process

An informal seminar following Mr. Schmidt's talk included:

Mary Doeble, City and Regional Planner, Metropolitan Planning Council, Boston

Justin Gray, Project Director, Low Income Housing Demonstration, The Institute of Public Administration, New York

Paul Opperman, Consulting City and Metropolitan Planner, Adams, Howard and Opperman, Cambridge, and Senior Lecturer, Department of City and Regional Planning, Massachusetts Institute of Technology

Ian Terner, Instructor in City Planning, Department of City and Regional Planning, Harvard Graduate School of Design

November 17, 1966

Brian J. L. Berry, University of Chicago

Merging cartographic and statistical systems

An informal seminar following Dr. Berry's talk included:

Michael Woldenberg, Research Assistant, American Geographical Society

Julian Wolpert, Assistant Professor, Department of Regional Science, University of Pennsylvania

John Kain, Assistant Professor of Economics, Harvard University

December 1, 1966

William Warntz and Howard T. Fisher

The scope and organization of a basic text in quantitative mapping

An informal seminar following Mssrs. Warntz's and Fisher's talk included:

Daniel Conway, Chief Information Systems Specialist, Regional Planning Council, Baltimore

George Lewis, Professor and Acting Chairman, Department of Geography, Boston University

Paul Procopio, Professor of Landscape Architecture, University of Massachusetts

William Nash, Professor and Chairman, Department of City and Regional Planning, Harvard Graduate School of Design

December 8, 1966

Robert Barraclough, Tri-State Planning Commission

Graphic display in transportation studies

An informal seminar following Mr. Barraclough's talk included:

Robert Murphy, Chief Transportation Planner, Boston Redevelopment Authority

Robert Keith, Director of Service and Systems Planning, Massachusetts Bay Transportation Authority

Leon Cole, Assistant Professor of City Planning and Urban Design, Harvard Graduate School of Design

John Meyer, Professor of Economics and Chairman of the Doctoral Program in Planning, Harvard University

Waldo Tobler, Brian Berry, and William Warntz were all speakers in 1966, showing that Fisher was trying to exhibit some of the cutting-edge of spatial analysis to a campus that had not had a geography department for 18 years. Horwood was invited, but did not attend.[22] Fisher—an architect with strong connections to the artistic traditions of the design world—was seeking allies from among the leaders of the movement for quantitative methods in geography and establishing linkages between Harvard and the University of Washington that did not pass through Northwestern. The visits from Warntz and Allan Schmidt led to posts at the Laboratory for both. Fisher also discussed various plans to give adjunct appointments to others, including Berry.[23] These luncheon seminars helped build interaction at Harvard connected to a community of international scholars and planning professionals. The list of discussants shows a broad reach to nearby institutions. For at least one of the invited discussants, Robert Aangeenbrug, who became organizer of the Second International Symposium on Computer-Assisted Cartography (known as AUTO-CARTO II) and the World Computer Graphics Association, this connection to Harvard figured in his professional credentials to the end of his career. Fisher, a design professional without a doctoral degree, understood how to build a network of influential allies.

STAFFING THE LABORATORY

In addition to specifying the director, the proposal to the Ford Foundation called for three senior specialists, three intermediate specialists, and five other staff.[24] The plan was to hire all these positions to start for the academic year 1966–1967. The first senior specialist was meant to focus on "factual information, its gathering, manipulation and analysis," according to the proposal. This person was presumed to come from urban geography with a strong mathematical orientation—in short, one of the quantitative revolutionaries. This person was expected to be associate director and to become director when Fisher would retire in 1968. Things turned out more or less as planned. Warntz, a research scholar at the American Geographical Society in New York, joined the Laboratory as associate director in fall 1966. His research program in spatial analysis will be covered in chapter 4. Warntz's mathematical approach to geographic phenomena had a markedly theoretical flavor. Unlike the quantitative geographers from Washington, he did not spend a lot of time on statistical hypothesis testing. Like Fisher, he found surfaces fascinating.[25] Warntz came with active grants or arranged to have some start as soon as he arrived. With these funds, Warntz was able to hire three research fellows: Frank Rens, a student of Waldo Tobler; Ernesto Lindgren, a Brazilian who had just finished an undergraduate degree in mathematics at Harvard; and Michael Woldenberg, a PhD student from Columbia University about to finish in physical geography (he had also spent a year at the University of Chicago).

Rather than hiring a specialist in statistics, decision theory, and computer science as proposed for the other two senior specialists, Fisher rounded out the Laboratory with connections to each of the academic departments in the School of Design. Allen Bernholtz was a link to Architecture, Peter Rogers was a link to City and Regional Planning, and Carl Steinitz (whose PhD was in urban planning from MIT) was assigned to work with Landscape Architecture. Schmidt, a geographer and planner who had taken Fisher's short course at Northwestern, was recruited to the Laboratory from a research job at Michigan State University in the spring of 1967. The list of staff for 1966–1967 in the *Red Book*,[26] lists 29 employees with various titles; far above the 12 predicted in the Ford Foundation proposal. Helen Mansfield, given the lofty title of Director of Extension Studies, took charge of the SYMAP correspondence courses (see chapter 2) with some staff to handle the mail. About 10 of the employees were students in part-time positions. While the Ford Foundation proposal had simply mentioned hiring planning professionals with advanced degrees, Fisher had quickly discovered that his freshman seminars gave him access to some of the most inquiring minds on the campus. At other universities, the graduate students are a selective group, but at Harvard, the undergraduate population is at least as selective as the graduate students. Harvard College undergraduate students were frequent recruits for all sorts of jobs at the Laboratory throughout its history. Since Harvard had no geography department and no courses on cartography, these students would have no direct training in the substantive work of the Laboratory. An interest in computing and graphics was usually enough background.

In addition to the staff and students, Fisher also wanted to bring a wider range of professionals to the Laboratory. He asked other institutions and agencies to send a staff member to the Laboratory for an extended period. There were fewer of these long-term visitors than desired, but one unplanned connection had an influence. The Census Use Study began operation in New Haven with very little time to prepare for the test census on April 1, 1967. Donald Cooke and William Maxfield, two recent graduates of Yale University, neither with any geographic training nor a lot of programming experience, found themselves in charge of making maps with the Address Coding Guide data that was fundamental to the "mail-out/mail-back" 1970 census. Since they had little experience, they rushed into a huge challenge without much idea of all the ramifications. They implemented the topological theory suggested to them by a staff mathematician, James Corbett.[27] This innovation was called DIME (Dual Independent Map Encoding), and is a key development for future work at the Laboratory and across the GIS community. These developments responded directly to the charge from the Census' Advisory Committee for Small Area Data. The challenges to Cooke and Maxfield were not just a matter of theory and innovation. Just as the test census tabulations had been returned to them in New Haven, the management of the Yale computer center decided to cut off access to the university computer. The Census was deemed a threat to personal privacy. Of course, the Yale administration that made this decision was in some ways anticipating the threats of increasingly sophisticated targeted marketing, but at the time the Census Use Study staff had to scurry around to find computers to finish their work. They came to Harvard and MIT and formed some personal ties that survived over the years.

The universe of people engaged in computer mapping and spatial database construction was a very small world in 1965–1967. The Laboratory at Harvard had some kind of connection to most of the active groups engaged in this work. It is pointless to ask what came first, since all the efforts were so closely linked.

TRAINING CONFERENCES

Fisher's proposal to the Ford Foundation had emphasized training for professionals in planning and related disciplines. He had held two "Short Courses on Synagraphic Mapping" through the University of Chicago Continuing Education Center, the first over December 9–10, 1964, with 34 attendees, the second over September 18–19, 1965, with 48 attendees. These events paralleled the ones presented by Horwood in 1962 at the University of Southern California, and in 1963 at UC Berkeley, the University of Pittsburgh, Northwestern, and Yale.[28] In this period, the National Science Foundation and other granting agencies promoted such training conferences as the series of "Summer Institutes of Cartography," operated from 1962–1965 at the University of Washington.[29] The faculty for all these events were drawn from a common pool of experts. At Northwestern in 1963, Garrison held a summer institute on "Quantitative Methods in Geography," during which Horwood presented his mapping programs. This is the event that attracted both Fisher and Roger Tomlinson[30] to Horwood's technology. Joining in on this conference circuit, Fisher was invited to present his SYMAP work at the 1965 summer institute in Seattle. As another example, during the period 1962–1967 when Tobler was a professor at the University of Michigan, he attended seven different summer institutes on a variety of subjects, in addition to the 1964 Short Course conducted by Fisher in Chicago and the 1967 Training Conference conducted by the Laboratory in Cambridge. Once Fisher obtained his Ford Foundation grant, he wasted no time organizing similar events, and inviting speakers from the same community.

Although originally planned for the first year of operations, a training conference required considerable advance planning, and the two-week event did not occur until May 8–19, 1967.[31] The training courses were held in the basement classroom of Memorial Hall, followed by a two-day conference at the Hotel Continental in Cambridge. Fisher lined up some presentations from outside the Laboratory staff, including Cooke from the Census Use Study, Tobler from Michigan, and Ivan Sutherland (a Harvard computer scientist pioneering in computer graphics). Many of the presenters were graduate students at Harvard and elsewhere, including David Sinton (see sidebar in chapter 3), and Joel Morrison, then a PhD student at the University of Wisconsin and later a professor there. The largest group included the Harvard undergraduates in Fisher's freshman seminar, notably Donald Shepard (see chapter 2). This training conference attracted 160 participants, many of them graduate students on full or partial scholarships paid by the Ford Foundation funds. (At other such events of the period, even those funded by the National Science Foundation, the students paid out of their own pockets.) Fisher was able to attract prominent cartographers and geographers by paying for travel and registration.[32] The scholarships for graduate students were an astute technique to bring a new generation in contact with the SYMAP technology. The recipients of these scholarships include people who would become academic leaders by the late 1980s, such as Michael Goodchild, Bruce MacDougall, Mark Monmonier, Harold Moellering, Gerald Rushton, Ben Niemann, and Fraser Taylor. Goodchild became director of NCGIA (National Center for Geographic Information & Analysis); MacDougall worked with Ian McHarg and became professor of landscape architecture at the University of Massachusetts; Monmonier wrote *How to Lie with Maps;* Moellering chaired the National Committee for Digital Cartographic Data Standards; Rushton became a prominent spatial analyst; Niemann, a landscape architect, was a key player in the Wisconsin Land Records movement; and Fraser Taylor became the president of the International Cartographic Association. This list shows how such events can influence a whole generation of academics—potential leaders in their various disciplines.

In 1967, at the time of this conference, no one had used the term "geographic information system" in print, though there would be three distinct uses of it in the next year.[33] The community was clearly ready for the term, and gathering 160 people together shows that there was plenty of interest throughout the United States, Canada, and Great Britain. This conference was meant to train users of SYMAP, a simple tool, ready to be installed at university computer centers. This event concentrated on the details of making it work. Perhaps quite importantly, the Laboratory distributed source code permitting local modifications and extensions as well as conversions to the diverse mainframes present at different institutions.[34] SYMAP was itself in flux at the time of the conference. Shepard presented a session about his new interpolation algorithm, but version V was not ready for distribution for another year (see chapter 2). Perhaps this set the pattern for software distributors to tout new features long before they are available for distribution. Yet, more than the mechanics of SYMAP, this event looked forward into uncharted territory, the prospects of major analytical use of computers for many disciplines.

Influenced and influential

While it is true that Howard Fisher did found the Laboratory for Computer Graphics at Harvard Graduate School of Design with a grant from the Ford Foundation, the process was not a simple linear track, but involved a web of interconnections with a community of others doing similar work. There was collaboration and competition, as in any human enterprise. The new Laboratory was certainly not the first place to do this kind of work. The influence of the organization derived from the promise of the technology, not a studied plan of development. The newly founded Laboratory opened a number of possibilities, each developing simultaneously.

In reflecting on these initial events surrounding the Laboratory, a few analytical lessons can be drawn. While the maxim holds that timing is everything, Fisher and SYMAP were not first; and yet being first was not crucial. Although the Ford Foundation had earlier worried that the timing was wrong ("the bloom was off the rose"), they gave the money anyway. At the time, it was not so clear what was going to become important later or which persons would later become influential. Certainly the personalities in this story played a role, but again they were not entirely determining. As the next chapters will demonstrate, there was a hybrid environment that mixed theories of spatial structure with the artifacts of the emerging computer technology. Again, it was not clear in the beginnings which features were going to be important. In the analysis of other scientific and technological changes, scholars like Michel Callon and Bruno Latour have documented the role of hybrid networks of people, institutions, and technical artifacts.[35] Actors in these networks enhance their control over the development by making themselves "obligatory points of passage"—key locations by which the flows of knowledge, technology, and academic credit were regulated. For a period, the Laboratory that Fisher founded became exactly such a confluence—a mixture of inconsistent, even conflicting, tendencies and exciting new directions.

NOTES

1. Material on Howard Fisher, used in this and later chapters, comes from the collection of the Harvard University Archives, under call number HUG (FP) 62. The material was donated to Harvard in 1981 by Howard Fisher's wife, following his death. Each of 23 boxes contains documents and file folders. I will refer to papers by HTF Papers with box number and folder, when available. Fisher's CV, dated February 1977, is in box 6. The archivists placed this note in the catalog: "The Fisher papers were received in the Archives in a fairly disordered state and in great bulk. An attempt was made to select only the more important papers for retention. The bulk of the papers retained have been arranged in a general alphabetic sequence."

2. Fisher's attendance at Horwood's training course is documented in many sources: James Dougenik and David Sheehan, *SYMAP user's manual* (Cambridge, Mass.: Laboratory for Computer Graphics and Spatial Analysis, Harvard University, 1976); Kenneth Dueker, "Edgar Horwood and URISA," in *Proceedings, URISA* (Orlando, Fla.: URISA, 2000); William Beyers (one of Horwood's teaching assistants in 1963), personal communication, 1999.

3. Howard Fisher, two page description of SYMAP, February 28, 1964 (HTF Papers, box 11, folder: Northwestern): "Objectives: To produce rapidly and economically graphic displays showing aggregated data applicable to human communities (such as for social, political, economic and other factors). The program is equally suited to isolate data as in any other connection (such as for rainfall, geologic substrata, etc.) wherever variable values occur at irregular locations." Northwestern University press release from December 9, 1964, cites Fisher and Mrs. O. G. Benson (Betty) as originators.

4. Brian Berry, personal communication, 2004.

5. Northwestern University, press release, December 9, 1964 (HTF Papers, box 11, folder: Northwestern); attendance list for 1964 and September 18–19, 1965 (box 5, folder: Chicago).

6. HTF Papers have many letters with prominent cartographers (including Arthur Robinson, George Jenks, and John Sherman), often arguing on terminology.

7. Howard T. Fisher, *Mapping information, the graphic display of quantitative information* (Cambridge, Mass.: Abt Books, 1982). Prior draft material appeared as *Harvard papers in theoretical cartography*, Papers 1–4 (1978). Fisher presented draft material as early as 1967 at the first Training Conference HUG (FP) 62.50, Transcripts, session 9A.

8. Louis Winnick's letter to Fisher, dated January 28, 1965 (HTF Papers, box 8, folder: Ford Foundation, Before the Grant), acknowledges Fisher's letter and replies "Although some of the bloom is off the rose (a number of schools are playing with the technique), we'd still be interested in a proposal along the lines previously indicated."

9. The failure to make arrangements at Northwestern and Chicago are covered in a few sources. Jack Meltzer, director Center for Urban Studies, University of Chicago, draft memo, December 23, 1964 (HTF Papers, box 3, folder: Chicago). This memo requests that Fisher be appointed half-time, splitting his time between Chicago and Harvard. This request was refused, and Fisher ended up full-time at Harvard. Fisher, letter to Meltzer, March 11, 1966 (same folder). Also, Fisher memo, May 1974, recounts Fisher's retrospective version of events (box 7, folder: Laboratory). Also, Brian Berry, personal communication, 2004.

10. "Proposal for an educational and research grant relative to computing science and systems analysis applications to city planning," September 28, 1965. The positive response was in a letter from Joseph McDaniel, Secretary of the Ford Foundation, to Harvard President Nathan Pusey, dated December 14, 1965 (HTF Papers, box 8, folder: Ford Foundation).

11. "Computer map-making," Harvard press release, February 23, 1966.

12. Howard Fisher, in a letter to Horwood dated April 13, 1964: "As you know I am entirely in your debt for an introduction to the computer, and whatever I (have) done that is worthwhile should be credited to your stimulation" (HTF Papers, box 23, folder: University of Washington).

13. Edgar Horwood, Clark Rogers, Arnold R. M. Rom, Norma Olsonoski, William L. Clark, and Stevenson Weitz, "Computer methods of graphing, data positioning and symbolic mapping: A manual for user professionals in urban analysis and related fields" (Department of Civil Engineering, University of Washington, 1963).

14. Materials on Horwood derive in part from Kenneth Dueker, "Edgar Horwood and URISA," in *Proceedings, URISA* (Orlando, Fla.: URISA, 2000).

15. Stephen Kinzy, "Horwood's short laws," *Urban and Regional Information Systems Association Journal* 4 (1992): 85–86.

16. There are copious sources on this era in geography, starting with Ronald J. Johnston, *Geography and geographers: Anglo-American human geography since 1945* (London: Edward Arnold, 1979); Richard Morrill, "Recollections of the 'quantitative revolution's' early years: The University of Washington 1955–65," in *Recollections of a revolution: Geography as spatial science*, ed. Mark Billinge, Derek Gregory, and Ron Martin, 55–72. (London: Macmillan, 1984). Interpretations of the "revolution" remain controversial, see, for example, Trevor Barnes, "Retheorizing economic geography: From the quantitative revolution to the 'cultural turn,'" *Annals of the Association of American Geographers* 91 (2001): 546–565.

17. Waldo R. Tobler, "Automation and cartography," *Geographical Review* 49 (1959): 526–534.

18. The trajectories of all these scholars have been verified with assistance of Brian Berry, Richard Morrill, Kenneth Dueker, and William Garrison, personal communication, 2004.

19. William L. Garrison, R. Alexander, W. Bailey, M. F. Dacey, and D. F. Marble, "Data system requirements for geographic research," in *Proceedings, Third Goddard Memorial Symposium*, 139–151, (Washington, D.C.: American Astronautical Society, 1965).

20. David S. Simonett, "Future and present needs of remote sensing in geography," CRES Report 61-12 (Center for Research, Engineering Science Division, University of Kansas, 1966). (Supported by NASA Contract NSR 17-004-003). D. N. Thomas and Duane Marble, "Use of remote sensors in urban information systems," *Technical Report 1 to Geography Branch, Office of Naval Research, Task NR 389-143 Contract 1228-37* (Northwestern University, 1965).

21. Brian J. L. Berry, Richard L. Morrill, and Waldo R. Tobler, "Geographic ordering of information: New opportunities," *Professional Geographer* 16, no. 4 (1964): 39–43.

22. Exchange of letters between Fisher and Horwood, April and May, 1966 (HTF Papers, box 23, folder: University of Washington).

23. Howard Fisher, letter to Horwood, September 27, 1966 (HTF Papers, box 23, folder: University of Washington); exchange of letters between Fisher and Berry, November and December, 1966 (HTF Papers, box 3, folder: Berry).

24. Proposal to the Ford Foundation, pages 8–9.

25. A clear example of this fascination was Warntz's early collaboration with Stewart: John Q. Stewart and William Warntz, "Macrogeography and social science," *Geographical Review* 48 (1958): 167–184.

26. List appears on page 11.0, at the start of the listing for 1966–1967. *Red Book* was a loose-leaf publication giving short summaries of Laboratory projects (produced annually from 1965–1972). William Warntz, and Allan Schmidt, eds. *Red Book: Projects of the Laboratory for Computer Graphics and Spatial Analysis,* (Cambridge, Mass.: Laboratory for Computer Graphics and Spatial Analysis, Harvard University, 1969–1974)

27. Donald F. Cooke and William H. Maxfield, "The development of a geographic base file and its uses for mapping," in *Proceedings, Fifth Annual Meeting* (Garden City, N.Y.: URISA, 1967). Described later in Donald Cooke, "Topology and TIGER: The Census Bureau's contribution," in *The history of geographic information systems: Perspectives from the pioneers,* ed. Timothy W. Foresman, 47–57. (Upper Saddle River, N.J.: Prentice Hall, 1998).

28. Dates and attendance for these events from Fisher Papers, and particularly from Waldo Tobler's CV (HTF Papers, box 22, folder: Tobler).

29. Nicholas R. Chrisman, "John Sherman and the Origin of GIS," *Cartographic Perspectives* 27 (1997): 8–13.

30. Roger Tomlinson, personal communication, 2004.

31. Complete files on this event, including transcripts of sessions, are in the Harvard Archives: HUG (FP) 62.50.

32. HTF Papers contain letters to various colleagues, offering scholarships to their best students. For example, Arthur Robinson's letter to Fisher, dated May 5, 1966, requests a scholarship for George McCleary (box 23, folder: Wisconsin).

33. The first publication in a reviewed publication is accepted to be Roger Tomlinson, "A geographic information system for regional planning," in *Land Evaluation,* ed. George Stewart, 200–210. (Melbourne: Macmillan, 1968). In the same year, Samuel Arms, "Computer mapping in selected geographic information systems," in *Proceedings, Sixth Annual Meeting,* 218–221, (Clayton, Mo.: URISA, 1968). The question about earlier citations includes internal reports and draft material, but the term also had some signs of use at Northwestern around the time that Tomlinson had visited with Garrison and Marble: Michael F. Dacey and Duane F. Marble, "Some comments on certain technical aspects of geographic information systems," ONR Contract Nonr 1228(35), Task 389-142, Technical Report 2 (Department of Geography, Northwestern University, 1965). A letter from Terry Coppock, University of Edinburgh, to Howard Fisher following the 1967 conference (June 10, 1967) demonstrates that draft versions of Tomlinson's paper were already in circulation (HTF Papers, box 7, folder: Edinburgh).

34. Laboratory for Computer Graphics, various price sheets and program descriptions, (HTF Papers, box 1, folder: Availability of SYMAP).

35. Bruno Latour, *Science in action* (Cambridge, Mass.: Harvard University Press, 1987); Bruno Latour, *Pandora's hope* (Cambridge, Mass.: Harvard University Press, 1999); Michel Callon, ed., *La science et ses réseaux: Genèse et circulation des faits scientifiques,* (Paris: La Découverte, 1989).

TWO

SYMAP
Packaging thematic maps

The original reason for creating the Laboratory for Computer Graphics was the software package known as SYMAP. SYMAP remained for many years the best-known thematic mapping package distributed around the world. Its output—on the line printers of the day—was quite crude, but tho cartographic models and transformations were rather sophisticated. SYMAP sparked innovations at the basic programming level as well as for specific applications to major social and environmental problems.

A mapping program with many faces

Howard Fisher envisioned a computer program that would provide a new way of seeing things together as a whole. Part of this motivation comes from a designer's sense of seeing patterns, and part of it comes from a *gestalt* philosophy that the whole was greater than the sum of its parts. Most of all, he wanted planners to place specific local facts in a spatial context through improved visual presentations. The program SYMAP lived up to that vision as much as the efforts of the programmers could deliver, considering the limited graphics capabilities of the hardware available in the early days of computing. The features of SYMAP were to some extent a response to user demands, but for the most part simply represented the limit of what was possible using computers with constrained memory and a programming language that treated numbers, not text. The combination of capabilities in the package reflects the rich interaction of unbridled theory and practical application at the Laboratory.

SYMAP, as early as the 1964 prototype developed at Northwestern,[1] employed a vector data model for its input with a collection of points, lines, and areas in some coordinate space—a basemap. These objects had thematic values attached to them with a presumption of many sets of values for each basemap collection of geometric objects. For most purposes, these values would be classified into as many as 10 classes. The default classification used equal intervals from the minimum value to the maximum, but the program allowed quantiles (equal number of geographic objects per class) or manual specification of the classification intervals.[2]

By the time the program came to Harvard in 1965, a map could be produced at various sizes with different symbolism, legends, titles, and other finishing touches. Because the line printer displays printed one size of character at fixed spacing across the lines and down the page, maps were cellular (raster) images with each character position filled by a particular symbol. SYMAP could either fill the objects in the choropleth style, or it could interpolate three ways: nearest neighbor, inverse distance weighting, and trend surface. The automated calculation of interpolation was quite novel, since the prior programs required the user to provide the linkage from each point to its nearest neighbors. SYMAP searched for the nearest neighbors and allowed considerable control over the mathematics of inverse distance weighting. Alternatively, it could fit a trend surface with various degrees of algebraic complexity.

The coordinate system was assumed to be planar, but the program

> **The words of SYMAP**
>
> Fisher coined the word synagraphic from the Greek roots of "together" and "graphics (writing)" because he wanted to emphasize "seeing things together." The program was thus SYnagraphic MAPping. While the word synagraphic saw little use, SYMAP, pronounced with a short *i*, became synonymous with computer mapping.
>
> Fisher also coined new words for the map types of SYMAP. Instead of the reasonably common "choropleth," he introduced "conformant," since the map symbols conform to the object. He coined the term "proximal" for a nearest-neighbor interpolation that is essentially the Voronoi/Thiessen polygons. These terms did not gather much of a following. In contrast, Fisher used the descriptive word "contour" when cartographers were inventing a million variants of isopleths for each kind of attribute (isobars, isohyets, isobaths, isodapanes, isochrones, and on into the night). Fisher's terminology did not find favor with most of the established cartographic academics of the era, so most textbooks continue to use the more established terms.

offered a flexible system of data windows and viewports that permitted changes in scale. This flexibility was quite an improvement over the fixed-integer coordinates of Horwood's programs (described in chapter 1). SYMAP established the basic functions that any subsequent cartographic display program has had to provide ever since: separating the base geometric data from the thematic attribute, scaling the map to different sizes, and permitting distinct graphic treatment of the same source material.

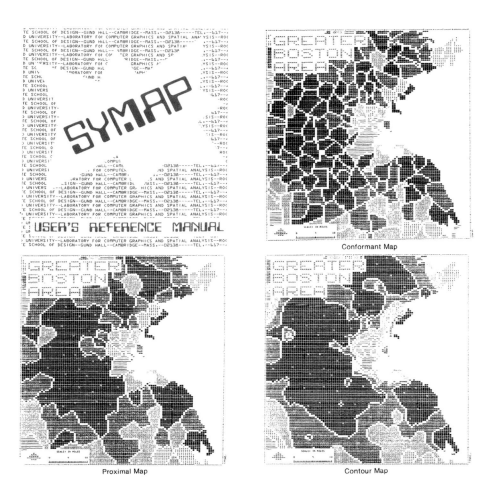

Conformant Map

Proximal Map

Contour Map

▲   Three basic map types from the cover of the SYMAP manual: conformant, proximal, and contour.

(Source: SYMAP Manual, 1975, front cover; LAB-LOG 1978, Harvard University Graduate School of Design)

How did SYMAP work?

The computers of the era were run in batch mode, meaning that jobs were staged and controlled by operators. Operators usually wore white coats and walked on raised floors, looking down on the users who presented their card decks over a wide counter. This crew kept mere users at a distance from the precious (and temperamental) hardware. Computing operated like a service industry, much like a dry-cleaners. Beyond the counter, under the supervision of the operators, card reading devices slurped the cards in, or, occasionally, crumpled them into unusable accordion folds. Dropping a deck of cards could require a week's work to reassemble the sequence. In this period, Harvard had a single computer for nearly all academic users. It occupied a special place in a special Computing Center building with raised floors for all the cables and copious air conditioning (then a bit of a novelty in the Northeast). Most Laboratory staff punched their cards in the Laboratory, then dropped them off at the Computing Center a few buildings away. Later on at night, they might just stay at the Computing Center in hopes of quicker turnaround.

For most of the SYMAP period, a complex operating system called OS/360 staged the jobs to run on the IBM computers that ran at Harvard and a majority of other universities. The Job Control Language (JCL) of OS/360 was exigent. Each job had to specify where every file was and how it would be handled. Small errors in specifying these JCL commands would lead to the whole job being rejected. The notorious data definition (DD) statements provided quite amazing flexibility but virtually no defaults. One had to know such things as the track size in bytes on that particular model of disk, or the exact blocking factor for each tape. One had to allocate file sizes in tracks or cylinders, a level of arcana hidden from the user in modern operating systems. The concept of a permanent directory of files in hierarchical subdirectories was developing on more interactive prototype systems at MIT, but the typical university mainframes provided no permanent storage beyond cards and tapes.

Programmers of SYMAP

As with any project that lasts for many years, it is difficult to give credit to everyone involved. In the code for the definitive 5.20 version, Fisher is listed as "originator." The following programmers are listed: Betty Benson, Marion Manos, Donald S. Shepard, Robert Russell, Nancy Peyton Gresham, Kathleen M. Reine, and James A. Dougenik. In 1963 and 1964, Benson wrote the versions operational at Northwestern University; she never worked at the Harvard Lab. When it arrived at Harvard, Russell mistakenly numbered that version "3" (as a decimal number, not a roman numeral), though Fisher estimated it may have been the tenth version of the code.[3] The list is not entirely in chronological order, since Russell appears to have joined the Lab a year earlier than Manos. Russell served as lead programmer with Manos working for him. Both of them were involved in creating version IV, the original Laboratory product. Shepard started work on the interpolation algorithm while in Fisher's freshman seminar in spring 1965; this capacity triggered the move to version V. Dougenik was hired as an undergraduate to rewrite the SYMAP manual in 1974. He took the novel approach of writing the manual first. He provided a logical presentation of what the program should do, then fixing the code to make it so. His version was the 5.20 (yes, the version numbers had moved back to digits), which was distributed in 1975 and remained the definitive version. Though uncredited, programmer Kathy Kiernan added the capability to calculate the index of dispersion/concentration for data points (option 28). This measure used the average distance to nearest neighbor, calculated by a simple nested loop comparing all points to all others. Who knows how many other programmers at the Laboratory may have done some work on the project?

When the program had run, the output was spooled to a printer, then that pile of continuous perforated paper would be delivered into a cubbyhole for the user to collect. Turnaround was a key measure of productivity. The whole of Harvard University was using one computer, at least in the early days. Often only one job could be turned around in a day. Obtaining three turnarounds in a day was considered special treatment, and the best to be hoped for.[4] Often the turnaround would consist merely of a terse note that your job control cards were incorrectly specified. There were strange little messages such as "MAIN does not exist but has been added to the dataset" which, despite the ominous tone, meant that the program would run. Slim listings were usually the sign of simple mistakes, but sometimes if the program misbehaved there would be a massive core dump—hundreds of pages long—produced when the program terminated in some error state. Programmers could spend days digging through the thick pile of paper searching for the cause. Carl Steinitz recalls that the first SYMAP output from the Delmarva Project (see chapter 3) took 30 submissions before the basemap emerged.[5] Some of those involved debugging the basemap, but many of them were procedural job control parameters. It took considerable persistence to use computers in this era and some sense of vision to see their potential for productivity. The catch-phrase "plug and play" was far in the future.

INPUT TO SYMAP

The input to the program was structured in packages with an implied, but partial, order:

▶ A-OUTLINE

▶ A-CONFORMLINES

▶ B-DATA POINTS

▶ C-OTOLEGENDS

▶ C-LEGENDS

▶ D-BARRIERS

▶ E-VALUES

▶ E1-VALUES INDEX

▶ F-MAP

The ordering allowed users to create a basemap through retention of earlier packages and then to produce subsequent maps with changes only to thematic values and display options. There were two parallel tracks for input, indicated by the two packages at the A level. The OUTLINE provided a single polygon covering the area to be mapped. The thematic mapping was confined inside this polygon; outside was given a uniform symbol (usually blank). If the outline polygon was omitted, the data points would be mapped inside a rectangular window just large enough for the data points. An OUTLINE was intended to lead to DATA POINTS for the interpolation procedure (producing either a contour or proximal map). The alternative was a conformant map, Fisher's term (as noted earlier) for what other cartographers called choropleth. The CONFORMLINES allowed a collection of points, lines, and areas to be filled with symbolism. For most applications, these collections were coverages of polygons.

Legends were cosmetic features that could be specified in two spaces. The LEGENDS were directly tied to rows and columns, hence in a given scale of output (like Horwood's programs). OTOLEGENDS could include basemap features like rivers or highways as reference for the thematic maps, or cartographic additions such as north arrows as if they were objects in the world. The OTOLEGEND objects were provided in the coordinate system of the basemap and then transformed onto a given scaled output.

The interpolation process used for contour maps could accommodate barriers that could modify the spatial searching for neighboring values. Though a technological feat, the BARRIERS package was rarely invoked. Most users had difficulty relating the automated logic of inverse distance weighting to the tricky permeability factors required for barriers.

All maps required some thematic VALUES. Basemap information could be reused with successive sets of thematic values. For example, a basemap of census tracts could be shown with population density, then an index of poverty, then average rental costs—each would just require a new E-VALUES package. Although the basic package expected to find cards with a single value for each object, more complex calculations could be triggered by invoking a FLEXIN subroutine. FLEXIN had to be written in FORTRAN and linked with the SYMAP object code for that particular production run (using a JCL procedure). For someone with some programming skills, it provided a way to calculate densities or the kinds of algebraic manipulations permitted by Horwood's software.

The INDEX provided a way to cross-reference between packages of objects placed in different orders. For example, the CONFORMLINES of municipalities could be created in alphabetic order and the attributes in Census FIPS code order (alphabetic by county). It was a bit tricky and thus not heavily used. It was more common to reorder the cards in the values package to match the order in the basemap. There was a field for an identifier

▲ "The Technique: Making a computer map is a matter of a few simple steps. This student, preparing a map of Boston, first uses the manual digitizing board to establish coordinates of the controlling points on the 'source map,' and enters the information on special coding forms. Next he transfers the information from the coding forms to punch cards. The Laboratory is fortunate enough to have a keypunch in its offices. All other peripheral equipment, with the exception of the new electronic digitizer and the teletype, is at the Computing Center. To have a record of his work in a form that is easy to check and store, the student lists his deck of cards. The machine reads the holes made in the cards by the keypunch and prints the corresponding characters on a special sheet. After listing the deck he will check the sheet against the coding forms to catch errors in keypunching."

(Source: Harvard Graduate School of Design Association newsletter [HGSDA] Supplement 1967, page 3)

on each object, but the program could not match an unsorted list to another list. It was just too much to expect from the memory-limited programming approach of SYMAP.

When SYMAP was conceived, there were no resources of digitized information, thus no formats for importing basemaps from elsewhere. The input was expected to come on cards, with one card for each point to keep it simple to maintain. Since a high degree of resolution was not required for the line printer display, digitizing was a pretty crude affair. The original manual and the correspondence course limited the discussion of input to the low-technology of a ruler on the source map.

The F-MAP package specified the output product with what were called "options," controlling elements such as the size of map, the symbolism, and the class intervals. The format for specifying each option was tied to specific columns on the input cards. This produced the potential for unintended results. Option 1 governed the size of the output map, in inches in both dimensions, down and across. The format permitted maps of truly gigantic proportions (millions of inches). To limit the potential damage, there was a special option to permit maps of more than a few pages—to guard against a mistake in entering the map size. The options were meant to have reasonable defaults, though many seasoned users had their preferences well-honed and sacred decks of cards to ensure there would be no keypunch errors (and loss of turnaround).

OUTPUT FROM SYMAP

Fisher wanted to produce a packaged piece of software to be used at many installations, as opposed to higher quality output available at only a few locations. There had been earlier efforts at high-quality cartographic output, including David Bickmore's Experimental Cartographic Unit (ECU)[6] at the Royal College of Art in London. Edgar Horwood at the University of Washington had written a package for mapping using the line printer, which any computer center of the time could be expected to have, and seeing this program gave Fisher the idea to write his own package with a mind toward wide distribution.

A SYMAP contour map of Boston being printed. The printer ▶ operated at 20 lines per second, so the map was printed in less than a minute. The operator then had to collect all the output from the printer and separate out this particular job before it would be delivered to the user. Only in staged pictures could a user watch the printer at work. *(Source: HGSDA Supplement 1967)*

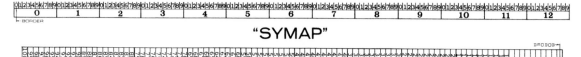

"SYMAP"

▲ A SYMAP ruler (not to scale due to format limitations). Scale on top is in tenths of inches across the page. Scale on bottom for vertical dimension is eight lines per inch. *(Source: Harvard Laboratory for Computer Graphics)*

Each line was printed all at once by the impact of print slugs onto the paper through a carbon ribbon (not so different from the typewriters of the era). The print slugs had the characters of the alphabet, originally in uppercase, but eventually the extended character set on the IBM 360 system permitted lowercase characters (though the keypunch devices made it difficult to input them). All characters were the same width and height, 10 characters per inch across the line. (Yes, all measurements were in inches, internationally.) The lines were 130 characters long, leading to the invention of the world's only 13-inch ruler, the SYMAP ruler, distributed with each correspondence course package (see page 37).

Printers usually were set to print six or eight lines per inch down the paper. A few special models could produce a square cell of 10 per inch by 10 per inch. These required remachined print heads, something that the grid-oriented projects found necessary to their work, but were not as critical for SYMAP's vector model.

The range of graphic symbolism produced by a line printer could be substantially enlarged by "overprinting," the ability to stop the paper from advancing, allowing additional printing on the same line. This capability required a $75 option for modifying the printer hardware to allow for rudimentary business forms and to underline text characters.[7] The printer used the first character of a line for carriage control; a blank meant a regular new line, a "1" meant a new page, and a "+" meant the paper would not advance, allowing overprinting. SYMAP permitted up to four character strikes on a particular cell of the map. Dark areas were often produced by overprinting the four characters OXAV in one cell, though there were proponents of MWI* to produce the darkest coverage. One had to understand the physics of the device, a single period "." directed the whole energy of the hammer on a single spot, so it would be darker than a larger slug such as O or W. The best quality SYMAP output was produced with multiple-copy, carbon-paper forms with a dark carbon paper for the interior copies. The first carbon was often much darker than the top copy, which was printed with the reusable ribbon, not the fresh single-use carbon paper. Since more recent equipment moved away from impact printers, some of the physical side has been lost in the uniformity of laser printing.

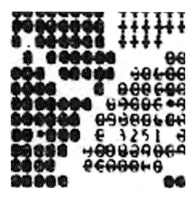

◀ Detail of overprinted symbolism.

(Source: SYMAP Manual, 1975, front cover)

AN EARLY APPLICATION: A MOVIE OF LAND-USE CHANGE

In March of 1967, just before becoming assistant director of the Laboratory, Allan Schmidt produced a motion picture generated from SYMAP output. This may be the earliest attempt to use automated cartography to display dynamic spatial information. Waldo Tobler's movie of the urban expansion of Detroit,[8] often described as the first such, was produced two years later.

Schmidt's movie portrays the urban expansion of Lansing, Michigan, where he was working at the Urban Regional Research Institute of Michigan State University. Every property transaction from 1850 to 1965 was coded by the square-mile section of the Public Land Survey System. To produce the SYMAP output, the percent of land in residential development was calculated for each five-year period. These maps were interpolated from centroids for each square mile, using the linear interpolation in SYMAP 3.

Each SYMAP output for a given year formed a square about 2 feet by 2 feet. Each map was hung in front of a movie camera and photographed, frame by frame in historical order. The sequence starts with a slow version of two minutes forty-five seconds, where each year had a number of frames on the film. Then the movie repeats the sequence more rapidly in forty-five seconds, and finally in five seconds with just one frame per year. The production values may not be great (the maps fade in and out of focus), but the film represents a milestone in the development of thematic cartography.[9]

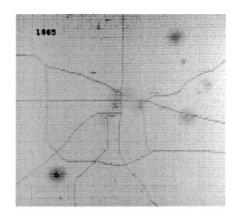

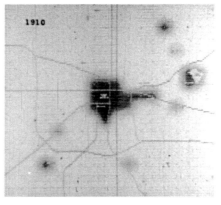

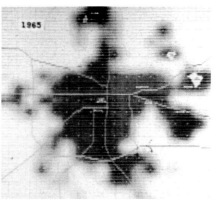

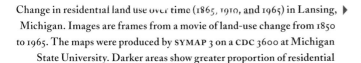

Change in residential land use over time (1865, 1910, and 1965) in Lansing, ▶ Michigan. Images are frames from a movie of land-use change from 1850 to 1965. The maps were produced by SYMAP 3 on a CDC 3600 at Michigan State University. Darker areas show greater proportion of residential land use. *(Source: Lansing Urban Growth Dynamics 1850–1965: A pictorial history of the expansion of the metropolitan area. SYMAP time-lapse prepared by the Urban Regional Research Institute, March 1967; produced by Instructional Media Center, Michigan State University. Used with permission of the Michigan State University Board of Trustees, and by permission of Allan Schmidt.)*

Programming SYMAP

At the level of source code, SYMAP was not an edifice of programming purity or particular elegance. As it expanded, it acquired a lumpy set of features that did not communicate much with each other. The conformant capability and the interpolation code were quite disconnected, though they used the same graphics options and cosmetics. While designed to support the mapping product, the programming of SYMAP demonstrates the limitations of the computers of the era, specifically in memory management and the column-bound user interface.

MEMORY MANAGEMENT

The computers of this era had limited memory, certainly by modern standards. SYMAP as distributed in 1968 could be operated in a computer with 128KB of main memory. That was considered a reasonably big machine at the time, though 256KB and even larger machines became common at large universities by the early 1970s. SYMAP gave itself a single work area using the FORTRAN convention of "blank COMMON," an area that could be made larger or smaller to fit the available memory. For conformant mapping, the program stored the basemapping data on a scratch file on disk; only the values were stored in main memory, one word per value. The interpolation algorithm stored the points in memory (two words, x and y), then added its searching data structures to this space (at the cost of three words of storage per point). The rest of this storage was used as a buffer to build the output map. The size of this buffer would establish the extent of a "section," a number of 130 character lines that could be fit into the remaining space. If the program had room for just one row, it would still valiantly continue. Each section was filled up with mapping symbolism by the appropriate subroutines, then output to the printer. Small sections caused a great amount of procedural overhead as well as revisiting all the data values.

Comments in the code mention a 1,000-point limit, but the limit actually depended on the amount of memory and the options chosen. In version 5.20, the workspace comprised 20,000 words (78KB of memory). This would permit a conformant map of full width across the printer (13 inches) to be about 19 inches long (at 8 lines per inch) in a single section. With 1,000 points to interpolate, the section would still be 14 inches long. Performance depended on the exact size of the map output, as well as the number of objects to map. SYMAP had the gymnastics of sections primarily to produce larger maps, since maps over 13 inches wide had to begin again on a new page with a new section, even if enough memory happened to be available. The program was built to chip away on section after section when the memory got clogged up with a large number of data points to interpolate or when a multipanel map was required.

Part of the reason for this complex programming was the unforgiving nature of the line printer. This device had no memory; it simply marked each line sequentially as commanded. There was no rewinding the printer and no backspacing over mistakes. Those who program in the era of video CRT tubes do not realize how incredibly dumb the older devices were. You couldn't simply draw the rivers in blue on top of the census tracts; you had to blank out the river cells and store the index to the river symbolism before you drew anything. With current computers, this work is done by the graphics card, using a buffer of special-purpose memory much larger than any university mainframe in the early days.

SYMAP was not entirely alone in the marketplace, and it was influenced by the competition in some small ways. For example, ESRI introduced a printer mapping package (AUTOMAP) around 1972 with claims that it was 12 to 16 times faster than SYMAP.[10] Responding to the challenge, SYMAP version 5.19 in 1975 added the option to save the calculated matrix of the map onto a magnetic tape or other media, allowing choropleth map production with changed attribute values to be much more rapid. This feature lagged ESRI by about three years.

USER INTERFACE

From the current perspective, it is hard to characterize SYMAP as having a user interface. What it did have was a set of expectations about the format of cards that made up the packages. While the "package" allowed the users to structure their work conceptually, the implementation was rigidly controlled by format rules. The program used the formatted READ statements of FORTRAN to control which columns of the card were interpreted for each variable. This procedure was quite averse to discovering alphabetic characters in numeric fields. Given a few innocent errors in the input deck, the program could choke on FORTRAN error messages and simply stop. For those errors that got by the watchful FORTRAN, there was some error checking internally, and if SYMAP detected errors, it would simply cycle through the control cards looking for either the end of the deck or a special CLEAR command that would restart everything. CLEAR was designed to permit multiple student decks to be batched together to save on overhead and to provide some chance that a later job would not be derailed by errors in an earlier one.

F-MAP			Package header card
INCOME PER CAPITA BY TOWN 1960			Title (printed below map)
SOURCE: US CENSUS			Title occupies three cards (no more, no less),
			so a blank card had to be included.
1	20.5	13.0	Map size 20.5 inches down, 13 across
3	6.0		Six classes
6			Value ranges: Since actual ranges were not provided, the program will produce quantiles; same number of towns per class.
9			Suppress histogram (options need not be sequential)
8			Suppress blank line around polygons
7			Symbolism option, on next four cards
.=IX*O	123456		Characters to symbolize 6 classes
*OMX	3456		and the data points in each class.
WA	456		Up to four levels of overprinting possible
V	6		
99999			End of package

▲　Annotated F-MAP package (card image on left). This would produce a map with six quantile classes, where the lowest class would be filled with periods and the top class overprinted with **OXAV**.

SYMAP specified the card format; there was little flexibility in the user interface. Yet, inside the format constraints, there were many ways for users to make a map product. Legends could be done in two different ways, tied to the map output or to the input coordinates. The same set of input packages could produce different results with only small changes of F-MAP options. For instance, the proximal map involved the same input as an interpolated contour map, and limiting the interpolation to use only a single neighbor (the nearest one) to provide the result. Similarly, the trend surface options were added to the package with another option for the mathematical complexity of the trend surface to fit. The user requested quantiles simply by giving a zero value to a numerical parameter of the option for user-specified value ranges (perhaps an odd way to do this). As one tries to figure this program out (and many have failed in this undertaking), it is fairly evident that there was no general structure to set up the major parameters for the map. Each new option was sort of tacked alongside the structure of a prior version. Internally, the old labels of the packages (prior to the imposition of the A, B, C ordering) remained as viable input. Overall, the program resembles an archaeological dig with many layers, relics of past civilizations dimly visible.

BRUTE FORCE PROGRAMMING

Most of the code for SYMAP was written without analyzing its algorithmic complexity. Shepard was concerned with how to locate the nearest points efficiently, and to do so he implemented a spatial index. The sorting routine used to index the data points (SORT) demonstrates a misunderstanding about complexity. His sorting procedure has a doubly nested loop structure. The inner loop runs down the list from I to the end and finds the lowest value, stored in K. Then K is put in the position I-1, operated by the outer loop. This is certainly a short amount of code for a sorting routine, but the nested loops set the number of comparisons by the formula: NITEMS squared divided by two. With some care, an improved algorithm could reduce the number of comparisons to NITEMS times the logarithm of NITEMS. For small numbers of input data points, the improvement would be fairly trivial, but at a few thousand, the difference would be quite noticeable. While Shepard tried to save computation time by indexing the points, he introduced a higher degree of computational complexity, reducing the effectiveness of the indexing. This kind of brute force programming was fairly standard in the early days of computing.

```
      SUBROUTINE SORT (ITEMS,NITEMS)
C   SORTS NITEMS ITEMS INTO ASCENDING SORT
      DIMENSION ITEMS(NITEMS)
      IF (NITEMS .LE. 1) RETURN
      DO 20 2,NITEMS
      K=I-1
      DO 10 J= I,NITEMS
 10   IF (ITEMS(J) .LT. ITEMS(K)) K=J
      IHOLD=ITEMS(I-1)
      ITEMS(I-1)=ITEMS(K)
 20   ITEMS(K)=IHOLD
      RETURN
      END
```

(Source: Harvard University Graduate School of Design)

INTERPOLATION IN SYMAP

To improve the interpolation as performed in Horwood's program, Fisher had implemented a kind of linear interpolation in which the user had to specify the nearest-neighbor relationships between points across the map and down the paper. This algorithm was implemented in the early versions at Northwestern University.

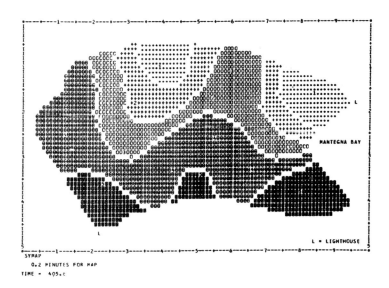

▲   A surface interpolated with SYMAP 3. Note the slightly uneven contour lines caused by the partitioning. *(Source: Red Book 1966, page I.3 , Harvard University Graduate School of Design)*

In his first two years at Harvard, Fisher conducted seminars for freshmen, showing them his work on SYMAP. Many of these students participated in Laboratory events, particularly the conference in 1967. Shepard, one of the freshmen, decided the improvement needed improving. His overhaul of the interpolation in SYMAP used a more mathematical framework that we now call "inverse distance weighting." He wanted a smooth surface that would also pass through each point exactly. He defined smoothness in calculus terms as having a first derivative (slope) at each point. These properties could be obtained by some form of weighted averaging that would depend on distance. Shepard conducted a number of experiments with the exponent of distance.[15] With the exponent of –1 (inverse distance), he described the effect as a generally flat surface, like a rubber sheet, poked up or down in the vicinity of the data points. The surface produced with an exponent of –4 resembled "a group of Arizona mesas—a large flat area surrounds each data point, separated by a fairly steep cliff from an adjacent plateau." He decided that an exponent of –2 was "visually pleasing and easy to read." Shepard's algorithm thus adopted the distance decay from Newton's Law of Gravitation.

William Warntz, a well-known proponent of the gravity model,[16] had presented his social physics approach to spatial analysis in a lunch seminar (see chapter 1) during the semester that Shepard was doing his exploratory work. It is not entirely clear if Shepard was influenced by Warntz or simply came to similar conclusions from his own study of the results of interpolation.[17] In any case, the undergraduate Shepard made a significant contribution to the state of the art in automated cartography.

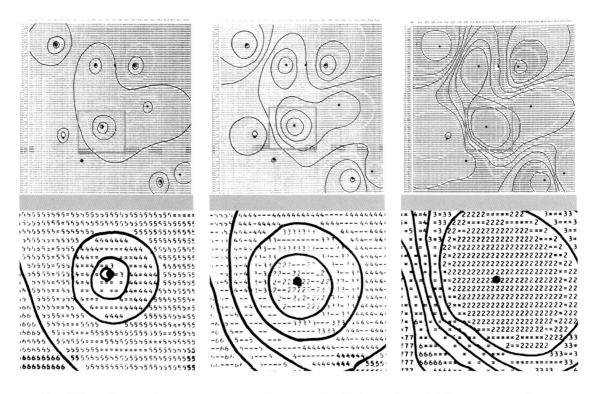

▲ Donald Shepard's interpolation experiments using the same neighborhood algorithm with different exponents of inverse distance weighting on a hypothetical surface: *(left)* exponent of –1; *(center)* exponent of –2; *(right)* exponent of –4.

(Source: Red Book 1966, p. I 8-I.11, Harvard University Graduate School of Design)

Shepard was not content with basic inverse distance weighting; it produced some mathematical properties that he deemed undesirable, particularly that the surface is flat in the immediate vicinity of each data point. To reduce this effect, he picked a specific distance (TRF in the code fragment below) and stitched in a polynomial. At the outer ring around a point, this function produced the same value as it would obtain at TRF using the other code. Nearer to the point, it maintains the trend of the slope measured to the nearest neighbors. This function was constructed to maintain the smoothness that Shepard desired. Shepard's algorithm also treated "intervening opportunity"—it downgraded the influence of a neighboring point if there was a closer point between it and the location being interpolated. This was done in the complex tangle of calculation around the line labeled 820 in the sprawling subroutine CLOSE. The result is the term W for each of the data points selected; W is based on S, the inverse distance effect, weighted by the proportion that this point contributes to the total of the terms ST, SA, and SB (cosine terms that treat the intervening opportunity). It is no wonder that only a very few people have ever figured out how or why this works. Other research centers were working on interpolation at this time, particularly the University of Kansas and its SURFACE II program. The features of SYMAP were state-of-the-art. Many current implementations of "inverse distance weighting" are much less sophisticated.

Code fragment from SUBROUTINE CLOSE

(from SYMAP 5.20, used with permission)

Situation: there are L1 points indexed in LIST1 within the search radius.

```
      SA=0.0
      SB=0.0
      ST=0.0
      DO 810 LK2=1.L1
      LK=LIST1(LK2)
C     ACTUAL DISTANCE ON DATA PATH = R2
C     DISTANCE INCLUDING BARRIER EFFECT = R3
      R2=SQRT(ABS(SHRTD(LK))
      R3=R2
      IF (NOWBAR) R3=SQRT((SHRTX(LK))**2+(SHRTY(LK))**2)
      IF (R2-TRF) 780,780,790
C     S(I) IS EFFECTIVE RELATIVE WEIGHTING DUE TO DISTANCE
  780 S(LK2) = 1.0/R2
      GO TO 800
C     THIS POLYNOMIAL IDENTICAL TO 1/R2 AT TRF
  790 S(LK2) A1*SHRTD(LK) + A2*R2 +A3
  800 QX(LK2)= S(LK2)*SHRTX(LK)/R3
      QY(LK2)= S(LK2)*SHRTY(LK)/R3
      SA=SA+QX(LK2)
      SB=SB+QY(LK2)
      SHRTD(LK)=R2
  810 ST=ST+S(LK2)
      DEN=0.0
C     RELATIVE WEIGHTING OF I TH DATA POINT ON LIST1 = W(I)
      DO 820 I=1,L1
      W(I)=S(I)*(ST*S(I)-QX(I)*(SA-QX(I))-QY(I)*(SB-QY(I)))
  820 DEN=DEN+W(I)
      RETURN
```

(Source: Harvard University Graduate School of Design)

Shepard's programming also allowed barriers to interpolation. Since the program would be searching for the nearest points around a given location, it was possible to impose an additional constraint by adding some value to a search that crossed a particular line. If the value was large enough, it was effectively impervious, so all neighbors would come from only one side of the barrier. These barriers were added in 1967–1968, following discussions with Warntz and Ernesto Lindgren on the properties of geodesics (direct paths across surfaces) (see chapter 4). Adding barriers added complexity to the code, but it also allowed for much more reasonable interpolation. The exact strength of a barrier would depend on what variable was being modeled. Apart from bridges, a river could be a large barrier for human interaction but of little consequence for air pollution, for example. Barriers are now available in some current software packages, but not given too much treatment in textbooks or user manuals.

In 1976, two users had independently complained of trouble with barriers. After a substantial effort in tracking the effect of barriers in the intricate searching technique, Jim Dougenik isolated the bug and fixed it with just a few lines of correction. The newsletter *Context* reports this success: "Inefficiencies which previously made the D-BARRIERS package costly have been diagnosed and brought under control. SYMAP runs which use the package will still require greater computation that those without BARRIERS (especially if the output map is large), but can now be submitted without fear of runaway processing time."[18]

COMPUTER MAPPING AS AN AID IN AIR POLLUTION STUDIES: A MAJOR APPLICATION OF INTERPOLATION

The development of the interpolation algorithm for SYMAP was closely linked to a major project funded by a contract from the U.S. Public Health Service between 1967 and 1969. John Goodrich, a research associate at the Laboratory and an urban planner by training, took charge of the project, with participation from a number of Laboratory staff.[19] The main task involved combining point samples of air pollution measures (over time) with demographic variables. It was a job for interpolation. Shepard perfected his interpolation algorithm and produced an undergraduate thesis[20] that considered the environmental consequences of different fuels for power plants at different locations. Jack Dangermond, a student in the master's of landscape architecture program, spent many late night hours at the Computing Center producing the maps for the Southern California, Puget Sound, and Connecticut regional studies.[21] The study of St. Louis, Missouri (performed by Shepard) was used as a test bed for the next-generation plotter-based program SYMVU, providing impressive visualization of the quantities of air pollution at different times of day (see chapter 5). The modeling work was done by SYMAP's interpolation capability.

The air pollution data for Los Angeles County produced by Dangermond demonstrates the utility of barriers in an actual application. He knew that the air pollution in that area got trapped by the San Gabriel Mountains, so he created a barrier along the ridge line. The real trouble was the uneven (and inadequate) distribution of air pollution monitoring stations in this early phase of environmental monitoring. More stations would eventually fix that problem, but SYMAP was designed to generate useful cartographic output from the limited measurements available. The experience that Dangermond gained from his one year working at the Laboratory provided the basis on which he founded the Environmental Systems Research Institute (ESRI). The fledgling nonprofit company did more air pollution studies in their first year, as well as a computer-generated movie inspired by Schmidt's movie of Lansing, Michigan.[22]

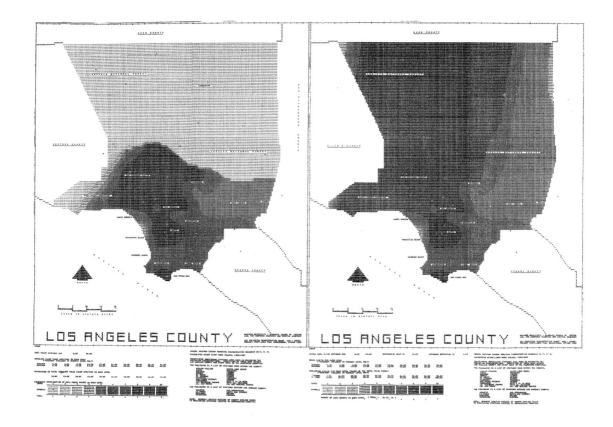

▲   Interpolating air pollution data with and without barriers. The map on the right, produced without barriers, extends the data from the more heavily urbanized area north into the desert, which had fewer sampling stations. The map on the left, produced with a barrier along the crest of the mountains, limits the interpolation to the primary airshed where the sampling was done. SYMAP by Jack Dangermond. *(Source: California Study, Computer Mapping as an Aid in Air Pollution Studies, Volume Two Report I, figure I-1, ed. John Goodrich)*

Dead ends in SYMAP development

Like other large projects, the SYMAP program grew through a variety of activities, planned and unplanned. The program that arrived at Harvard was labeled version 3. Version IV, constructed on the IBM 7094 system, included Shepard's interpolation replacing the older interpolation and its requirement for users to input connectors between adjacent points. (As noted earlier, the version numbers switched in and out of roman numerals.) Distribution of version IV was guarded due to concerns about bugs and integrating features developed separately. Meanwhile, the computing environment was shifting. Another version was produced for the new IBM 360 line, an upgrade that required major software migration and the use of the powerful OS/360 operating system. The FORTRAN changed in some implementation details between these two platforms, and memory requirements were substantially larger to support different library routines for such devices as disk and tape. Version V was distributed for the 360 environment, leaving the 7094 computer unsupported. The Laboratory was learning about the influence of major vendors on programming.

In this process, some options and developments were attempted only to be left behind. For example, a whole type of map display called the "conformant dot map" was clearly operational from the example below, dated spring 1966, but not released in any distribution version. It appears that each polygon was filled by a set of dark black dots randomly located inside the polygon in proportion to the quantitative value of the polygon (or its density, the difference is not apparent in this small demonstration example).

Later on, the roman numeral for version V was dropped for a decimal series of maintenance revisions numbered from 5.01 to 5.20. A version 6 was under construction during 1969 and 1970, with some new features, but eventually the distribution version absorbed most of the advances without changing over to 6.0. The decision to avoid changing the version number meant that there would not be a charge for users to upgrade. Maintenance versions were distributed for free, or for the price of a replacement tape copy. A change to 6 would have gone along with a special upgrade fee, and users would pay only if the new version offered substantial improvements.

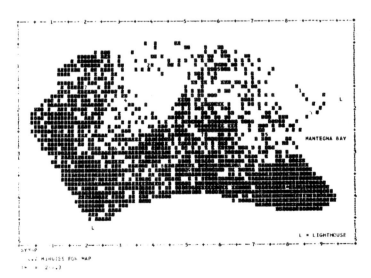

◀ **Conformant dot map.** *(Source: Red Book 1966, page I.3, Harvard University Graduate School of Design)*

At the height of the mainframe era, there were several alternatives to IBM. Many universities had selected another vendor, usually on strictly technical grounds, but also related to special discounts offered to capture a large research university account. Local programmers specialized in conversion from IBM-based programs into the local FORTRAN. There were 60-bit word machines from Control Data (6400, 6600, and so forth), 48-bit word machines from ICL and Control Data (3600), 36-bit word machines from Univac and Digital Equipment, as well as close copies of the IBM hardware from Xerox, Systems Development Corporation, General Electric, and others. The Burroughs machines were decimal, not binary, leading to many differences. In 1973, the Laboratory knew of 24 distinct conversions of SYMAP,[23] and probably many more were made after 1973. Harvard did not maintain a library of these conversions, since the tape formats were usually inscrutably incompatible with the IBM worldview. Once a site had purchased the program from Harvard, it would arrange to get the converted version from a site that had already made the conversion. This informal network of support was fueled by zealous attachment to a particular brand of hardware at user institutions, as well as the Laboratory's policy of distributing source code.

Correspondence course

Fisher had run short courses at Northwestern in December 1964 and September 1965. These events, which had registered 32 and 48 participants, respectively, provided the model for the much larger events that would be funded by the Ford Foundation grant. But nothing could reach planners from all over the world as well as a correspondence course.

The correspondence course consisted of instructions in several manila envelopes, one SYMAP ruler, and a set of maps for the fictitous geography of "Mantegna Bay" (informally Mag Bay)—an island roughly the shape of Jamaica. Each registrant would read their lesson and code their homework on coding forms—character-by-character for each 80-column card image. Attached to a dozen data collection zones, the thematic variables quantified such things as per capita consumption of macadamia nuts. These values would be rendered in the conformant zones, interpolated to a surface, or shown as proximal maps based on the calculated centroids. After completing the first lesson, students could open the second envelope and compare their coding form visually with the correct answer. The whole course assumed that the student would have no access to a computer or to SYMAP. The next exercise (also in the second envelope) would be sent to Harvard for correction and to be submitted to SYMAP. The Lab staff would keypunch the cards as specified on coding forms in the exercise and submit them to produce map output. Those who successfully completed the course were given certificates, as well as discounts for purchasing new versions of SYMAP.

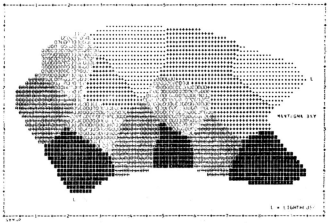

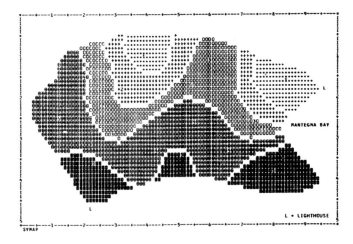

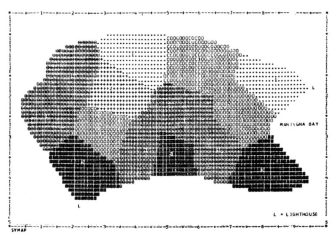

◀ *Top to bottom:* The fictional geography of Mag Bay displayed in the conformant, contour, and proximal map types.

(Source: SYMAP description, Red Book 1966, pages I.3, I.4, Harvard University Graduate School of Design)

The course material was later upgraded with less hypothetical data from the state of Connecticut, at first using information from Schmidt's contract work with the Federal Housing Administration (1967). In 1969, the correspondence course was expanded to include examples from the air pollution studies covering Connecticut, the work of Dangermond and John Goodrich. Mag Bay still lived on in the SYMAP manual and in subsequent Laboratory programs as test data.

Many planners were introduced to computer mapping through this correspondence course. Instructors at many universities used this material to teach computer cartography (as it was called in the 1970s). Continued sales of SYMAP manuals through university bookstores into the 1980s demonstrate this widespread influence.

Average lot size by town of ▶ Connecticut, produced by Allan Schmidt and John Kidwell, fall 1967. The original map was 23 inches by 26 inches in two panels (vertical strips), since the printer was 13 inches wide. This illustrates the use of the option to shade polygon boundaries with dark symbolism. It was more common to use white space for the boundaries. *(Source: Red Book, page III.38, Harvard University Graduate School of Design)*

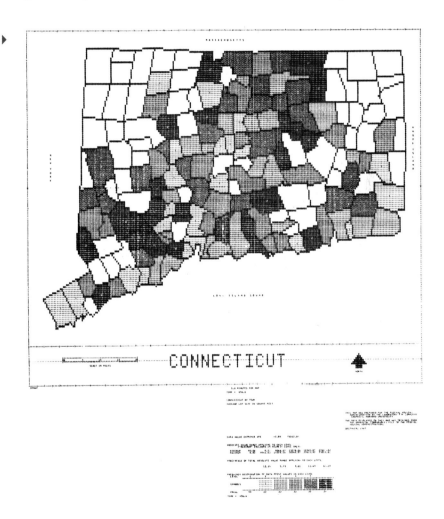

NOTES

1. Two-page description of SYMAP, February 28, 1964 (HTF Papers, box 11, folder: Northwestern)

2. The fullest description relates to the definitive version, 5.20: James Dougenik and David Sheehan, *SYMAP user's manual* (Cambridge, Mass.: Laboratory for Computer Graphics and Spatial Analysis, Harvard University, 1976); see also, Allan Schmidt and Wayne Zafft, "Progress of the Harvard University Laboratory for Computer Graphics and Spatial Analysis," in *Display and analysis of spatial data,* eds. John C. Davis and M. J. McCullagh, 231–243 (London: John Wiley and Sons, Inc., 1975). (Has a good summary of capabilities of all Laboratory products of 1975.)

3. Howard Fisher, letter to Daniel Conway, January 29, 1968 (HTF Papers, box 5, folder: Conway). In response to question about version 1 of SYMAP, Russell called what arrived from Northwestern version 3, but it was more like 10.

4. Howard Fisher, memo to Robert Russell and Donald Shepard, October 28, 1966 (HTF Papers, box 11, folder: Laboratory).

5. Carl Steinitz, personal communication, 2004.

6. David Rhind, "Personality as a factor in the development of a discipline: The example of computer-assisted cartography," *The American Cartographer* 15 (1988): 277–290.

7. "Mr. Berry" from IBM Corporation describes a $75 modification to the standard printer to allow it to overprint (HTF Papers, transcripts of conference, session 9D, page 117).

8. Waldo Tobler, "A computer movie simulating urban growth in the Detroit region," *Economic Geography* 26 (1970): 234–240.

9. A clip of the Lansing movie is on the CD that accompanies this book.

10. Letters between Fisher and Jack Dangermond, 1972 (HTF Papers, box 6, folder: Dangermond).

11. "Program user list," internal document, July 20, 1978.

12. Pricelist, July 1967 (HTF Papers, box 1, folder: Availability of SYMAP).

13. 1973, 1977, 1980 prices from the LAB-LOG catalogs from those dates.

14. Software sales in 1986 from internal documents, broken down by program.

15. Donald S. Shepard, "A SYMAP interpolation algorithm," in *Red Book,* I.8-I.11 (Laboratory for Computer Graphics and Spatial Analysis, Harvard University, 1966).

16. William Warntz, "A new map of the surface of population potentials for the United States," *Geographical Review* 54 (1964): 170–184.

17. The published form of the interpolation algorithm: Donald Shepard, "A two-dimensional interpolation function for irregularly spaced data," in *Proceedings, Twenty-third National Conference,* 517–524, (Association for Computing Machinery, 1968). Also appeared as *Harvard papers in theoretical geography,* no. 15, (Laboratory for Computer Graphics and Spatial Analysis, Harvard University, 1968).

18. *Context,* no. 8 (May 1976), 13.

19. John Goodrich, ed., *Computer mapping as an aid in air pollution studies,* two volumes with many "reports." (Cambridge, Mass.: Laboratory for Computer Graphics and Spatial Analysis, Harvard University, 1970). The project was funded by Demonstration Grant 68A-2405D, National Air Pollution Control Administration, U.S. Public Health Service.

20. Donald Shepard, "A load-shifting model to reduce exposure to air pollution caused by electrical power generation" (honors thesis, Harvard College, 1969).

21. Paul Jack Dangermond, "California study," in *Computer mapping as an aid in air pollution studies,* vol. 2, report 1,ed. John Goodrich (Cambridge, Mass.: Laboratory for Computer Graphics and Spatial Analysis, Harvard University, 1970). Also, report F, Connecticut study; report H, Puget Sound study.

22. Jack Dangermond, letter to Fisher, July 27, 1970 (HTF Papers, box 6, folder: Dangermond).

23. *Context,* no. 4 (June 1973), 2.

THREE

Environmental Planning

One group at the Laboratory, led by Carl Steinitz, applied computer mapping to issues of environmental planning, closely coordinating their work with the instructional program of the Department of Landscape Architecture and other research projects. In 1967, a major regional study was conducted for the Delmarva Peninsula, a project that clarified many of the challenges for an early GIS. An annual series of such studio projects has continued in the Department of Landscape Architecture ever since. The requirements of this analytical work led the team to deviate from the vector-based approach of SYMAP. Their grid analysis alternative has had a huge influence on professional practice and instruction.

Setting the scene

Howard Fisher's 1965 proposal to the Ford Foundation emphasized the gathering of factual information about urban planning. In the text of the proposal, the word "environment" does not appear. As an architect, Fisher had a perspective on planning that did not address the problems of the environment, particularly as articulated by the discipline of landscape architecture. Yet, Fisher understood that his new Laboratory had to engage each of the academic departments in the Graduate School of Design. The work begun at the Laboratory would lead to significant contributions in environmental planning.

Environmental issues emerged rapidly a few years later, an emergence usually attributed to Rachel Carson's influential book *Silent Spring*, Earth Day, and related political movements in the public consciousness.[1] However, in professional and academic circles, the environmental movement had deeper roots. In 1967, Charles Harris in the Department of Landscape Architecture at the Graduate School of Design assigned several students to document the techniques used by a range of practitioners for environmental analysis and design. With some funding from the Conservation Foundation, three eminent practitioners came to Harvard to describe their work and techniques.[2] The goal was a critical evaluation of these techniques so that the students could select the most appropriate for their work. This process assembled representatives from each of the projects that we now identify as the origins of GIS. Angus Hills, a soil scientist and forester from the Ontario Department of Lands and Forests, presented his hierarchical land evaluation technique. It was strongly linked to geomorphic land units, and a set of presumptions about the linkage between geomorphology, soils, vegetation, and ecological carrying capacity. Hills's mapping system served as the framework for the Canada Land Inventory,[3] an ambitious project to assess the potential for agriculture, forestry, wildlife habitat, and recreation across Canada. The maps of this inventory directly assessed suitability of each polygon for the particular use. (By contrast, a modern inventory would perform the assessment as a second step, using more basic multipurpose source materials.) The boundaries of each polygon in the inventory were interpreted from aerial photographs, and many polygons had mixtures of suitability (such as 20 percent at level 5, 50 percent at level 4, 30 percent at level 3). In effect, the map recorded a complex environmental assessment performed by the cartographer.[4] Hills's work fits into the focus on land evaluation evolved by an international collection of environmental scientists over a few decades. The paradigm for this group was that a comprehensive evaluation required collaboration of multiple disciplines, discovery of the hierarchy of "land systems" in a region, then production of a single map as the result. Researchers at CSIRO (the Commonwealth Scientific and Industrial Research Organisation) in Australia took the lead in developing this technique and promoting it in various United Nations workshops throughout the 1960s.[5]

In Ottawa, a project for converting the Canada Land Inventory to digital form was the first to use the term "geographic information system."[6] This system, piloted by Roger Tomlinson, was called CGIS (for Canada GIS), often regarded as the origin of the modern GIS. Yet of the three techniques presented at Harvard in 1967, Hills's was the one that needed a GIS the least. The analytical work was mostly performed in the process of compiling the maps. Each of the CGIS layers depended on expert photointerpretation. In addition, to create the wildlife and recreation maps, a cartographer produced buffers and other spatial transformations with manual drawing tools. The financial justification for Tomlinson's computer system hinged on the estimated effort to tabulate the areas of the polygons on the compiled maps and their overlays. In Hills's presentation at Harvard there was little discussion of the computer system then being constructed in Ottawa.

The other two practitioners were Philip Lewis from the University of Wisconsin and Ian McHarg from the University of Pennsylvania, both landscape architects. Both advocated assembling maps from a variety of sources using transparent overlays. In contrast to Hills, they focused on the analytical process that led to the evaluation of suitability. There was no presumption of a hierarchy of land systems.

McHarg's book *Design with Nature*[7] inspired the environmental movement and has been regarded as one of the foundations of later GIS practice. In his presentation to the Harvard students, McHarg emphasized the importance of environmental processes, flows, and changes. He also suggested an exhaustive collection of all possible data sources, often a prohibitive undertaking in this era. Despite the grand overview, his technique boiled down to separate maps of suitability overlaid to produce a composite. How all the variables would be combined was not entirely specified; it would vary for each application.

Lewis, who served as "invited critic" at the Graduate School of Design that year, had conducted statewide inventories of recreational potential for Illinois and Wisconsin.[8] He emphasized "environmental corridors," the connectivity provided by the river network and other linear patterns. Lewis also advocated using multiple transparent map layers to identify landscape patterns. In general, Lewis made do with available information, selecting key variables that he had connected to the corridor scheme. In contrast to McHarg's approach, Lewis saw suitability in a setting of connectivity and larger neighborhoods. This element has been somewhat under-appreciated in the treatment of GIS history.

As a conclusion to their report on the three visitors, the Harvard researchers observed that none of the methods was complete enough as presented. They also proposed the use of arbitrary grid cells as the basis for an information system that could handle changes over time and support computerization. The report's conclusion cited Carl Steinitz and parallel work at Cornell.[9]

Transparent overlays, in themselves, were not new; the Graduate School of Design faculty included Jacqueline Tyrwhitt, who had featured map integration as a part of the textbook for the Town and Country Act in Great Britain in 1950.[10] Homer Hoyt made substantial use of transparent overlays in 1936 for housing surveys of Richmond, Virginia. For that matter, as Steinitz and his students described in 1976, there were examples of map overlay in the field of landscape architecture stretching back to Warren Manning in 1913.[11] What is important is not who was first, but how these well-known techniques came together at the moment when computer techniques were being developed. Lewis and McHarg preached the integration of diverse sources, a key element for GIS development. McHarg's approach was interpreted by some to imply a cumulative overlay of black and white maps representing limitations.[12] Any area left uncovered by the black zones of this simplified technique had no restrictions to the particular land use. In fact, McHarg, in his book as in his presentation at Harvard, used a variety of combination techniques, though specified somewhat imprecisely. Both McHarg and Lewis put substantial faith in the integrative role of the designer in looking at the whole and seeing patterns, a role that still defies direct translation to computer software.

The visits to Harvard from these three prominent landscape planners provided a survey of the state of the art to the group that emerged at the Laboratory. This interaction and sharing of techniques shows that it is fruitless to choose one or another as the origin of GIS. There was a collective process of communication spanning decades of experience, and rapid transfer of innovation between dispersed centers of activity.

Doing projects

Howard Fisher had expected that the Laboratory would become closely linked to the instructional process in planning and other disciplines at Harvard. This linkage succeeded most directly with the Department of Landscape Architecture. Research in the Laboratory setting merged with the teaching mission for environmental planning. Carl Steinitz (see sidebar), who was initially appointed both in the Laboratory and Landscape Architecture, started off doing projects with the aid of computer mapping. The work on technological innovations combined with research and consulting on environmental analysis and on models of urbanization and change. Each year, Steinitz's studio project course would direct its attention to another region and to the concerns of different clients. This practical project would provide the framework to continue to test the limits of current technology.

Carl Steinitz

Trained as an architect at Cornell University, Carl Steinitz worked in design firms and entered the PhD program at MIT specializing in urban design. He studied with Kevin Lynch (author of *The Image of the City*) and produced a dissertation on the connection between elements of the built environment and people's perceptions.[13] It was a time of expansive possibility in planning and architecture, with the idea that environmental meaning could be decoded by examining congruence between urban form and activity patterns across cities. The crucial question was whether the relationships could be perceived and understood by people living in cities. Yet, to decode all the kinds of connections required coding many variables and examining many potential patterns of connection. At a lunch in 1965, Steinitz sat next to Howard Fisher, who talked about the ability to make many maps rapidly with a computer.[14] From that conversation, Steinitz realized how computer mapping could provide crucial support for his research work, using SYMAP to make dozens of grid-coded map layers for his dissertation. The 1,800 one-acre cells covering downtown Boston became the statistical units for his analysis, prefiguring his long-term association with gridded environmental analysis.

Steinitz was hired in 1966 by both the Laboratory and the Department of City and Regional Planning. By the next year, he moved the academic affiliation to Landscape Architecture. He rose rapidly to become full professor by 1973. Virtually every year of the past 40 years he has conducted a studio project course that allows students to address complex environmental planning problems around the world. In 1967, he saw the potential for computer technology to assist in answering the question, "What can our future landscape be like?" He has continued to ask this question.

▲ Carl Steinitz explaining the Delmarva Project in 1967. *(Source: HGDSA Supplement 1967)*

DELMARVA PROJECT

In 1967, both the City and Regional Planning and Landscape Architecture departments chose to work on the Delmarva Peninsula (Delaware, Eastern Maryland, and a tip of Virginia) between Chesapeake and Delaware bays. This work involved some local groups, but the main client was the Conservation Foundation in Washington, D.C. Carl Steinitz applied SYMAP to this enterprise. This was the integration between the Laboratory and the Graduate School of Design that Fisher had assumed would occur.

The Delmarva Project had all the components of any GIS enterprise: base layers, computer-generated intermediaries (built on models applied to the base layers), and results. The base layers included topographic maps, soil maps, airphotograph interpretation, and the census for county-level statistics. (In 1960, there were not many tabulations for fine geographic detail outside cities.) The 14 counties, the shoreline, and the roads were entered as vector objects, but most of the environmental sources were coded according to grid cells 2 miles by 2 miles. The land use was recorded as the percentage of the cell that was forest or agriculture. The topographic relief was recorded as an "average" elevation in this flat terrain. In SYMAP, these grid cells were treated as areas, displayed by 20 cells (five across, four down due to the rectangular proportion of the standard printer typeface). Because the shoreline and roads were treated as vectors, the resolution does not appear to be as crude as a 2-mile grid would imply.

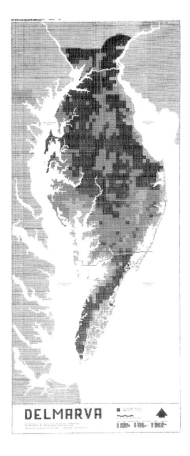 

◀ Soil potential for agriculture (left) compared with percent in agriculture (right). *(Source: Computer output 1967, photoreduced. By permission of Carl Steinitz, Harvard University Graduate School of Design)*

Steinitz realized that the computer could be used to construct layers as well as to display them. Following the interest of William Warntz in the gravity model of interaction, the project calculated a "population potential" for each grid cell. (The word "potential" here does not involve time; it is not a model of future population. Rather, it adopts the concept from physics of a field of interaction. While traditional demographic maps deal with the characteristics at that place, this field considers the influence of the whole region on each point. Environmental planners hoped to use it to deal with remoteness and traffic models.) Another layer, the wildlife potential map, used a detailed survey from a small area to establish correlations to cover type that could then be used to extrapolate the distribution over the whole area. From these examples, it is clear that the computer supported complicated analytical techniques; it was much more than a device to carry out the superposition of black-and-white layers on a light-table.

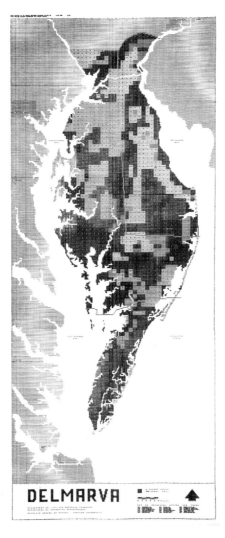

◀ **Potential for wildlife,** a map layer constructed from a limited local survey used to establish correlations to other distributions known for the whole study area. *(Source: Computer output 1967, photoreduced. By permission of Carl Steinitz, Harvard University Graduate School of Design)*

The main results of the Delmarva Project were produced by a map overlay of all the factors. First, each factor was rescaled so that the numerical values ranged from 0 to 9. Suitability for a particular use was assessed using a sum of factor scores with each factor weighted for its importance to that particular use. Different weightings demonstrated the different objectives of various interest groups. For example, the weights chosen to represent the interests of conservationists placed the highest value on forest density, coastal beach dunes, and high wildlife potential, with lower weights for prime agricultural soils and indented coastlines. Agricultural interests were represented by highest weight for the best soils and lower weights for most of the other factors. The students and faculty doing this project did not adopt any of the three models presented by Hills, Lewis, or McHarg. Perhaps due to the nature of the study area, the environmental constraints were not considered to be sharp black-and-white distinctions. Rather than solutions dictated by environmental constraints alone, this project allowed scope for the broader considerations that were the basis for the students' plans.

Areas for conservancy (based on ▶ criteria of conservationists) (left) contrasted with the areas preferred by agricultural interests (right).

(Source: Computer output 1967, photoreduced. By permission of Carl Steinitz, Harvard University Graduate School of Design)

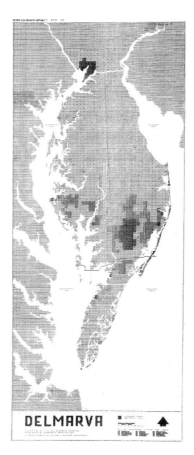

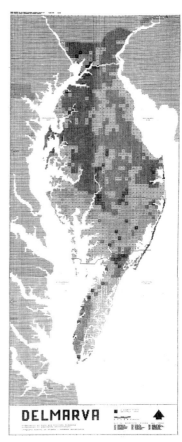

At the start of a course, a professor never knows which student will master the material, let alone how important one specific person may later become in the discipline. In the fall term of 1968, Steinitz brought the studio project to the Boston region with a course that built a grid-cell database of six thousand cells (1/9 square kilometer—fairly crude by current standards).[15] The class had twenty-three students. One was Jack Dangermond, who had completed a master's degree at the University of Minnesota the year before. His thesis for that degree cited the report about the visit of the three landscape planners (Hills, McHarg, and Lewis). Dangermond wanted to come to Harvard to learn more. As mentioned in the previous chapter, he worked as a student assistant on the air pollution study. Dangermond was fascinated with making maps using computers. He worked late nights with a personal energy (and caffeine consumption) that continues to this day. With two other students, Timothy Murray and Wayne Tlusty, Dangermond took on a project for the "America the Beautiful Fund" to plan recreational facilities in East Boston (perhaps one of the toughest locations to beautify).[16] While at Harvard, Dangermond made it clear to any who would listen that he saw a commercial role for these tools, and that he planned to go back to his hometown of Redlands, California, to set up this business. The one year in the Landscape Architecture program, working with Carl Steinitz and the Laboratory, had an influence on the development of ESRI in the management of projects as well as the technology.

◀ From left, Carl Steinitz, Peter Rogers, Jack Dangermond, and Wayne Tlusty participating in an "Urbanization and Change" class in 1968 in the basement of Robinson Hall at Harvard University. *(Source: photographer unknown; photograph from the collection of Carl Steinitz, used with permission)*

HONEY HILL AND ENVIRONMENTAL RESOURCE ASSESSMENT

As the explosion of public interest in the environment continued, political events moved very fast with passage of the National Environmental Policy Act (NEPA) and many similar local laws across the United States. Despite all the interest, there were no guidelines or procedures on how to conduct an environmental assessment. In 1969, Carl Steinitz and Peter Rogers, working with a group of landscape architecture students, took on a contract with the U.S. Army Corps of Engineers.[17] The study area was called Honey Hill, surrounding a flood-control reservoir near Swanzey, New Hampshire. They used a range of different techniques: traditional design (best professional judgment), linear programming, and simulation.

As one of the experimental methods, they developed alternatives to the weighted scores that had been used in Delmarva (and that would be used in many projects thereafter). For Honey Hill, they came up with a sequence of three-by-three matrices that permitted the team to provide nonlinear outcomes that depended on the interaction of variables, not just the sum of the values. These matrices were hard to fill in, but they do demonstrate the spirit of exploration of the period.

Projects such as Honey Hill developed expertise in evaluating natural resources and environmental interactions. Steinitz, David Sinton, and Allan Schmidt produced a report to the Public Land Law Review Committee in 1970 that provided a *General System for Environmental Resource Analysis*.[18] This document, coupled with many project reports in the public domain, influenced the development of environmental analysis (and regulation) in the United States and beyond. Multifactor environmental analysis executed on a computer became the expectation for high-profile public decisions, including the siting of nuclear power plants.

URBANIZATION AND CHANGE: MOVING OUTSIDE THE LABORATORY

Steinitz and his group of colleagues and students took on a study of urbanization south and east of Boston. This work began with student-sized projects in an area called Little's Creek. They combined simulation of potential growth with environmental assessment of its effects. After presenting this work in book form,[19] they obtained a major grant from the National Science Foundation (NSF). The study area expanded to include a number of municipalities, and the software was enhanced to include a number of new analytical capabilities.

All of this expanded activity occurred after the Ford Foundation grant had finished, after William Warntz had left Harvard, and after the Laboratory staff had begun to disperse (see chapters 4 and 6). This landscape architecture group also left the Laboratory. The NSF project had an office adjacent to the Laboratory, but the story of that project does not belong in this history of the Laboratory as such.

> **David Sinton**
>
> Originally from Northern Ireland, David Sinton arrived at Harvard as a master's student in planning. In 1967, he worked on the Delmarva Project with Steinitz and was hired as a graduate student assistant at the Laboratory. For a few years he was a research associate, doing the programming for GRID and project support for many diverse applications. He was assistant and associate professor of landscape architecture from 1969 to 1980. After leaving Harvard, he spent many years at Intergraph and is currently with Harris Corporation in Florida, working on spatial technology solutions for clients such as the U.S. Census Bureau.[20]

Software lineage: On from GRID

In the Delmarva Project, overlay analysis was produced by generating an attribute value for each point that represented a grid cell center, leading Steinitz and Sinton, his student assistant, to question the need for the vector model. Simple grid cells would be easier to conceptualize and manage. They also argued that, at sufficient resolution (and substantial computing cost), a grid could approximate any vector representation. Sinton pulled the conformant map production capability from SYMAP IV (SUBROUTINE FLATON) and spliced on a simple, grid-based input system. The result was called (somewhat unoriginally) GRID. GRID was sold by the Laboratory starting in 1969. Sinton rewrote GRID as IMGRID for landscape planning projects in the 1970s, this new more interactive package becoming the springboard for many software developments up to current commercial products.

Software to perform environmental analysis with grid cell data was probably developed independently at more sites than other more complex data structures. Since the basic concept had many origins, the exact order of appearance does not matter. What is interesting to track is how basic technical solutions turned into markers that can distinguish between different approaches. In this early era, computer memory was at a premium; the large computer mainframes had storage capacities much smaller than a megabyte (in 1966 more like a quarter that size). Each programmer had to compromise on the number of bits to assign to each cell. In the remote sensing arena, they settled on an eight-bit (one byte) storage unit for each cell. Some, like a software team at University of Wisconsin–Madison working on a package called GRASP, adopted a single bit (bit planes) for each cell.[21] In implementing the program GRID, Sinton started with the paneled mapping system of SYMAP that worked through the matrix incrementally, using a full computer word (four bytes) to each cell. The SYMAP programmers had various reasons for this profligate use of memory: first, standard FORTRAN did not provide for half-word entities, and each cell after interpolation contained a floating point attribute value that required four bytes. In GRID, Sinton reduced the memory use by switching to a two-byte integer, using FORTRAN code that would only work on the IBM line. This technical choice forced users to discretize floating point attributes, but with 32,767 possible values, it was much less limited than the one-bit or one-byte approaches. In addition to the size of the value stored in a cell, systems differed in the way that cells were organized. GRID had each layer arrive separately, while remote sensing systems had various formats of interleaving either by row or by cells (or pairs of cells) due to hardware limitations on the satellite sensor systems.

IMGRID

For the NSF project, Sinton decided to replace GRID with a totally rewritten system, called IMGRID. The turn toward an interactive package was in part prompted by resistance from some students to spend so much time learning programming and entering data and so little time doing planning. IMGRID de-emphasized map production, and favored analytical manipulations (what was later to be called map algebra). It moved on from the single theme of SYMAP to treat many distinct map "layers" at once. Each cell had its own record in a disk-based random access file (a proto-database) with room for over a hundred values for each cell. It was particularly easy to access all the values for a single cell, thus this software was designed for operations like weighted overlays. This organization did mean that the whole database had to be read to access any specific map. Operations based on neighborhoods had to be performed in memory, then written back into the database. IMGRID operated on the IBM mainframes and used the "short" two-byte integer hardware extensively. All attributes were coded into the limited resolution (32,767 possible values, no fractional values).

Dana Tomlin, while a graduate student in landscape architecture, worked under Sinton's supervision to code a set of algorithms for neighborhood operations and more complex operations. Using the immediate neighbors of a cell, for a start, various mathematical functions could compute the average value (a smoothing function), a minimum, a maximum, or whatever else was needed. By spreading outward from specified cells, a generalized set of buffers could be produced, within the limits of the cell resolution. At the more computationally demanding end, a viewshed operation was taken from the public-domain program VIEWIT[22] by the U.S. Forest Service.

TOWARD MAP PACKAGE AND BEYOND

The "Tomlin subroutines" of IMGRID used the IMGRID data structure only for storage. Tomlin restructured the input and output, going back to the single map per file organization of GRID. This one file per layer approach was much more flexible and expandable than Sinton's random access database. Tomlin wrote procedures that moved on from cell-by-cell overlay to variants of neighborhood analysis. He did continue to use two-byte integers to store each value. This development, continued while Tomlin was a PhD student at the Yale School of Forestry, created the Map Analysis Package (more commonly known as MAP or "MAP package"),[23] a program that went through many versions designed for many platforms from mainframes to minicomputers to the early generation of PCs. Originally written on an IBM mainframe, MAP could be easily ported to the early 16-bit minicomputers that appeared around this period. These computers came along with interactive timesharing access, a huge revolution in computer access for students as well as researchers. For some time in the 1980s the Laboratory was a distributor of MAP,[24] but MAP had many centers of distribution, unlike SYMAP, which was distributed solely by the Laboratory.

Another group of graduates from landscape architecture at Harvard around 1975 saw a commercial potential in loading IMGRID capabilities into a microcomputer that could be located in the user's office. Lawrie Jordan and Bruce Rado teamed up with Nick Faust, a professor at Georgia State University, to reprogram IMGRID for these small computers.[25] They founded a company called ERDAS in Atlanta (recently bought out by Leica Geosystems), and developed a sophisticated package of remote sensing and spatial analysis software that owed much to a common origin in Sinton's original GRID.

Tracing these linkages forward to the current day takes us away from the story of the early Laboratory for Computer Graphics, but it demonstrates the impact of the innovations at Harvard.

This book will stick to the Laboratory as an institutional entity, but it is quite apparent that the boundaries were frequently challenged. The environmental planning component of the early Laboratory incorporated itself much more successfully inside the Graduate School of Design, specifically in the Department of Landscape Architecture.

NOTES

1. Rachel Carson, *Silent spring* (London: Penguin, 1962).

2. Landscape Architecture Research Office, Graduate School of Design, Harvard University, *Three approaches to environmental resource analysis* (Washington, D.C.: The Conservation Foundation, 1967).

3. Environment Canada, brochure on Canada Land Inventory (Ottawa: Lands Directorate, ca. 1980). While Hills's method called for a single integrated map, CLI produced separate suitability maps for different uses (agriculture, forestry, recreation, and wildlife). Hence, CGIS required an overlay function.

4. G. Angus Hills, "The classification and evaluation of land for multiple uses," *Forestry Chronicle* 42 (1966): 1–25.

5. Jack Mabbutt and G. A. Stewart, "The application of geomorphology in resources surveys in Australia and New Guinea," *Revue de Géomorphologie dynamique* 14 (1963): 97–109; C. S. Christian and G. A. Stewart, "Methodology of integrated surveys," *Aerial Surveys and Integrated Studies,* (Toulouse, France: UNESCO, 1968), 233–280; G. A. Stewart, ed. *Land evaluation* (Melbourne: Macmillan, 1968).

6. Roger Tomlinson, "A geographic information system for regional planning," in *Land Evaluation*, ed. G. A. Stewart, 200–210 (Melbourne: Macmillan, 1968).

7. Ian McHarg, *Design with nature* (Garden City, N.Y.: Natural History Press, 1969).

8. Phillip Lewis, *Recreation in Wisconsin* (Madison, Wis.: State of Wisconsin, Department of Resource Development, 1963); Phillip H. Lewis, "Quality corridors for Wisconsin," *Landscape Architecture Quarterly* January (1964): 100–107.

9. Carl Steinitz, *Computer mapping and the regional landscape,* unpublished manuscript (Laboratory for Computer Graphics, Harvard Graduate School of Design, 1967). At Cornell, Donald Belcher was also exploring computer-based inventories.

10. Jacqueline Tyrwhitt, "Surveys for planning," in *Town and country planning textbook,* ed. Association for Planning and Regional Reconstruction (London: Architectural Press, 1950).

11. Carl Steinitz, Paul Parker, and Lawrie Jordan, "Hand-drawn overlays: Their history and prospective uses," *Landscape Architecture* 66 (1976): 444–455; Warren Manning, "The Billerica town plan," *Landscape Architecture* 3 (1913): 108–118. John Cloud has presented a series of talks about Homer Hoyt's use of overlay in the 1930s, as well as other accounts of the use of overlay in Nazi Germany. He contends that there is a "mystery" of "curiously uncontested origins" of the overlay method (for example, John Cloud, "Overlays of mystery: The curiously uncontested origins of analog map overlay (abstract)," in *Annual Meeting,* (Chicago, Ill.: Association of American Geographers, 2006). In historical research, one can always discover more antecedents. The question is which ones were actually known and functional at the time. This account demonstrates what the people at Harvard knew about and talked about.

12. Lewis D. Hopkins, "Methods of generating land suitability maps: A comparative evaluation," *American Institute of Planners Journal* 43 (1977): 386–400.

13. Kevin Lynch, *The image of the city* (Cambridge, Mass.: MIT Press, 1960); Carl Steinitz, "Congruence and meaning: The influence of consistency between urban form and activity upon environmental knowledge," (PhD thesis, MIT, 1967).

14. Date of lunch from Carl Steinitz, "Geographical information systems: A personal historical perspective, the framework for a recent project, and some questions for the future," in *European conference on geographic information systems* (Genoa, Italy: EGIS, 1993).

15. "Boston: Metropolitan Core," in *Red Book,* IV.43–IV.48 (Laboratory for Computer Graphics and Spatial Analysis, Harvard University, 1968).

16. "A systems analysis model for community open-space and recreational planning," in *Red Book,* IV.29– IV.33 (Laboratory for Computer Graphics and Spatial Analysis, Harvard University, 1968–1969). "Project directors" listed as Timothy Murray, Jack P. Dangermond, and Wayne Tlusty.

17. Timothy Murray, Peter Rogers, David Sinton, Carl Steinitz, Richard Toth, and Douglas Way, "Honey Hill: A systems analysis for planning the multiple use of controlled water areas," Institute of Water Resources 71-9; NTIS AD 736 343 & 344 (Army Corps of Engineers, 1971). Also in *Red Book,* v.29–v.33 (1969–1970).

18. Carl Steinitz, David Sinton, and Allan Schmidt, *A general system for environmental resource analysis,* Report to the Public Land Law Review Commission, Washington, D.C. (Cambridge, Mass.: Steinitz Rogers Associates, Inc., 1970).

19. Carl Steinitz and Peter Rogers, *A systems analysis model of urbanization and change: An experiment in interdisciplinary education.* (Cambridge, Mass.: MIT Press, 1970).

20. Bernard Niemann and Sondra Niemann, "Lines of code and more: David F. Sinton," *Geo Info Systems* (November/December 1993): 58–62; David Sinton, "Reflections on 25 years of GIS," *GIS World,* special insert (1991).

21. Kent S. Butler, William A. Gates, and Brent H. McCown, *A resource management system, GRASP: Description of a land resource data base,* IES Report 88 (Institute for Environmental Studies, University of Wisconsin–Madison, 1976).

22. M. R. Travis, G. H. Elsner, W. D. Iverson, and C. G. Johnson, *VIEWIT: Computation of seen areas, slope and aspect for land-use planning,* Technical Report PSW-11/1975 (USDA Forest Service, 1975).

23. C. Dana Tomlin, "Digital cartographic modeling techniques in environmental planning," (PhD thesis, Yale University, 1983); C. Dana Tomlin, "A map algebra," in *Harvard Computer Graphics Conference,* vol. 2, 1–46 (Cambridge, Mass., Harvard Graduate School of Design, 1983).

24. C. Dana Tomlin, "The IBM-PC version of the Map Analysis Package," *Internal report LCGSA-85-16* (Laboratory for Computer Graphics and Spatial Analysis, Harvard University, 1986).

25. Nickolas Faust, "Raster based GIS," in *The history of geographic information systems: Perspectives from the pioneers,* ed. Timothy Foresman, 59–72 (Upper Saddle River, N.J.: Prentice Hall, 1998).

FOUR

Spatial Analysis

The Laboratory added "Spatial Analysis" to its title in 1968, sparking many of its most important innovations. Spatial analysis took on many forms at the Lab. It had some highly theoretical components, and some detailed studies with specific programming to support them. William Warntz set the original direction by establishing a theory of the topological structure of surfaces, and this theme continued through most of the Laboratory's developments. The results can be traced in current GIS practice. In addition, issues of spatial allocation cut across all the disciplines working at the Lab. As usual in interdisciplinary work, some of the most important influences were not the ones anticipated.

Abstract visions

Fisher's Laboratory fits into a larger set of movements that changed the role of science in society. World War II and the effort to build nuclear weapons placed academic physicists in the unexpected position of conspiring to destroy the planet. The Cold War accelerated expenditures on science and development. At the same time, the university system expanded rapidly to accommodate new waves of veterans and, later, their children.

In reaction to the Manhattan Project, John Q. Stewart, an astronomer at Princeton University and president of the American Physical Society, sought a way to place physics in the service of immediate human goals. He proposed a "social physics," particularly applying mathematical models of gravitation to the study of aggregate social behavior. His wartime books on navigation included maps of the "population potential" of Europe and the United States, applying the gravity model.[1] Stewart's turn toward social issues had little impact on the influence of big money, huge equipment, and ever-more esoteric theory in physics, but it resonated with enough social scientists to make "social science" a part of the post-war redevelopment of American academic life.

Disciplines that studied people—sociology, anthropology, geography, psychology, and economics—had been around for 50 years or more. Each sought to become more "scientific"—interpreted as a need for demonstrable theory and more mathematical treatment of quantitative data. Theory and numbers were often conflated, and hard numbers were expected to lead inexorably to harder theories. Fisher, in his proposal to the Ford Foundation, aligned himself with this trend by emphasizing the role of factual information for planning. He also sought out research scholars who shared these goals, using the luncheon seminars and conferences mentioned in chapter 1.

When the Laboratory for Computer Graphics started operations in early 1966, the discipline of geography was being swept by a "quantitative revolution." Some of the shock troops of this movement had dispersed from the University of Washington to positions around the United States, but they were not the only members of the movement. At the American Geographical Society in New York City, Warntz worked directly with Stewart applying the mathematics of surfaces to macrogeography (a term that Stewart and Warntz[2] proposed for this form of rather abstract spatial analysis). Howard Fisher invited Warntz to speak in the first series of lunch speakers in spring 1966. Warntz came to Harvard by the fall of 1966 with the title of "Professor of Theoretical Geography and Regional Planning." He fulfilled Fisher's plan to appoint a geographer specialist in "factual information" as associate director. According to that plan, when Fisher retired in 1968, Warntz became director of the Laboratory. To signal the expanded scope of the theoretical purview of research, Warntz appended "and Spatial Analysis" to the name of the Laboratory.

William Warntz in 1967. In this staged picture, Warntz is pointing at a ▶
photograph of the physical model constructed from his calculations of
the population potential surface for the United States.

(Source: HGSDA Supplement 1967)

Geography at Harvard

When William Warntz was appointed to the faculty of the Department of City and Regional Planning in 1966, he asked for the title of "Professor of Theoretical Geography." This was a fair description of his academic specialization, but it was taken as a vindication by geographers. Just 18 years previously, Harvard University had disbanded its Department of Geography in a move that has been revisited again and again, particularly by geographers.[3] The reasons for closing the department and handing the elegant building that housed the Institute of Geographic Explorations to the Harvard–Yenching Library have been the subject of much recrimination. The official report from Harvard included intimations that geography involved mere description, and had no theoretical basis. In the dominant high-minded scientism of the post-war era, under the leadership of Harvard president James Bryant Conant, the lack of theory was damning.

The loss of the Harvard Department of Geography was just the first of many wounds to the discipline of geography. Eventually, geography disappeared from many of the well-established private universities where it had been first founded in the United States. William Morris Davis, one of the founders of the Association of American Geographers and first president of that organization in 1904, spent his whole career at Harvard. Geography found a new base at public universities farther west, but the loss at Harvard remains a story told over and over with varying versions. These retellings usually leave out the possibility that geography could have been restored after a gap of less than twenty years.

Warntz had a clear sense of the history of geography at Harvard. His appointment was taken as a signal that geography would return. Warntz planned first to establish a base in the Graduate School of Design, allied with the Department of City and Regional Planning. The Laboratory would become the research center, but eventually there would be a restoration of the Department of Geography. In partial response to the crucial matter of funding, Warntz and his assistants compiled a list of all the endowments of the Institute of Geographical Exploration to be restored. At its most expansive, the plan also hoped to retake the building that used to house that institute with its many maps carved in stone around the roofline alongside the names of classical geographers.

As with any wild dreaming of regaining the territory of some past empire, reality intruded. Harvard proved a more complex place than imagined. Warntz was not able to mobilize the forces (and funds) to advance the cause of geography. This complex story is a reminder that history is not inexorable; Harvard did, by some measure, accept that geography did have a theoretical component by appointing a professor of theoretical geography. The director of General Studies did commission course outlines for a number of course offerings with titles like "Introductory Geography"—from a number of Laboratory staff. The process was quite frustrating, and in the end fruitless. Formal titles and plans for courses are not enough to rebuild all the institutional network of support required to reconstitute a department.

In 2006, the combination of research and teaching interests across the Harvard campus had changed the tide. Harvard announced the creation of a "Center for Geographic Analysis," connected to the Institute for Quantitative Social Science. This development occurred outside of the Graduate School of Design in the Faculty of Arts and Sciences. Ironically, the newly named director of the center, whose research uses GIS for the history of China, has an office in the Harvard–Yenching Institute building. The university used the title "Harvard Returns to Geography" for the conference to launch this center.

Prior to his arrival at Harvard in 1966, Warntz was a fellow of the American Geographical Society (AGS) in New York. He used the term "geographic analysis" to describe his research. He had a strong string of publications in geographic journals,[4] and some existing research contracts that he brought to Harvard, particularly a grant from Evelyn Pruitt's geography program at the Office of Naval Research to study the properties of surfaces. While at AGS, Warntz hired Ernesto Lindgren, a Brazilian student in physics with strong mathematical training, and Michael Woldenberg, then a PhD student at Columbia University. This team moved with Warntz to the Laboratory in 1967. Frank Rens, who had studied with Waldo Tobler at the University of Michigan, joined them. In 1968, Warntz became director of the Laboratory and amended the name. For whatever combination of reasons, he did not stick to the term "Geographic Analysis," but used "Spatial Analysis" instead. At the time, this might not have been seen as a move of weakness. New interdisciplinary movements used a variety of different terms, so that "spatial" addressed a broader community than "geographic." Geography was challenged by the emergence of "regional science," and the planning community felt more connection to their common role in manipulating space. Around this time, Peter Haggett wrote a major book on "locational analysis" and collaborated on another on "network analysis." Many quantitative geographers collaborated on an important book edited by Brian Berry and Duane Marble titled *Spatial Analysis* that appeared in 1968.[5] Warntz was broadening the scope by adopting a focus on spatial relationships, and on the fundamentals of geometry.

To Warntz, spatial analysis implied the study of surfaces and the mathematical structure of spatial distributions. He brought along his contract with the Office of Naval Research for this highly theoretical enterprise, and hired a number of research assistants, postdoctoral fellows, and staff. In short order, this group produced

---

Another spatial analyst: Walter Isard

Warntz was not the only research scholar from the spatial analysis movement at Harvard in this period. Walter Isard spent much of his time during 1966–1968 working in an office over a theater in Harvard Square. He had the title of "Research Professor of Landscape Architecture" in the Graduate School of Design. Isard worked with landscape architects on the interaction between the environment and the economy at the same time that the Delmarva Project was under way (see chapter 3). Isard, a PhD graduate of the Harvard Department of Economics in 1949, had founded a Department of Regional Science at the University of Pennsylvania. His book, *Location and Space-Economy* (based on his PhD dissertation), was considered a major statement of the theoretical basis for approaching geographical and planning issues.[6] The *Papers of the Regional Science Association* became a major outlet for those working on spatial analysis. By this period, Isard had moved on to interregional applications of input–output analysis and integrating environmental concerns into economic analysis, but still had a considerable influence on a growing group of young modern geographers through his leadership in the Regional Science Association. Isard did not have a formal relationship to the Laboratory, but his presence demonstrates that the work at the Laboratory was not a fluke of personalities. These issues were in the air. The Laboratory for Computer Graphics was not the only center of activity, and other futures were possible. Isard asked the Graduate School of Design to found a Department of Regional Science, a request that went no further than Warntz's desire for a renewed geography presence.

Regional science did not emerge as an alternative to academic geography; there are no departments of regional science left. Walter Isard had grand visions—visions that he was not able to constrain within the discipline of regional science. He went on to found a second interdiscipline of peace science at Cornell University.

research reports. The *Harvard Papers in Theoretical Geography* includes more than 50 papers, most produced in the "Geography and the Properties of Surfaces" series, though some were placed in a "Geography of Income" series.[7] The distinction was mostly between sources of funding. The properties of surfaces work was supported by grant 00014-67A-0298-0004 from the Office of Naval Research. The geography of income was supported by grant GS-2833 from the National Science Foundation. Some papers broached abstruse mathematical theory (like the "Sandwich Theorem," about the topology of entities); some were morphological (like "Law and Order in the Human Lung," which applied stream ordering and geometric series analysis to a wide set of branching networks).

SURFACES: THEORY AND PRACTICE

Research on surfaces was the buzzword of the late 1950s and early 1960s. Each of the three grand American cartographers of this period—Arthur Robinson, George Jenks, and John Sherman—had published articles about surfaces or surface presentations. It was considered important to distinguish between the data measured and the underlying distribution. Confusingly, the word "surface" was used in this context to refer to the superficial, as opposed to the "deep" structure. In most disciplines, some form of this structuralist interpretation took hold. Noam Chomsky brought this distinction into prominence (as applied to the analysis of grammar and language) to provide some glue to the disparate social sciences, but the spirit of the age had already communicated the excitement of an abstract approach. So, to some extent, Fisher and Warntz were not unusual in stressing surfaces in their approaches to spatial distributions.[8] What was important for the Laboratory and its role in the intellectual debate was that Warntz took the interpretation of surfaces to a more fundamental level. Not only did he point out that the distribution might have an underlying continuity, but that the properties of the surface provided useful results for applications in wildly divergent disciplines.

While everyone else was struck by the numerical properties of surfaces, and saw their work as quantitative geography, Warntz's approach to surfaces started out with a recognition of topology. This fits into the importance placed in mathematics on invariance under transformation. The most fundamental properties are not those that depend on the particular values of numbers. Citing the work of mathematician Arthur Cayley (1859) and physicist J. Clerk Maxwell (1870), Warntz described the topology of surfaces. He adopted the terminology of the better known Maxwell (peaks, pits, passes, pales, ridges, courses, hills, and dales), but the argument about slope-lines and the indicatrix comes directly from Cayley.[9] This long-established (hundred-year-old) mathematics was still a fresh idea in geography.

Warntz was primarily interested in thematic surfaces covering a wide range of distributions such as population potential (human interaction viewed as gravitational fields), prices, income, and continentality. All these surfaces had ridges, passes, hills, and dales just like the 3D terrain of elevation above sea-level. His work on continentality demonstrates the abstraction implicit in his view of distributions. He was not content with the simple binary logic of water and land. He conceived of a continent as having some core bulk of land that was far from seas. All continents were not equal, but exhibited a degree of continentality. The surface of continentality was drawn on a projected map of the world, and also on a globe with plastic tape for the contours and the surface-specific lines.[10] This was a work of the broad brush of a theorist, and not calculated at any significant resolution owing to the lack of a detailed world shoreline database at this date, and to the complexities of calculating the generalized surface on a sphere.

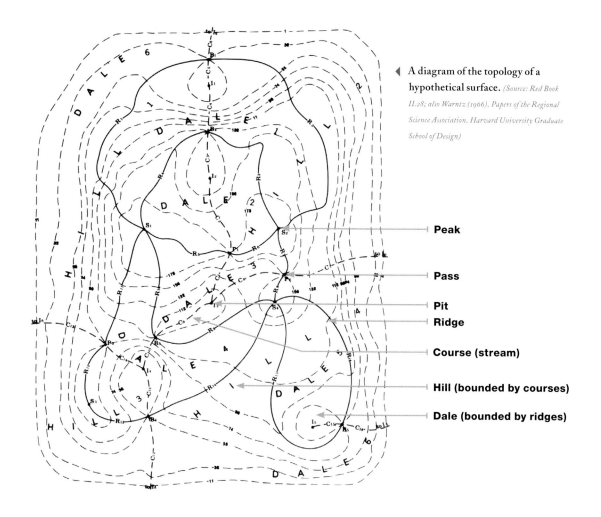

A diagram of the topology of a hypothetical surface. *(Source: Red Book II.28; also Warntz (1966). Papers of the Regional Science Association, Harvard University Graduate School of Design)*

Peak

Pass

Pit
Ridge

Course (stream)

Hill (bounded by courses)

Dale (bounded by ridges)

While others treated a surface as a thematic display of a distribution of numbers, Warntz saw the surface as a way to interrelate various properties of the distribution. Force, energy, and potential are given explicit meaning relative to the slope of a surface of the appropriate phenomenon, based on Stewart's gravitation analogue. Like other geographers of the period, location theory and central place theory were seen as the important intellectual agenda. If the correct surface were constructed, the hills and dales could be directly interpreted as market areas, zones of influence, and other geographic regionalizations. In 1968, Tom Peucker (now spelled Poiker) spent a semester at the Laboratory. He had written a PhD thesis in Germany on adjustments to location theory and central place theory for nonhomogeneous surfaces. The early work had all been done on the simplicity of a (hypothetical) uniform plane that was not even present in paradigmatic Iowa, the case study in one of August Loesch's classic works. Peucker came to the Laboratory with an ability to deal with complex surface problems. The international research agenda appeared to be directed toward adjusting simple theories to more and more complex settings.

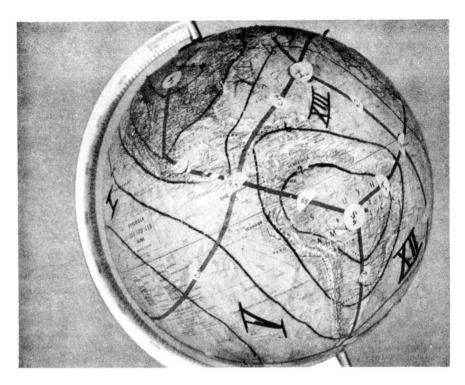

▲　Continentality of the world showing contours, ridges, and course lines. The highest peak is in Asia; the lowest pit is in the Pacific Ocean. Ridges link the continents; Panama is a "pass" where the ridge from North America to South America dips to its lowest point. *(Source: Red Book V.66, figure 3, Harvard University Graduate School of Design)*

Ironically, the primary outcome of studying the topology of surfaces was not to be applied to economic patterns or human settlement. Instead, the idea of surface-specific lines, particularly ridges and course lines, was applied to the structure of topographic surfaces. From a cartographic perspective, the surface of the earth remained a huge project to map. Much more money was expended on mapping the topographic surface than anything more theoretically interesting. Peucker, from his home base at Simon Fraser University in British Columbia, assembled a team that developed the triangular irregular network (TIN) data structure. His group had substantial interaction with the Laboratory in the next phase of the Laboratory (1970s). Jim Little, programmer of the ASPEX surface display program, joined Peucker along with Rob Fowler, who had programmed for David Sinton and Carl Steinitz. Randolph Franklin, a programmer for some of the early TIN work, came to Harvard for a PhD. Underlying the TIN approach originally was the idea that surface-specific lines were more important to preserve than other terrain information.[11] It is an argument about what could be generalized and what had to be invariant.

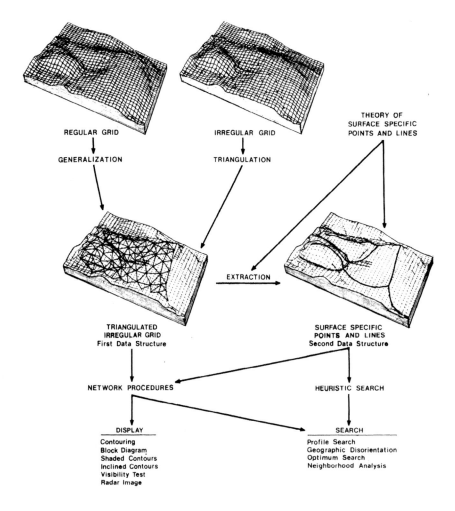

REGULAR GRID

IRREGULAR GRID

THEORY OF
SURFACE SPECIFIC
POINTS AND LINES

GENERALIZATION

TRIANGULATION

TRIANGULATED
IRREGULAR GRID
First Data Structure

EXTRACTION

SURFACE SPECIFIC
POINTS AND LINES
Second Data Structure

NETWORK PROCEDURES

HEURISTIC SEARCH

DISPLAY

Contouring
Block Diagram
Shaded Contours
Inclined Contours
Visibility Test
Radar Image

SEARCH

Profile Search
Geographic Disorientation
Optimum Search
Neighborhood Analysis

▲ The proposed Geographic Data Structure, showing the source of surface samples in a regular or irregular form, the triangular irregular "grid" (later network), and the surface-specific topological structure. *(Source: Peucker and Chrisman 1975, figure 9)*

LEAST COST PATHS OVER COMPLEX SURFACES

As a bomber navigator during World War II, Warntz had learned "pressure pattern flying," taking winds into account to find the fastest path. Perhaps this experience provided an impetus for all of his research on surfaces, since it figures in Stewart's text on navigation that Warntz used. The aircraft of the era were mostly unpressurized, so they had to stay down in the stormy troposphere. It was only after the war that pressurized aircraft could fly higher in the much smoother stratosphere. The practice of pressure pattern flying relied on weather maps that displayed isobars (lines of equal pressure). Winds in the northern hemisphere tend to flow clockwise around high-pressure cells, more or less parallel to the isobars. Navigators were equipped with paper maps, rulers, and slide rules, a much different technology than the geopositioning now so readily available. The weather maps, particularly over large oceans, were mostly surmise, and the navigator was called upon to adjust flight plans to account for the changes in conditions. Warntz used the question of choosing the shortest time path for a transatlantic flight as a way to open up a more general problem that he saw as a critical contribution from geography to "truly unified knowledge."[12]

Calculating a path across a complex surface was not a new problem, born in an era of aviation. The study of the refraction of light between two media is fundamental to optics (seventeenth-century physics), and the applications to geographic analysis are also long-established. American and British locational analysts point to various studies from the era of railroad construction in the late nineteenth century that attempted to provide a mathematical solution to the angular deflection that a small city might exert on a railroad line between two major hubs. One nineteenth-century work was translated from the German for the *Theoretical Geography* series.[13]

There was plenty of theory for this kind of calculation, but it amounted largely to hand-waving in undergraduate lectures. To actually apply these theories in a realistic setting was much more complicated than it seemed. Warntz demonstrated some graphical methods that worked with contour maps of the accumulated costs or the vectors of displacement of a wind field.[14] From 1967 though 1969,

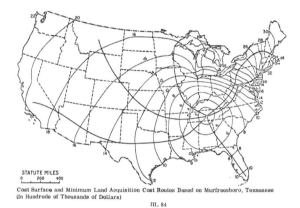

STATUTE MILES
0   200   400
Cost Surface and Minimum Land Acquisition Cost Routes Based on Murfreesboro, Tennessee (In Hundreds of Thousands of Dollars)

III. 84

▲   Cost surfaces for construction of interstate highways showing least cost paths from Lewiston, Montana and Murfreesboro, Tennessee. *(Source: Red Book III.84, Harvard University Graduate School of Design)*

Lindgren produced a series of papers on the least cost path problem. His arguments were based on a geometrical construction of normals to isolines (lines of constant cost). At the end of one paper, he quotes a sage geometer from the hazy past of mathematics to support his use of the geometric method:

"To operate with algebra is like navigating with a compass. To operate with geometry is like navigating with a compass, looking at the coastline."[15]

In a later paper, Lindgren had to admit that there were substantial flaws in his constructions: "Let us just say that the fog was heavy and visibility nil when we proposed the solution which appeared in Paper number 6."[16] Lindgren's geometry did not provide a direct implementation in the programming languages of the period.

Eventually, the computer opened a new method of practice, but not based on Lindgren's graphical constructions. Despite the complexities of programming required, the interpolation algorithm in SYMAP (see chapter 2) was elaborated to introduce barriers—artificial alterations to the distance metric of the space. The barriers changed the values of distance used to compute each interpolated value. Current software capabilities that construct least cost paths over surfaces can be traced back to this theoretical work at the Laboratory. Dana Tomlin's work on IMGRID and MAP package (in the 1970s) implemented an iterative exploration across the cost surface, accumulating the total cost surface using Dykstra's pivot point algorithm (incrementally pixel by pixel).[17] While applied in the field of environmental planning and landscape architecture, the theoretical work arose from other disciplines. The interaction between disciplines is a major contribution from this period in the history of the Harvard Laboratory. More efficient algorithms have been developed in later decades,[18] but the speed of recent computers and availability of cheap memory have blunted the importance of innovations of this kind.

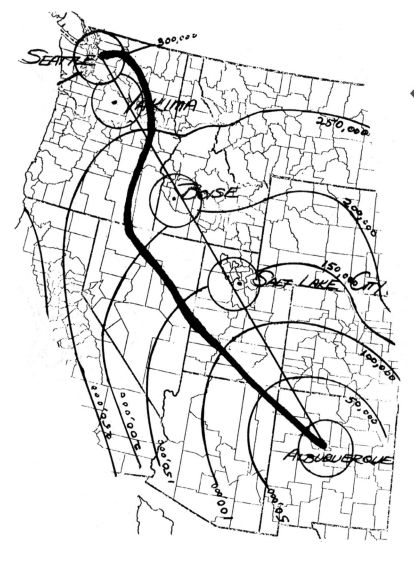

◀ Minimum man-boom flight path for a supersonic transport, Albuquerque to Seattle.

(Source: Red Book V.73, Harvard University Graduate School of Design)

EVEN MORE ABSTRACT MATHEMATICS: THE SANDWICH THEOREM

At the end of Warntz's tenure as director of the Laboratory in June 1971, he and his research team produced "Harvard Paper in Theoretical Geography" number 44, titled *The Sandwich Theorem—A basic one for geography*.[19] This paper applies some abstract mathematics to a geographical problem. The various components of the paper demonstrate the combination of skills in this part of the Laboratory, and give an idea of the research process.

This paper had five distinct sections, with separate authorship. Warntz wrote the first, an unnumbered introduction of four pages. The Sandwich Theorem can be stated in a short piece of mathematical language:

"Given any three sets in space, each of finite outer Lebesgue measure, there exists a plane which bisects all three sets."

To translate and apply it to geography, this asserts that any three thematic distributions (the Lebesgue measure refers to some property like population, income, or area) can be bisected by a single plane. On a map, this would mean a line. On a globe, the plane would slice through the solid to produce a great circle (if it passed through the center of the earth) or a small circle. Warntz was interested in regionalization—a geographical procedure to divide a distribution into distinct objects. The divisions would equally divide any distribution, producing a geographic median (the midpoint of the distribution). He connected this basic capability to problems such as redistricting where a series of equal-sized objects needed to be created. Of course, most political districts do not use straight line boundaries. Warntz was interested that there were many possible dividing lines.

Why is this called the Sandwich Theorem? The idea is that you might have three distributions: one the bread, another the butter, another the meat of a sandwich. You may have been faced with sharing such a sandwich with your sibling. How do you divide it equally between two suspicious and hungry boys? Could it be possible to divide the bread equally, but not the meat? This mathematical theory just presents an existence proof. No matter how badly distributed, there does exist a single straight cut of the knife that will divide the bread, the butter and the meat equally. Like all existence proofs, it is a bit infuriating; it does not necessarily tell you where to slice the sandwich.

Following the introduction, there was a translation from French to English of Hugo Steinhaus's article (see sidebar, next page) from 1945, filling twenty-six unnumbered pages. This is a typical piece of mathematical writing with lemmas and proofs. The problem leading to the Sandwich Theorem is attributed to Steinhaus, who phrased the problem as dividing a cake among n people; the case of $n=2$ was solved by one of Steinhaus's students in 1933. One can imagine this eminent mathematician hiding from the Nazis throughout the long world war, refining his arguments and preparing a paper for publication as soon as peace restored mathematics to its proper place in the world.

Thirty pages into the report, the page numbers start at one with a section by Lindgren, titled "A geometric analysis concerning the sandwich theorem." He argues that the theorem is "nothing more than a simple conclusion drawn from the study of angles" (p. 6). At the end, he talks about producing a program to implement the construction of sandwich divisions using two approaches advanced by mathematicians. In the next section, Eduardo Lozano (a recent graduate of the School of Design) presented a simple algorithm that maintains a cutting line perpendicular to the x-axis. The following section presented a technique that varied the angle around the first distribution until the division was equal enough. This algorithm was written by Luisa Bonfiglioli, a mathematician at the Israel Institute of Technology in Haifa.

Part IV of the report presented an implementation of Bonfiglioli's approach in a program written by Kathy Kiernan. She used the counties of the 48 conterminous states as the study area, with 1960 data of population and income borrowed from the work of David Neft at the University of Pennsylvania (also a student of Warntz while at Columbia University). Neft had published work on centrography (measures of the mean center and dispersion) of various spatial distributions for the United States. This data had been used by Warntz to estimate

Hugo Steinhaus: early spatial analyst

When taking abstract mathematical research into an applied field like geography, it is not at all clear which ideas will be more fruitful than others. While some of the movement for a quantitative geography simply applied statistical techniques to geographic datasets, Warntz's spatial analysis group reached more deeply into mathematical theory, finding great attraction in Hugo Steinhaus's basic work on divisions of sets, retermed the "Sandwich Theorem" by Lindgren. Warntz inspired some of his undergraduate students to produce their thesis work by borrowing from other works of Steinhaus. For example, Stephen Selkowitz, of the class of 1970, wrote a paper[20] on locating antipodal points with the same pair of attribute values. Steinhaus and his students had generated an existence proof of this construct years before.

The work of Steinhaus and his colleagues has provided a starting point for some notable advances in automated cartography and spatial analysis. Steinhaus and his student Julian Perkal did work on epsilon sets that provided the basis for the use of a tolerance in overlay software (see chapter 8). Also, Steinhaus's question *"How long is the Vistula River?"* was the starting point for Benoit Mandelbrot to write *"How long is the Coast of Britain,"*[21] and thus to develop the theory of fractals. While the Sandwich Theorem remains a mathematical curiosity, fractals became a huge academic enterprise, sparking doctoral dissertations, articles, symposia, and whole careers.

Steinhaus (1887–1972) was born in the Carpathian Mountains region of Poland (then a part of the Austrian Empire), studied at Lwow, then received his PhD in 1911 at Göttingen under the supervision of renowned mathematician David Hilbert. His work was strongly influenced by the visiting Henri Lebesgue, not the star-studded faculty at Göttingen. When Poland was recreated, Steinhaus joined the faculty at Lwow. The mathematical community in this city met in the Scottish Café, known for good pastries and marble tables to write on with their pencils. They produced a list of the hundred top problems in mathematics that Steinhaus published after the Second World War. (The "sandwich problem" was problem 123; the group didn't stop at 100.) For an intellectual of Jewish origins, the political climate of the 1940s was dangerous. After hiding out in the mountains during the German occupation, Steinhaus joined the faculty at Wroclaw. As an applied mathematician, he dealt with early game theory, probability of paternity, and a collection of mathematical problems called *Mathematical Snapshots*.[22] Unlike his more Platonist colleagues, Steinhaus believed that mathematics provided a universal language for the world around him, not some remote esoteric universe. In that philosophical belief, Steinhaus provided guidance to the spatial analysts at the Laboratory and around the world.

the population potential surface of the United States, and the 3,070 cards were parked on the Laboratory's mountable disk pack for other projects. (Population potential, measured in people per mile, is a theoretical surface of the gravitational "energy" that the whole population would exert on each given location, just as gravitational potential sums up the attraction of all bodies in a physical setting.) Kiernan's code used a common numerical programming technique of searching for a minimum by successive halving of the search space. As long as the distribution is reasonably continuous, this algorithm will find solutions quickly. The program had one main section that read the data and put the current attribute into the arrays in the correct locations. Then the main program invoked a routine called FIB to explore the search space. (The name of the routine is a small homage to Fibonacci, the major Italian mathematician of the thirteenth century and long associated with iterative expansion of series.) FIB used FUN (the actual division calculation) to evaluate how much of the attribute was to the left or right of a particular dividing line. FIB would split the difference in the appropriate direction to locate a 50–50 split as closely as possible. Since there were only 3,070 county data points, it is not possible to get the sum of population or income to split perfectly. This is just due to the discretization, not any flaw in the mathematics of the theorem. The implementation of the splitting lines used the somewhat unstable $Y = mX + b$ form, not the more tractable $aX + bY + c = 0$ form. Practically, this means that vertical lines would not be quite as accurately calculated; however, the searching strategy was probably robust enough to not be bothered. It is interesting that all this geometric work was done on latitude–longitude coordinates as if they were planar. This produces a bias in the direction of lines (roughly related to the cosine of latitude). In line with common usage at the time (and a certain North American flouting of mathematical conventions), west longitude was treated as positive. This meant that the trigonometry was flipped over, but that didn't change the operation of the algorithm. There is no report on how much computer time it took to produce these solutions. Each trial had to evaluate all 3,070 counties all over again. There is no record of how many iterations it took to decide on the best-fit cutting line. By 1971, floating point calculations were fairly rapid, and central-processing intensive jobs were not particularly costly.

When he left the Laboratory, Warntz moved to the University of Western Ontario to become chair of the Geography Department. He continued to work on spatial analysis until his death in 1988. In the 1980s, Warntz was writing the manuscript for a book to be titled *Distance in the Man-made Environment;* it did not get published, though he had some correspondence with Penguin Books on possible publication.

MORPHOLOGY OF STREAMS AND BRANCHING SYSTEMS

Ten of the papers in the *Theoretical Geography* series concerned the study of branching systems, particularly streams. Much of this work was produced by Michael Woldenberg, a physical geographer who arrived at the Laboratory with a fresh PhD from Columbia University. Woldenberg attempted to integrate the human geography of central place theory with the physical geography of river systems and glaciers.[23] The common thread was the study of branching ratios and other measures of networks and hierarchies in trees and other natural structures. This spilled over to include the branching networks inside the human body in the best-known title *Law and Order in the Human Lung,*[24] coauthored by a team of physiologists from Birmingham, England. The reference to the famous Nixon-era slogan uses the technical meanings of stream-ordering and the supposed laws of central place theory, all applied inside the human body. The combination was startling, to say the least. Streams are ordered in a number of different ways, but the idea is to capture the different spatial arrangements of branching. These relate to the physical geography of the substrate, the hydrological regime of the region, and an overall energy-minimizing constraint. Woldenberg produced some detailed studies of specific streams, and overarching theoretical treatments of hierarchy and branching systems. A common measure is the "Strahler order" of the stream, a measure that starts at 1 at the headwaters and increases whenever two same-order streams join.

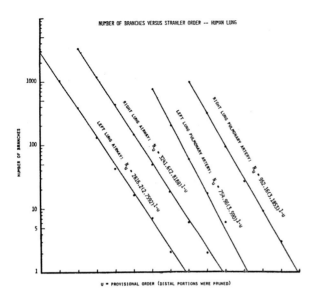

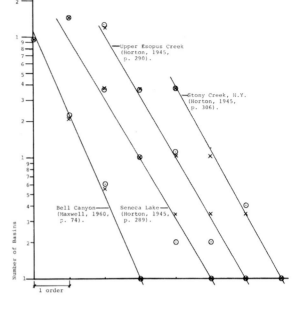

▲   Regression line plots from the study of the airways of the lung and the arteries serving the lung (left) and a series of river basins (right). In both studies, the Strahler order of the stream is compared to a measure of the area drained. *(Source: Harvard Papers in Theoretical Geography, number 41, figure 3; paper 13, figure 3.)*

Warntz connected his theory of surfaces to this analysis of branching networks, an important connection often overlooked by the narrowness of professional specialization. One element of this work was the search for ratios that remain constant over space or time. Warntz developed a measure (called Q, in homage to Stewart) to measure the correspondence of the ratio of population potential and income over a century or more. The principles of allometry from biology were connected to his geographic analysis. Geoffrey Dutton, then a planning master's student who was drawn into the Lab for what was to become a long and varied path of research, worked with Warntz on this analysis. Whereas much of the other work appeared only in the internal reports of the Laboratory, in 1973 Dutton edited a special issue on allometry in *Ekistics*,[25] a journal with a wide range of interests dealing with human issues in design.

Many scholars expected that the use of geometric measures and numerical computing would bring together the previously distinct human and physical components of the discipline. William Bunge's book *Theoretical Geography* was taken as the beginning of a geography directed toward spatial laws. Woldenberg is one of the few scholars who actually attempted to bridge the divide; he wrote about systems of cities and river systems within the same article. Sadly, the branches of geography are now even more divided over method and theory than they were in the 1960s. The spatial laws proved hard to find, and the discipline of geography moved in other directions.

Space allocation

At the peak of activity (1968–1970, more or less), the Laboratory had 45 official employees, plus numerous visitors and hangers-on. Many discussions were informal, cutting across the seeming divisions of discipline, funding source, or topic of application. Pure mathematics sounded exciting, and provided a common framework to guide the discussions.

One issue attracted substantial interest by teams that cut across disciplinary origins. It concerned the spatial allocation of functions in a building or on a site, a concern of architects and other designers at the conceptual stage of design. Each team formulated the problem slightly differently, and some software was written to implement some of these algorithms, though not taken to a polished level for distribution.

GRASP: GENERATING PLANS

Eric Teicholz, a master's student in architecture at the Harvard Graduate School of Design, produced a program called GRASP for his thesis project in 1968. GRASP (Generation of Random Access Site Plans) generated floorplans with a combination of architecturally relevant constraints and a random component. The program worked with modules of 15-by-15-foot rectangular building parts, including exterior and interior walls. The constraints included a distinction between sheer walls and wet walls, no windows on the inside of the building (actually more tricky than it might sound), assured solar access (one hour of sunlight on December 21), and no bedroom windows facing living room windows within 45 feet. These rather specific constraints were developed for the kind of modular housing

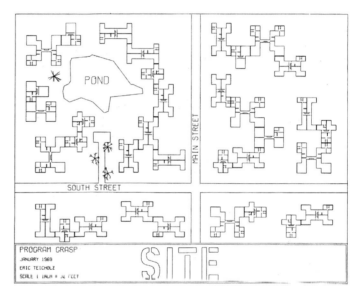

▲ Examples of the output of the GRASP program (January 1968), a part of **Eric Teicholz's master's project.** *(Source: Red Book IV.55, Harvard University Graduate School of Design)*

made popular by the Habitat experimental project associated with the Montreal Expo in 1967.

GRASP produced vector graphics that looked like rudimentary architectural drawings, produced on plotters and refresh graphics screens. The Laboratory did not have any of these expensive devices; instead, Teicholz worked on the interactive PDP-1 graphics computer controlled by Ivan Sutherland. Sutherland's Sketchpad system (see chapter 5) opened up a world of graphic interaction just beginning to be recognized. Teicholz joined a highly creative and competitive collection of interdisciplinary graduate students tied together by an interest in graphics.

Teicholz became a research fellow at the Laboratory, and continued to work on architectural visualization (a program called OTOTROL; see chapter 5) and practical space allocation programs linked to cost estimation and the scheduling of construction projects. In 1968, working with Perry, Dean, and Stewart, a local architecture firm, Teicholz developed COMPROGRAPH, a suite of programs for architecture offices that included a schematic approach to space allocation. Sliding away from the Laboratory for a few years, he did a substantial amount of work in the private sector with his firm Design Systems. This company produced a vector graphics architectural design package for the PDP-15 called ARK-2 that bundled the capabilities of OTOTROL, COMPROGRAPH, project-planning (critical-path) algorithms, and some cost-estimation software. During this commercial development period, Teicholz continued to teach graphic design and computer usage in architecture, and returned to the Laboratory full-time as associate director in 1972.

◀ Eric Teicholz operating a gantry-style OTOTROL digitizer (1967). The OTOTROL hardware used bar-code readers to measure the movement along both axes, rather than the electronic cursor of more expensive digitizing hardware. *(Source: HGSDA Supplement 1967)*

RUMOR: RANDOM GENERATION OF PLANS

Allen Bernholtz, hired as the research associate with connections to the Architecture Department, worked with Kathy Kiernan, the programmer who worked on SYMAP and on the spatial analysis grant projects (see earlier this chapter), to produce a program called RUMOR in 1968–1969. Given a matrix of the desired distances between pairs of functions (living room to dining room, living room to bedroom, kitchen to dining room, and so forth) this program would generate random floorplans. Rather than building its own graphics display, the program generated SYMAP input packages. The RUMOR output was submitted to SYMAP to produce the visible results. RUMOR made no attempt to screen out bad plans or to impose constraints.

Bernholtz also experimented with packaged programs for architectural space allocation of a more mathematical nature imported from other centers.

LOKAT: ANOTHER PROGRAM TO GENERATE PLANS

Bernholtz continued his work on space allocation through 1969 and 1970 with a project called LOKAT (pronounced "locate"). In contrast to the purely random strategy of RUMOR, LOKAT provided mechanisms to enforce certain relationships (largely topological constraints: "must be together," "may be together," "must be apart"). Each function had a differential buffer, and controls specific to the circumstances. The results were scored with a measure of goodness of fit to the desired distances. LOKAT continued to use SYMAP as its output interface.

The LOKAT project had some participation from a design firm (Perkins & Will in White Plains, N.Y.) working on hospitals and other complex building projects. Bernholtz moved on to a faculty position in Canada, and produced a LOKAT II with support from the National Research Council of Canada in 1970 and onward.

OPTIMIZING A MATRIX

Underlying the calculation of spatial allocation, the matrix of relationships may or may not have a clean projection into two dimensions of a plan. Ernesto Lindgren recognized the basic mathematics. With Carl Steinitz, he wrote a paper[26] that provided a serious consideration of the spatial transformations to collapse the N-dimensional matrix of distances between each activity and the two or three dimensions of a real building plan. As with much of Lindgren's work, he had a geometric solution, involving projection of the multidimensional space onto the drawings. Although this approach was not coded into a computer program, it shows the cross-fertilization between spatial analysts and designers.

Much later on, around 1976, Dutton did some more work on allocation using a spatial strategy. His ALLOC program was designed for assigning demand to service centers based on proximity. It was run for coronary care centers in Massachusetts and Sweden, as well as the industrial facilities of the Air Products Corporation. This practical turn reflects the changes that the Laboratory went through following the Warntz years.

NOTES

1. John Q. Stewart, *Coasts, waves and weather* (Boston: Ginn and Company, 1945); John Q. Stewart and Newton L. Price, *Marine and air navigation* (Boston: Ginn and Company, 1944); John Q. Stewart, "The development of social physics," *American Journal of Physics* 18 (1950): 239–253.

2. John Q. Stewart and William Warntz, "Macrogeography and social science," *Geographical Review* 48 (1958): 167–184.

3. Neil Smith, "Academic war over the field of geography: The elimination of geography at Harvard, 1947–1951," *Annals of the Association of American Geographers* 77 (1987): 155–172; Saul B. Cohen, "Reflections on the elimination of geography at Harvard, 1947–1951," *Annals of the Association of American Geographers* 78 (1988): 148–151.

4. For example, William Warntz, "Transportation, social physics and the law of refraction," *Professional Geographer* 9, no. 4 (1957): 2–7; William Warntz, "Transatlantic flights and pressure patterns," *Geographical Review* 51 (1961): 187–212; William Warntz, "A new map of the surface of population potentials for the United States," *Geographical Review* 54 (1964): 170–184; William Warntz, "The topology of socio-economic terrain and spatial flows," *Papers, Regional Science Association* 17 (1966): 47–61.

5. Peter Haggett, *Locational analysis in human geography* (London: Edward Arnold, 1965); Peter Haggett and Richard J. Chorley, *Network analysis in geography* (London: Edward Arnold, 1969); Brian J. L. Berry and Duane F. Marble, *Spatial analysis* (Englewood Cliffs, N.J.: Prentice Hall, 1968).

6. Walter Isard, *Location and space economy: A general theory relating to industrial location, market areas, land use, trade and urban structure* (Cambridge, Mass.: MIT Press, 1956).

7. A complete listing of the *Harvard papers in theoretical geography* is contained on the CD that accompanies this book.

8. McHaffie argues that surfaces provided an important metaphor, but the user community was also prepared to accept it. Patrick McHaffie, "Surfaces: Tacit knowledge, formal language, and metaphor at the Harvard Lab for Computer Graphics and Spatial Analysis," *International Journal of Geographical Information Science* 14 (2000): 755–773.

9. William Warntz, "The topology of socio-economic terrain and spatial flows," *Papers, Regional Science Association* 17 (1966): 47–61; William Warntz and Michael Woldenberg, "Concepts and applications: Spatial order," *Harvard papers in theoretical geography 1* (Laboratory for Computer Graphics and Spatial Analysis, Harvard University, 1967); Arthur Cayley, "On contour and slope lines," *The London, Edinburgh and Dublin Philosphical Magazine and Journal of Science* 18 (1859): 264–268; J. Clerk Maxwell, "On hills and dales," *The London, Edinburgh and Dublin Philosphical Magazine and Journal of Science* 40 (1870): 421–427.

10. "Global index of continentality," in *Red Book*, V.62–V.67 (Laboratory for Computer Graphics and Spatial Analysis, Harvard University, 1970); Chistopher W. Warntz, "The continent problem-geography and spatial variance," *Harvard papers in theoretical geography 9* (Laboratory for Computer Graphics and Spatial Analysis, 1968).

11. Thomas Peucker, Mark Tichenor, and Wolf-Keiter Rase, "The computer version of three relief representations," in *Red Book*, VI.93–VI.94 (Laboratory for Computer Graphics and Spatial Analysis, Harvard University, 1971); Thomas Peucker and Nicholas Chrisman, "Cartographic data structures," *The American Cartographer* 2 (1975): 55–69; Robert Fowler and James Little, "Automated extraction of irregular network digital terrain models," *Proceedings of an International Conference on Computer Graphics and Interactive Techniques*, (Chicago Ill.: ACM-SIGGRAPH, 1979).

12. *Red Book* (Laboratory for Computer Graphics and Spatial Analysis, Harvard University, 1968), III.82. This source cites William Warntz, "Transatlantic flights and pressure patterns," *Geographical Review* 51 (1961): 187–212; William Warntz, "A note on surfaces and paths: Applications to geographical problems," *Discussion paper 6* (Ann Arbor: Michigan Inter-University Community of Mathematical Geographers, 1965).

13. Eduard Lill, *Das Reisegesetz und seine Anwendung auf den Eisenbahnverkehr* (Wien: Commissions-verlag von Speilgelhagen und Schurich, 1891); Thomas K. Peucker, "The law of travel and its application to rail traffic, translation of Eduard Lill 1891," *Harvard papers in theoretical geography 25* (Laboratory for Computer Graphics and Spatial Analysis, Harvard University, 1969).

14. *Red Book* (Laboratory for Computer Graphics and Spatial Analysis, Harvard University, 1968), III.85–III.86.

15. C. Ernesto S. Lindgren, "A minimum path problem reconsidered," *Harvard papers in theoretical geography 28* (Laboratory for Computer Graphics and Spatial Analysis, 1969), 10.

16. C. Ernesto S. Lindgren, "The use of geodesic curvature in the determination of geodesic lines," *Harvard papers in theoretical geography 29* (Laboratory for Computer Graphics and Spatial Analysis, 1969), 3–4.

17. C. Dana Tomlin, *Geographic information systems and cartographic modeling* (Englewood Cliffs, N.J.: Prentice Hall, 1990).

18. David H. Douglas, "Least cost path in GIS," *Research note 61* (Department of Geography, University of Ottawa, 1993).

19. William Warntz, C. Ernesto S. Lindgren, Katherine Kiernan, Luisa Bonfiglioli, and Eduardo Lozano, "The sandwich theorem—A basic one for geography," *Harvard papers in theoretical geography 44* (Laboratory for Computer Graphics and Spatial Analysis, Harvard University, 1971). Contains a translation of Hugo Steinhaus, "Sur la division des ensembles de l'éspace par les plans et des ensembles plans par des cercles," *Fundamenta Mathematica* 33 (1945): 245–263.

20. Stephen E. Selkowitz, "Geography and an existence theorem: A cartographic computer solution in the localization on a sphere of sets of equally-valued antipodal points for two continuous distributions with practical applications to the real earth," *Harvard papers in theoretical geography 21* (Laboratory for Computer Graphics and Spatial Analysis, 1968).

21. Benoit Mandelbrot, "How long is the coast of Britain?" *Science* 156 (1967): 636–638.

22. Hugo Steinhaus, *Mathematical snapshots,* new revised ed. (Oxford: Oxford University Press, 1960).

23. William Warntz and Michael Woldenberg, "Concepts and applications: Spatial order," *Harvard papers in theoretical geography 1* (Laboratory for Computer Graphics and Spatial Analysis, Harvard University, 1967); Michael Woldenberg, "Spatial order in fluvial systems: Horton's laws derived from mixed hexagonal hierarchies of drainage basin areas," *Harvard papers in theoretical geography 13* (Laboratory for Computer Graphics and Spatial Analysis, Harvard University, 1968).

24. Michael Woldenberg, Gordon Cumming, Keith Harding, Keith Horsfield, Keith Prowse, and Shiam Singhal, "Law and order in the human lung," *Harvard papers in theoretical geography 41* (Laboratory for Computer Graphics and Spatial Analysis, Harvard University, 1970).

25. Geoffrey Dutton, ed. "Size and shape in the growth of human communities" *Ekistics* 36, no. 215 (1973).

26. C. Ernesto S. Lindgren and Carl Steinitz, "Graphical representation of a matrix with application in spatial location," *Harvard papers in theoretical geography 33* (Laboratory for Computer Graphics and Spatial Analysis, Harvard University, 1969).

FIVE

Graphic Expressions

Though its early efforts relied on the line printer as its graphic output device, the Laboratory also produced software for the vector graphics devices of the day. OTOTROL explored architectural rendering of three-dimensional objects with wireframe drawings; SYMVU displayed surfaces with profile lines correctly hidden from a vantage point; CALFORM filled polygons laboriously with plotter pens for choropleth mapping. These efforts brought the Laboratory closer to the cutting edge of computer graphics.

Computer graphics

The title "Laboratory for Computer Graphics" was a bit deceptive. Howard Fisher had not conceived it as a center to develop general techniques for drawing pictures with computers. He had much more specific goals in mind, mostly related to an overhaul of thematic cartography, as described in the earlier chapters. It was he who had adopted the line printer as an output medium, tying the logic of SYMAP (see chapter 2) to a crude cellular display technique. At other centers such as David Bickmore's Experimental Cartography Unit at the Royal College of Art in London, the reproduction of top-quality cartography took priority. The costs were high, and the devices were not available anywhere else. In contrast, Fisher was making a calculated tradeoff, dependent on the technology available at that particular time. Yes, the line printer produced low-resolution graphics, but it was fast and universally available. Fisher's choice tapped an immediate market, but it also excluded access to the highest-quality products.

In the long run, such a tradeoff leads to stagnation. Research teams should predict how the world of graphics technology would evolve and position themselves ahead of these developments by building prototypes using more advanced technology. This strategy would fulfill the spirit of a "laboratory." Fisher did not restrict the Laboratory to the line printers, since dropping prices would bring new devices into the reach of a larger audience. Fortunately, other research groups at Harvard did have access to cutting-edge technology, and Laboratory members took the opportunity to experiment. The most striking images produced by the Laboratory in this period came from vector plotters, using either ink pens or beams of light. Beyond the high-quality graphics, these devices forced the programmers to rethink the structure of spatial data.

SKETCHPAD AND THE LURE OF INTERACTION

In 1966, as the Laboratory was being created, Harvard University hired Ivan Sutherland as an associate professor of electrical engineering. He had finished a PhD at MIT in 1963, based on his Sketchpad system—a revolutionary combination of a solid-state computer called TX-0, an interactive operating system, and a graphics screen.[1] The hardware was advanced, and the software was radically different from the mainframes of the era. Visual access to a computer was the most radical concept.

Sutherland had done this work at the MIT Lincoln Labs facility, a shadowy outpost where academic research melted softly into the military-industrial complex. This had been the site of radar research during World War II, of Norbert Wiener's research on gunnery that led to his 1948 book *Cybernetics*,[2] and of advanced computer hardware such as WHIRLWIND, with its ferrite core memory. Lincoln Labs had much to do with the early burst of electronics industry that developed in a ring along Route 128 around Boston. The TX-0 that Sutherland worked on, and its progeny TX-2, became commercialized as the PDP-1 and PDP-6 by the fledgling Digital Equipment Corporation. Sutherland integrated the computer with a graphic display, and overthrew the batch mentality in favor of interactive computing. It was a radical leap. The graphics appeared on a cathode ray tube, but not an ordinary television. These devices were vector graphics engines whose beam had to repaint the image 30 times a second to maintain the image. Consequently, it could only draw so many lines at a time. On the computer hardware side, the TX-2 also made big advances, with the enormous (for the time) memory of 320K bytes, all built from individual transistors. Integrated circuits were still a generation in the future.

Sutherland spent his mandatory military service working for the super-secret National Security Agency (NSA) and the Advanced Research Projects Agency (ARPA). ARPA gave this newly commissioned lieutenant a secretary and $15 million to spend on computer science research. Considering what Howard Fisher's $294,000 grant produced at Harvard in this era, $15 million was a lot of money. Given so much power so quickly, it is rather interesting that Sutherland left the military and took an academic post at Harvard. He wanted to stay close to the development of software and new applications of computer graphics.

Immediately on his arrival, Sutherland tried to build a team similar to the MIT development environment described as the origin of the computer hacker.[3] He toured campus to recruit students interested in computer graphics. The idea paralleled Noah's Ark, with at least one student from each school around campus. There were a bunch of "serious" science types, but Sutherland sought out any problem that used graphics. At the Graduate School of Design, Eric Teicholz, in the master's of architecture program, took up Sutherland's challenge.

Sutherland built a high-pressure environment with weekly review of progress. The single-user model of the hardware meant that this expensive equipment had to be allocated by 15-minute slots, day and night. He gave students "yen" to bid for time, and those working on the more successful projects got more yen, and hence better access to the equipment. Although the sponsors of this high-end equipment would not have appreciated it, this computer was best known for its wickedly addictive "Spacewar" game, written at MIT.

ARCHITECTURAL DRAWINGS BY COMPUTER: OTOTROL

Given access to the state of the art in computer graphics hardware, Teicholz developed a program to input an architectural drawing in two dimensions, to construct a three-dimensional model, then to draw "wire-frame" objects that could be rotated in any orientation on the display screen. Most of the programming had to do with conversion of coordinates from drawing to model to screen. The hidden line problem (the ability to calculate which parts of the three-dimensional objects would obscure the view of others) was a research topic of its own at the time, considered too ambitious for Teicholz's project.

Sutherland's high-tech equipment provided little support for graphic input from large documents such as architectural drawings or maps. Sutherland had developed his Sketchpad using a lightpen, a device that sensed the cathode ray as it drew a particular vector. The lightpen provided interaction on the screen, but not a way to draw bigger objects with higher resolution. The Harvard PDP-1 had experimental input devices such as Douglas Engelbart's early mouse, as well as a much more exotic 3D wand. To deal with large format documents, the digitizing table technology had been developed in the United Kingdom originally through the Experimental Cartography Unit. On his own budget, Teicholz purchased one of the early models from the Ototrol Corporation. It had a gantry construction with two ribbons of bar-coded plastic to measure motion in both the x- and y-axes (see photo in chapter 4). This device launched his career as a computer graphics professional.

Teicholz also had a connection to Fisher's Laboratory, as liaison to the Architecture Department. Using the program running on Sutherland's machine, he created a basic "space frame"—the intersection of three orthogonal planes. Produced on a photographic plotter, a series of rotations at small increments provided the image adopted as the logo of the Laboratory.

Teicholz called his program OTOTROL (an ambiguous choice, considering the name of the hardware company). It took three-dimensional line drawings (input from traditional plans and elevations) and produced views from any point in space. Hidden line algorithms would come later on larger computers. It was packaged up for distribution by the Laboratory in 1968, combined with a correspondence course just like SYMAP. The price was

Rotations of a three-dimensional space frame, produced ▶
by Eric Teicholz on a film plotter in 1967. The
highlighted rotation was adopted as the logo of the
Laboratory. *(Source: Context 1, page 1, February 1968, Harvard University
Graduate School of Design)*

similar to SYMAP ($320, or $200 for nonprofits), with a discount to those who attended the May 1968 Training Conference in Chicago on architectural graphics. The capabilities of OTOTROL and related software interested some local architectural offices. Teicholz took some leave from Harvard and spent a few years in the corporate sector developing a commercial venture—a dedicated architectural workstation with computer graphics and supporting software (ARK-2). This project combined the computer graphics display with a version of the space allocation software (GRASP) described in chapter 4. The design process focused spatial analysis of the functions to which a building would be put. The designer had access to an analysis of the materials required and the estimated cost of construction. Instead of designing a generic computer-aided design (CAD) system based on just the drawing, Teicholz had adopted the kind of vision that Howard Fisher had applied to thematic maps. It was way ahead of its market, in many ways.

Teicholz kept a part-time teaching role in computer graphics for architects and played the role of representing the potential of the Laboratory to design professionals. As the commercial venture closed down, he took the title of associate director of the Laboratory.

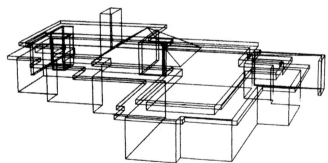

◀ Output from a perspective drawing program:
Architectural drawings could be rendered in
any 3D view, but only as wireframes (no hidden
surfaces). *(Source: Red Book III.2, Harvard University Graduate
School of Design)*

Plotting a revolution

Interactive computing with Sketchpad on a dedicated TX-2 computer was inaccessible to the community of planners and geographers who used SYMAP in the late 1960s. Computer centers were the primary locus for access to computing, and remained so into the mid-1970s. Scientific computer users at many universities were dissatisfied with the line printer as their only output device. The combination of physicists, chemists, and engineers could influence the managers of a computer center as a lone geographer or planner could not. Pen plotters became available at computer centers, and were often used to draw scatter plots and other forms of scientific diagrams.

Pen plotters were off-line devices driven by magnetic tapes. The instructions for the graphics were written onto the tape by the computer at computer speeds, then the tape was transferred to the plotter device where the pen had to be dragged across the paper. Some of the earliest plotters were large tables with the pen on a gantry that moved in both x and y directions, but the bulk of computer centers bought less expensive (and less space-consuming) drum plotters. Plotter paper on a long roll could be rolled back and forth using a sprocket feed. A single pen could be moved across the drum on the other axis of the paper. Early drum plotters were incremental, moving only one or the other axis at a time. Diagonal lines had to be constructed in small stairsteps. Advances in equipment permitted "zip mode"—true diagonal lines—and high-quality cartographic output.

The pen could be raised and lowered with electromagnets, producing satisfying thuds and klunks mixed with whirrings as the paper slipped back and forth along the drum. Watching a plotter was an impressive experience, though the current expectations of instant downloads would make it seem very slow to build up an image. The pens were the weakest link in what was a fairly complex hybrid human–computer system. Computer center operators were happy to slap in a ballpoint pen that could run for days without much attention. Mount a tape, punch a button, and return to find a roll of output. The resulting line work, though, was not adequate for reproduction. Higher-quality output required liquid ink pens, the same Leroy lettering pen nibs used for manual cartography during the period. While a cartographer could give the pen a little shake to get the ink flowing, a plotter had no such feedback. A short skip in the ink flow would leave a gap in the graphics, requiring a complete replotting. Most scientific users produced huge rolls of charts and graphs of fairly low density. Cartographic output would hammer away on a short stretch of paper, tying up the plotter for hours. Asking for a replot was not a great way to make friends among the operators. A partial solution to the pen problem involved doctoring the india ink with a drop or two of ethylene glycol; this helped a bit, but the pens then might drip ink in the wrong places.

Eventually, friction drives and plain paper replaced the sprocketed rolls and drums. Pen plotters also supported multiple pens in varying colors. They got much cheaper and no longer required a centralized facility. However, these developments could not reduce the basic burden of moving the paper and making each mark separately. This vector technology lost out to the PostScript printer (a raster marking engine driven by vector commands) and the raster screen display. The combination technology in the modern PostScript printer was present by 1968 or 1970 in the form of the "Geospace" plotter.[4] This device could expose a 40-inch-by-60-inch plot in a minute or two, but it took a half-hour or more of computer time to prepare the raster file from the vector input. Improved speed of processors and larger cheaper memory were the developments that rendered the plotter obsolete.

SYMVU: Surface displays

Howard Fisher and William Warntz were fascinated by surfaces. Each placed great importance on the shape and smoothness of spatial distributions. Yet SYMAP could only show 10 classes, separated by nine contour lines. Most surfaces require much more resolution to do them justice. Another display technology was required.

In 1967, Frank Rens came to the Laboratory. He was a University of Michigan graduate student working with Waldo Tobler on a PhD (completed in the fall of 1968). Rens brought with him a prototype program that drew perspective views of surfaces using a pen plotter. It required a matrix of the surface values as input, exactly the product of the SYMAP interpolation procedure. The SYMAP programmers were able to direct this matrix to a tape or disk file, to be handed on for a surface display. At the same time, the air pollution study performed for the U.S. Public Health Service (see chapter 2) provided ample resources to fund development of interpolation and surface display techniques. Rens worked on the programming of the package with staff programmers Lannon Leiman and Kathleen Reine. The resulting program was called SYMVU, a pastiche of SYMap and computerese VU for view. This usage shows that SYMAP had already become a brand, not directly dependent on Fisher's word "synagraphic."

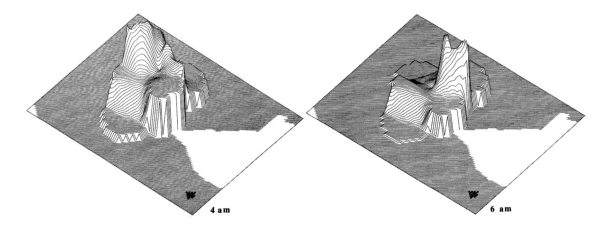

4 am   6 am

▲   Air pollution surface (2-hour SO_2 concentration) for St. Louis, Missouri, December 20, 1964 at 4 am and 6 am. Produced by SYMVU for the U.S. Health Service contract by Laboratory research staff. *(Source: Computer Mapping as an Aid in Air Pollution Studies, Volume One: Summary Report Appendix, figure b-3, ed. John Goodrich)*

SYMVU was made available in 1969, shortly after the release of SYMAP V, the version with the Shepard interpolation. Like the SYMAP package, it had been developed on the IBM 7094, but it outgrew that computer's memory. The version for the IBM 360 was the only version distributed. Sales of SYMVU were brisk, and startling perspective views became a signature of computer cartography, beginning with the reports of the air pollution study. The computer was now able to do something better than a manual cartographer could. With the appropriate pens and substantial patience in attending the plotter, the output was of publication quality.

SYMVU solved the hidden surface (or hidden line) problem, a topic of substantial interest in computer graphics at the time. The algorithm produced the perspective drawing coherently starting from the foreground and working away from the viewer. Parallel structure lines were traced across the matrix in order. The height values in the matrix raised the lines proportionately according to the perspective from a given vantage point. The position of the line on the drawing was recorded as a rising horizon in an array. Each new line was plotted only if it was above the lines already plotted. The new lines were intersected with the horizon line, so they emerged smoothly.

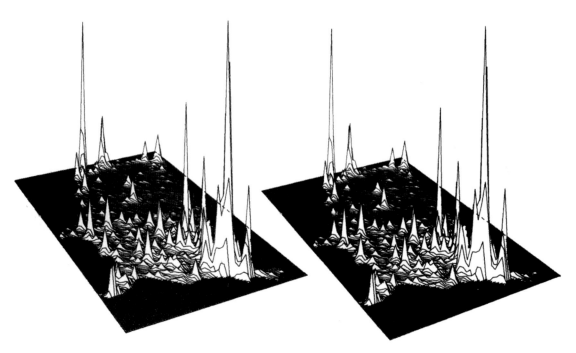

▲   Two images, produced at slightly different azimuths, can be used to produce a stereo pair. Viewed from a distance of about 6 to 8 feet, these pairs can be made to merge into a stereo image by moving your point of focus (with the aid of a finger held close in front of the nose). *(Source: Original produced by Geoffrey Dutton)*

While SYMAP could produce the matrix output in sections as it printed the map, SYMVU had to hold the whole matrix in memory. The original program could handle a matrix of only 130 cells by 130 cells. At 67K bytes, this matrix was considered large in a period when the whole computer (including operating system and various time-shared partitions) was limited to 128K or possibly 256K on the biggest university computers. Doubling the linear dimensions of the matrix in both axes would have taken just this matrix beyond the capacity of available computers.

SYMVU had a sneaky way of learning which area on the matrix was outside the study area. SYMAP recorded a floating point number for the height of the surface, but it stored the binary equivalent of "integer 25" in cells outside the study area. The value of 25 was the value used inside SYMAP for the background symbolism. This trick worked because the floating point number format produced distinct bit patterns, none of them looking like an integer 25. Such mixed mode storage was not very portable across different computers, but it worked as long as the matrix stayed in binary format without any translation. This approach to the background confirms that SYMVU was dependent on SYMAP to generate the surfaces. In graphic display using SYMVU, the background could be left blank or blackened with a hashing of linework. The user controlled the image by selecting a point of view. A given matrix could be drawn from various azimuths and altitudes, revealing different portions of complex surfaces since some areas would be hidden from particular perspectives. Most users would try a few different views, looking for the most dramatic orientation or the least hiding by foreground peaks. Due to the lag in plotting, a search for the best azimuth and altitude parameters was time consuming.

SYMVU demonstrates the informal manner in which intellectual property was treated in this period. While the original work was done at the University of Michigan, Harvard took it over and distributed it without any particular reference to the original work. Later, Adrian Thomas, a programmer, worked on SYMVU at the Laboratory and continued to work on it when he moved to the University of Edinburgh's Program Library Unit. The distribution version from Harvard by 1972 derived from an agreement between Harvard and Edinburgh.

SYMVU was very flashy, attracting attention from cartographers and noncartographers alike. A SYMVU output would go on the cover of many reports and books, just as it has on this book. However, the startling views were not always the most effective way to display routine thematic data. This is because the peaks shown in surface context did not make it easy to identify the source of the particular data item. And the perspective made a legend problematic to measure specific values. SYMVU played a role in cartographic display, but there was still a need for routine choropleth mapping on the plotter.

CALFORM: Choropleth maps on the plotter

If SYMVU is the flashy end of advanced computer graphics in 1969, CALFORM arose from a need to produce publication-quality graphics from more mundane choropleth data. The bulk of thematic cartography in that era, as in the current world, came from columns and columns of attributes attached to a common set of base polygons, often political subdivisions or census units. In Fisher's terminology, choropleth maps were called conformant, hence the FORM part of the word. The CAL syllable comes from the dominant plotter manufacturer, CALCOMP (for California Computing, originally). CALFORM was independent of SYMAP, using a different input data structure and user interface.

The first version of CALFORM was written around 1970 by a Harvard undergraduate student, Robert (Corky) Cartwright. He wrote it with 12 predesigned symbolism patterns that the user could select by number. The distribution version of CALFORM was reworked by Kathleen Reine and me. We discarded the 12 separate shading routines in favor of a single routine that slices a polygon into the lines to draw back and forth. This change added substantial flexibility in constructing shading; it also made the code smaller and simpler to maintain. CALFORM appeared in 1972 and had substantial distribution. Unlike SYMVU, though, it had competition from a number of similar packages produced at other universities in the United States and United Kingdom.

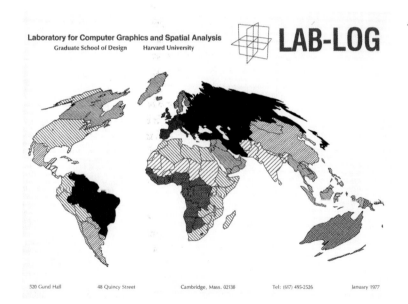

◀ CALFORM output as featured on the cover of the Laboratory catalog (LAB-LOG) in 1977 (without a legend). Shading shows classes of per capita rate of gross national product growth 1965–1972 by country of the world. The sinusoidal projection was performed by POLYVRT. (Country outlines from World Data Bank I as corrected and restructured by the Laboratory; attributes from 1974 World Bank Atlas; map produced by David Sheehan and Geoffrey Dutton, with cooperation of American Geographical Society.)

(Source: LAB-LOG 1977, cover, Harvard University Graduate School of Design)

Consequences for data structures

The pen plotters used by SYMVU and CALFORM offered much greater resolution than the line printers used by SYMAP. A set of polygons digitized for SYMAP might look correct on the line printer, but prove to have many small gaps and overlaps (slivers) when drawn on the plotter. The programming for CALFORM attempted to overcome this problem by moving away from the straightforward polygon outlines of the SYMAP A-CONFORMOLINES package. Instead of independent loops around each polygon (a data structure now called a shapefile), CALFORM worked through an intermediary, a "dictionary" of all the points to be used. Each polygon was constructed by reference to this common set of points. First, you entered all the points; then you specified each polygon as a list of point identifiers.

The point dictionary had been developed by some of the staff at the Laboratory to ensure topological consistency and to manage digitizing operations by numbering the points to be measured. They applied this practice manually to building databases for use in SYMAP, though the program didn't provide any support for the data structure. The points were digitized one to a card, with identifying numbers. Then the cards were duplicated a few times (in a grid city, a point could be used for four adjacent polygons at most). Polygons were manually assembled by pulling out the cards for the points in sequence around the polygon. CALFORM simply automated this procedure.

The point dictionary solved one problem, but created another. Instead of the local processing of SYMAP where each polygon could be treated without needing to know anything else, CALFORM required all the coordinates for a map to reside in memory. This was a serious limitation for large collections of polygons with complex boundaries. The point dictionary was a data structure that did not see much widespread use.

Yet, the act of numbering the points is the first step in developing cartographic data structures. In telling the story of the DIME files at the U.S. Census Bureau, Donald Cooke reports on a critical meeting where the high-flying theory of topology is boiled down to its essentials: "Do we number the nodes?"[5] The Census Bureau thought it needed to identify the areas (blocks and tracts) and the lines (the streets with addresses), but it was not clear that they had any use for identifiers for the points. The key to create the DIME structure was to recognize that each node was a distinct object that required an identifier. At Harvard, this practical step was similarly a start on the path toward more complex data structures.

Graphics online

The field of computer graphics was changing rapidly in this period. The plotters used by SYMVU and CALFORM were not that big a leap from the line printer, since they were still operated by the computer center as offline peripherals. Turnaround time was slower, since the output tape had to be transferred from the computer to the plotter. Due to consolidation of the Harvard facilities with MIT, the computer and the tape drives were a few miles away from the plotter. A courier service dropped the tapes off a few times a day. From the software perspective, the drivers were provided by the manufacturers of the particular device. There were no graphics standards; programmers had to modify the code to access the correct routines.

The future direction of information technology in 1972 seemed to be in the direction of broadband connections and video displays. Harvard, like many other institutions, invested in a cable system linking buildings. The Laboratory moved into video production with tapes designed for learning about SYMAP and SYMVU. The low-resolution imagery of broadcast television limited the application to cartographic display.

One competing technology for graphic display was the line of graphics terminals sold by Tektronix. Unlike the displays on the Sketchpad and the PDP-1 from Sutherland's era, these terminals had a storage screen, so the objects were drawn once, much as on a plotter. In 1973, the Laboratory first acquired a Tektronix 4012 which had a 12-inch (diagonal) tube and the revolutionary capability to show characters in both upper- and lowercase. The 4012 was originally connected to the Harvard PDP-10 using a dial-up modem operating at 300 bits per second with an acoustic coupler. A much larger 4014 arrived in 1974, and a dedicated line was installed that was able to transfer at what was considered to be the maximum rate possible using telephone lines—9,600 bits per second. Access to the hardware brought in a completely new approach to accessing computers interactively.

While a computer science undergraduate at Harvard, Jim Little had access to an interactive computer that had taken the place of the earlier IBM mainframe in the specially built space of Aiken Labs (named after Howard Aiken, whose Mark-1 electro-mechanical calculator sat outside). Harvard had given up running a mainframe, joining up with MIT to run ever bigger IBM 360s. The Computing Center itself had moved to a building that IBM used to occupy on Cambridge Street. The machine that took the place of the mainframe at Aiken was a PDP-10, manufactured by Digital Equipment. It was still room-sized and needed special cooling, but it no longer had a protective layer of operators. It had an operating system based on years of development at MIT that was designed by programmers for programmers. The timesharing options provided by IBM were limited by comparison. Unlike the Computing Center, the cost of access to the Aiken facility was a lump sum per year. The lure of interactive computing and the rapidity of interaction drew the development of new programs away from the batch world. It was a new world with no clear standards, but the speed of development and the rapid display of graphics made the Lab much more exciting. It also brought the promise of Sketchpad closer to delivery to regular computer users. (This computer was also connected to the fledging ARPANET using a special phone line and interface hardware to connect to the few other computers on what eventually became the world-spanning network.[6] The interactive access to computing was more crucial to the Laboratory's development than having access to a few other computer science laboratories across North America.)

ASPEX TAKES THE SCREEN FOR SYMVU

Once the Tektronix hardware arrived, the first idea was to convert SYMVU to operate on the screen. The FORTRAN code could be moved from the mainframe IBM to the timesharing world of the PDP-10, but the style of interaction would need to be changed. It didn't make sense to emulate cards, punching the commands in specific column positions. A whole new approach had to be developed, with keywords and a more tolerant style of interaction that announced errors to the user and permitted their correction.

The graphics changed as well. The limitations of the screen size required active windowing and clipping functions. The software provided by the manufacturer did not seem adequate, so the Laboratory staff wrote some drivers quickly. The devices were so simple that there was little difficulty getting the basic functions operational.

The conversion of SYMVU to the interactive mode of operation turned into a complete rewrite. The resulting program, called ASPEX (vaguely subtitled Automated Surface Perspectives), was operational inhouse during 1974, but didn't get polished for distribution until the end of 1975. The delays

▲ Jim Little, programmer of ASPEX, showing off a surface of U.S. population on the screen of the Tektronix 4012. Note the acoustic coupler in the background; the maximum rate of connection was 300 bits per second. *(Source: Context 5, page 5, November 1973, with the title "Jim Little at the controls", Harvard University Graduate School of Design)*

were annoying to some users, but the graphics terminal equipment was not so widely accessible throughout the user community as yet. ASPEX still depended on SYMAP to generate images; it had limited facilities to enter data. In terms of display, it went far beyond SYMVU in allowing the viewpoints down close to the surface, the precursor of the "flythrough" now expected of surface display modules. The departure of Little to Simon Fraser University slowed the process, but so did the production of a user manual and the other requirements for distribution. The requirements of this conversion—interactive command processing and graphics drivers—foreshadowed the next major phase of software development at the Laboratory (see chapter 8).

INPOM: AN EXPERIMENT IN CHOROPLETH MAPPING

Just as ASPEX was motivated as a conversion of SYMVU, the interactive environment also required a conversion of CALFORM. The project was assigned to Harvard undergraduate computer-science student Geoffrey Clemm, working with me as his cartographic advisor and CALFORM expert. Clemm wrote a program called INPOM (for INteractive POlygon Mapping). Rather than the keyword language of ASPEX, it used a dialog-style interaction. All commands had a descending set of queries, with options given as single letters in response to a prompt. Thus, each option managed its own interaction, asking questions and requiring responses from the user. The displays were shaded polygons, using a topological data structure of chains forming polygons. The program supported data input using the cross-hair graphic input available on the Tektronix. While the PDP-1 at Harvard had Engelbart's mouse, it was considered a bit of a curiosity. The cross hairs were directly on the screen, manipulated

◀ Choropleth map of Africa by countries, produced by INPOM. Thematic variable is gross national product per capita, 1970. This photograph shows the image as drawn on INPOM's normal display device, the Tektronix 4014 storage screen. *(Source: Tecktronix Graphics brochure, 1976; map produced by Nick Chrisman; base file from World Data Bank I.)*

by separate thumbwheels for *x* and *y*. It was a clunky and slow method of digitizing. Most maps were entered using a full-sized digitizing table instead.

The 3000×4096 resolution of the Tektronix 4014 made presentable thematic maps, if you got used to the one shade of green available. The program was demonstrated live over the ARPANET at AUTO-CARTO II (September 1975) using a dial-up connection to the local access to the network. The interactive mode of map making was exciting at the time, though functions like zoom have become entirely routine. The weakness of INPOM was its user interface. The few insiders knew all the options and could fly through the dialogs, making maps very rapidly. In preparation for distribution, the program was presented to some students for class work. They got quickly lost, and the program would crash for unpredictable reasons due to unexpected combinations of commands. Although it was announced for distribution, there was too much effort required to salvage it. Interactive thematic mapping required a more integrated design that was planned in the next phase of program development (see chapter 8).

▼ INPOM's zoom function allowed what was then revolutionary—the ability to select a point on the screen and zoom in rapidly. This illustration was a part of the marketing in the software catalog. *(Source: LAB-LOG 1977, page 15, Harvard University Graduate School of Design)*

 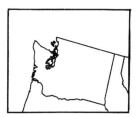 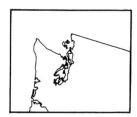 

NOTES

1. Ivan Sutherland, "Sketchpad: A man-machine graphical communication system," (PhD dissertation, MIT, 1964). Sources on Sutherland and Sketchpad abound on the Web.

2. Nobert Wiener, *Cybernetics or control and communication in the animal and the machine* (New York: John Wiley and Sons, Inc., 1948).

3. Steven Levy, *Hackers: Heroes of the computer revolution* (New York: Doubleday, 1984).

4. The U.S. Census Bureau made much of Geospace plotter in the New Haven Census Use Study. The capabilities of the device were discussed at Fisher's conference in 1967 (see transcripts, session 9C). Jerrold Rubin, "A Geospace mapping program," in *Proceedings, Sixth Annual URISA Conference,* 193–199 (Kent, Ohio, URISA, 1968).

5. Donald F. Cooke, "Topology and TIGER: The Census Bureau's contribution," in *The history of geographic information systems: Perspectives from the pioneers,* ed. Timothy W. Foresman, 51 (Upper Saddle River, N.J.: Prentice Hall, 1998).

6. Janet Abbate, *Inventing the Internet* (Cambridge, Mass.: MIT Press, 2000).

SIX

Decline and Rebound

By 1971, each of the main directions of the Laboratory's research had come to an end of some kind, each for their own reasons. Howard Fisher retired, the Ford Foundation grant finished; William Warntz departed, his grants closed out; the landscape planners went on to success through Landscape Architecture. For all these reasons, there was a sharp drop in staff and activity. Yet, the story does not end here. The Laboratory bounced back, overcame a negative evaluation by a faculty committee in 1974, and took some new directions.

Decline

In academic life, the most prevalent stories of successful researchers involve a "cycle of credit." If a given scholar has a certain amount of credit, he or she uses it to obtain some grants, which in turn permits hiring staff and students. If the work comes out well, this leads to publications, presentations, and more credit. In the upward spiral, this allows bigger grants, more students, bigger labs, and so on. The cycle also works in reverse. If credit declines, the pool of resources diminishes, and the probability of new grants fades.[1] In the case of the Laboratory, it is hard to pinpoint which component was causative (in either an upward or downward sense), since the cycle was so interlocking. Both upward and downward spirals operated in the early history of the Laboratory.

Howard Fisher started with some amount of credibility for his prototype SYMAP. He worked hard to turn that into the grant from the Ford Foundation, using his Harvard connections to render it more creditable. With solid flows of money, he hired staff and attracted students. Some of the staff brought along other research grants, and attracted more students. The expansion was rapid, going from three in the spring of 1966 to 36 in the fall of 1967. The expansive cycle continued until 1971 with a staff of more than 40, but then nearly all of the sources of funding dried up. The cycle reversed rapidly, and the staff diminished to about six by spring 1972. This sharp decline had a number of independent contributing factors, each of which is worth recounting.

FORD FOUNDATION GRANT FINISHED

The grant from the Ford Foundation was a prerequisite before Harvard would announce the Laboratory in the first place. Once in place, this grant supported staff, conferences, correspondence courses, and many other important activities described in chapters 1 and 4. The original proposal had requested funding for three and a half academic years. Nearly half the $294,000 was projected to be spent in the first year and a half (1966–1967). The actual hiring process lagged behind the schedule in the proposal, so the grant lasted a bit longer. Still, by 1970, the Ford funds were depleted.

Following his announced plan, Howard Fisher handed over the directorship in 1968 on reaching the mandatory retirement age (65). He made a transition from directing the Laboratory to working on his textbook for thematic cartography. He submitted proposals to the Ford Foundation to complete his book, and received $35,000 in 1971. He used these funds to hire some cartographers (Herb Height, Eliza McClennan, and Carolyn Weiss) to help him prepare the illustrations. This project continued for a few years, using as much manual technique as computer output. Fisher saw his contribution as map design, not in the analytical work that fueled the computer packages. Despite continued promises about publication dates, the book did not appear until 1982,[2] three years after Fisher's death.

In the original proposal, Fisher projected that the Laboratory for Computer Graphics would become a Laboratory for Computer Technology over time. This change in title was meant to accompany a transition toward support for the instructional functions of the Graduate School of Design, and a consequent source of funding from the School. Although Fisher had laid out this transition, the use of computers in the instructional work of the School was not large enough to justify diverting resources to such a purpose. Such a computer support facility did eventually appear, but not for over twenty years. The Laboratory required another strategy to survive.

WARNTZ DEPARTS

Fisher's departure had been planned from the start. His successor as director, William Warntz, was intended to ensure the Lab's future. The professor of theoretical geography, Warntz, lasted three years in the job. It was a stormy period at Harvard, what with student strikes, occupations of the administration buildings, and an overall political climate of challenging all authority. Warntz had come with plans to reestablish geography at Harvard (see chapter 4), but the politics of the Graduate School of Design and the university as a whole made such plans totally unlikely. Warntz was a research scholar much more than a politician. He wrote proposals to institute a course in general geography in the undergraduate curriculum, but the machinery of Harvard College found no place for that course in their structure. Unlike many other universities, Harvard places the undergraduate program in a much more central position. The graduate schools are largely professionally oriented, including the highly regarded schools of law, medicine, and business (the latter two both in Boston, not Cambridge). These schools have active research programs, but very limited connection to the central life of the campus and the academic departments. The Graduate School of Design was (and remains) a small and rather weak element of the university.

During the period that Warntz was director, the Laboratory prospered from a variety of sources. Warntz arrived with a substantial grant from the Office of Naval Research and obtained additional support from the National Science Foundation for his theoretical work.[3] Various Laboratory staff received support as IBM Fellows, through a grant administered by the Harvard Computing Center. Many projects were funded by public agencies or nonprofit groups. The largest was the air pollution study funded by the U.S. Public Health Service (see chapter 2). Yet, all of this money was short-term. It could have been sustained, but it required continued attention to writing new proposals and finding new project work. When the projects were completed, the students stopped getting support. Staff members tried to attach themselves to new projects, but when the money dried up, they left.

To some extent, the boom and bust of the research sector was a normal part of the academic world. Research empires built up over long careers could vanish very quickly. The younger members of the research staff, if they had their PhD, would just move into an academic job somewhere (hoping to build their own research empire perhaps in the future). Many of the Laboratory staff took this career path. Tom Peucker already had an academic job at Simon Fraser University. Carl Steinitz, although originally hired by the Laboratory, moved quickly to become attached to the instructional program at the Graduate School of Design. He took his student, David Sinton, along with him to provide technical support for his courses and research projects. Michael Woldenberg also moved from a research associate inside the Laboratory to teach in City and Regional Planning as assistant professor. He continued his research on the branching ratios of streams and other distribution systems (see chapter 4), but played no direct role in the Laboratory. Similarly, two of the research associates connected to the design professions, Allen Bernholtz and Eduardo Lozano, took jobs teaching architecture. Lozano came back to Harvard after a short venture outside but had limited connection to the Laboratory on his return.

The programming staff did not follow the path of academic jobs (at least right away). Through a connection to Tom Waugh, a programmer at the University of Edinburgh who spent a year at the Laboratory, Adrian Thomas and Kathy Kiernan found positions in the Program Library Unit in the Computer Centre at Edinburgh. This group revised SYMVU and eventually built GIMMS, a thematic mapping package. Many of the students involved at the Laboratory took up jobs that involved using geographic information in some fashion. Quite a few became influential in the GIS industry as it evolved, including the presidents of both ESRI (Jack Dangermond) and Caliper Corp. (Howard Slavin). If the history of the Laboratory ended here, there still would be much to show.

Warntz did not build close connections to the Department of City and Regional Planning (his official academic attachment in the Graduate School of Design). The leadership in planning placed greater emphasis on economic management, not spatial relationships. In a few more years, this department left the design-oriented Graduate School of Design to join the Kennedy School of Government, a graduate school of public affairs and management at Harvard. Warntz's spatial analysis was too abstract and his geographic discipline was not highly valued. In 1971, he took a position as professor and chair of geography at Western Ontario University in London, Ontario. Some grants moved with him; others trailed off with support for a student or staff member for a short period. His departure in May 1971 created a vacuum in leadership of the Laboratory; five years passed before a new director was named.

LANDSCAPE PLANNING MOVES

Of the threads of research at the Laboratory described in prior chapters, landscape planning developed most rapidly. Peter Rogers and Carl Steinitz had made firm links with the instructional program of the Graduate School of Design, through the Landscape Architecture Department. Steinitz, who had arrived in 1966 with his PhD just completed, rose to full professor by 1972. Tenure, a scarce commodity in the Harvard constellation of the period, came later. The consulting firm Steinitz Rogers helped establish standards of practice for the Environmental Impact Statements (EIS) required by the newly passed National Environmental Policy Act (NEPA).[4] Steinitz also maintained contacts with the Joint Center of Urban Studies at MIT. The Steinitz and Rogers integrative approach to urban change[5] attracted attention, leading to a major grant from the NSF through the Research Applied to National Needs (RANN) program. The first two years from 1972 were funded at $522,700, with additional funds in later years. Their modeling of urban change depended on computer analysis of gridded spatial data. The project geared up to employ dozens of students and staff, in the typical boom-town economy of academic life. Much of the work involved visual interpretation of air photographs, manual coding of grid cells, and keypunching of the results. David Sinton played a lead role in developing grid-based software to support the research projects and instructional demands. As described in chapter 3, Sinton's programming and that of his students set the course for a major portion of the current commercial software.

Some connections to the Laboratory were initiated by the students themselves. Students such as Bruce Rowland explored vector solutions to overlay and data input for their thesis projects in landscape architecture. Another landscape architecture student, Ted Driscoll, pursued his programming work on visual simulations, mixing grid and triangular representations of complex terrain using Laboratory facilities. The manual for the resulting program SOLARE appeared under the Laboratory imprint,[6] although Driscoll had not been funded by any Laboratory sources.

This activity was a direct outcome of work supported by the early Laboratory, but it did nothing for the Laboratory in its decline. The landscape planning group had already begun to distance themselves from the Laboratory a few years before (see chapter 3). Their projects were run through the Research Office of Landscape Architecture. The story of this research initiative deserves its own telling, in another volume. The result for the Laboratory was that a highly productive group left.

The residual Lab

While each of the distinct threads of events stripped away a piece of the Laboratory, some pieces remained. A few key staff members, clustered around Allan Schmidt, hung on as the budgets shrank. As a form of capital, they had the software. Sales of SYMAP and the other packages continued, providing a stable source of revenue. Some service contacts helped float the operations long enough to let the new directions emerge.

SOFTWARE SALES

What remained for the Laboratory was the revenue from software sales. The grants and research contracts may have dried up, but the reputation of the software grew. Specific sales figures did not survive, but by 1972 three of the remaining six staff members were working primarily to fulfill orders or to maintain the programs. In retrospect, it seems obvious that software is saleable, but this was an era when the largest computer corporations were still giving software away to sweeten the sales of hardware. The whole concept of academic software sales was new and unexplored. This novelty would lead to greater difficulties in the next phase of the Laboratory.

A (small) tub on its own bottom

Harvard University is a place of strong traditions, firmly convinced of the necessity of its way of doing things. Somewhere in the mists of time, some Harvard president used the story of a rising tide as the metaphor for his management of the institution. A rising tide might lift all boats, but they had to be sound on their own. This story was encapsulated using the phrase "every tub on its own bottom." This policy meant that there would be no subsidies from successful parts of the operation to float the less successful ones. Harvard administrators for over a century have repeated this story, often believing that they invented it themselves. It probably has its origins in John Bunyan's *Pilgrim's Progress*, a moral compass for Harvard's curriculum from the earliest days. Bunyan used the phrase "each vat must stand on its own bottom." A century later, in 1781, Charles Macklin used the exact phrase "each tub on its own bottom" in the play *The Man of the World.*[7] Whatever the source, this principle had become a part of an institution with a three-hundred-year perspective on survival and progress.

Originally, each graduate school was a tub. Each dean would have to balance a school's expenditures to match the revenues from tuition and research grants. Eventually, deans applied the same management technique down the hierarchy, but with some modifications (notably a tax on research grants to support overhead). With a rising stream of revenue in the early period, this policy allowed the Laboratory to expand. The dean was happy to collect the overhead from each grant and contract. When revenues diminished, the Laboratory was reminded that it was a tub on its own bottom. The dean's overhead fund could level out fluctuations from one year to another, but, in general, expenses had to conform to revenues.

SERVICE CONTRACTS

Faced with the budgetary shortfalls, laboratory staff actively explored contract work. Though not managing the Laboratory, Howard Fisher had built up his own staff of cartographers for his book project, and, to defray some of the staff cost, he opened the Harvard Mapping Service, an entity with ambiguous connections to the Laboratory. This group did some maps for such clients as the *New York Times* for its story on the migrations of African-Americans to the North. The products reflect Fisher's experimentation with display techniques.

Some of the projects done by regular Lab staff were small and low-profile—for example, David Sheehan's demographic analysis for the Girl Scout Council. In what we might now term "business geographics," this study identified which units were not reaching as high a proportion of the population. The clients were pleased with the spatial presentation of their tabular data. These kinds of projects mobilized the software, databases, and expertise of the Laboratory, but the demand was spotty and revenue barely covered staff costs.

Estimated Absolute Numbers

Estimated Rates Per Region

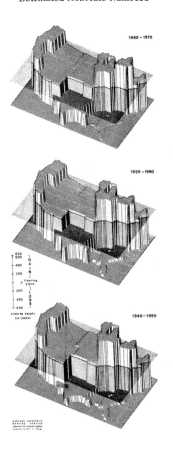

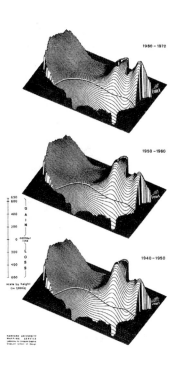

◀ Net black migration by nine census regions 1940–1970. SYMVUs produced by Harvard Mapping Service under the direction of Howard Fisher, 1971. These graphics show some struggle to present both population loss and gain, either in raw numbers or rates of change. The *New York Times* published a less complex version, without the floating plane. *(Source: Red Book, page VII.48, Harvard University Graduate School of Design)*

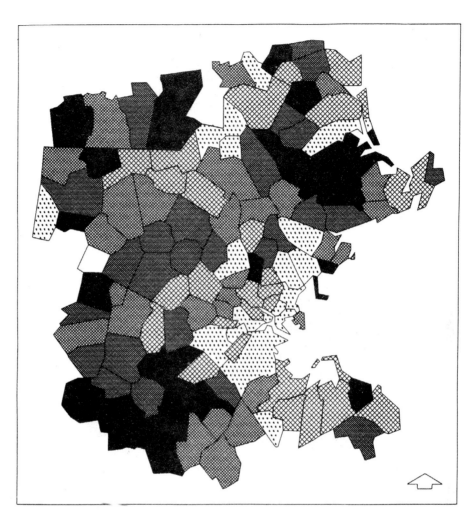

■	80.00 - 100.00
▨	60.00 - 79.99
▨	40.00 - 59.99
▧	20.00 - 39.99
⋯	0.01 - 19.99
□	0.00 - 0.00

% GIRLS 7-8 YRS OLD WHO ARE BROWNIES
GIRL SCOUTS OF THE USA MEMBERSHIP STUDY:
EASTERN MASSACHUSETTS REGION (DEC. 1972)

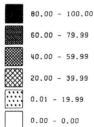 CALFORM output produced for the Girl Scout Council of eastern Massachusetts. Five equal-interval classes (plus one zero value) for percentage of girls aged 7 and 8 who have joined the Brownies by cities and towns of the council's service area in Massachusetts and southern New Hampshire. Produced by Geoffrey Dutton and David Sheehan, 1973. *(Source: Red Book, page VII.69, Harvard University Graduate School of Design)*

Other projects undertaken in this period required more analytical work, and were closer to research. Geoffrey Dutton developed a location-allocation model[8] to assess the number of beds in coronary care units in Massachusetts. The model revealed a rather large over-provision of beds, particularly in metropolitan Boston. This study attracted a subsequent study of the whole of Sweden, which demonstrated that there were insufficient beds for that population. The model could recommend the best locations that were inside the maximum radius for transport of coronary cases.

By far the largest contract involved the Defense Intelligence Agency (DIA). Robert Mercready, a geographer on staff at DIA, had spent a year at the Laboratory in 1968–1969. Since the Lab's offices were next to those of the Students for a Democratic Society (SDS), there was some gentle joking that he was a spy. Of course, real

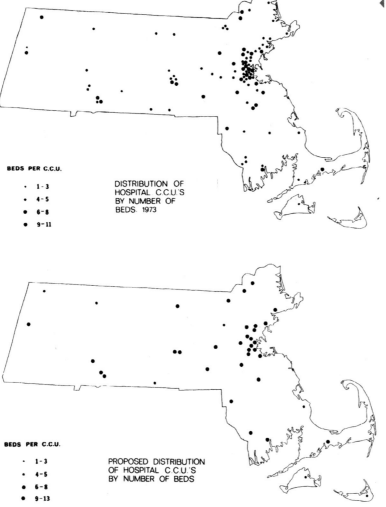

◀ *Top:* Existing distribution of beds in coronary care units, Commonwealth of Massachusetts, 1973; *bottom:* **Proposed distribution (note that this removes many of the smaller facilities, retaining regional capacity to respond at a given level of service). Maps produced by Geoffrey Dutton, 1973.** *(Source: Red Book VII.23, Harvard University Graduate School of Design)*

BEDS PER C.C.U.

· 1 - 3
· 4 - 5
● 6 - 8
● 9 - 11

DISTRIBUTION OF HOSPITAL C.C.U.'S BY NUMBER OF BEDS. 1973

BEDS PER C.C.U.

· 1 - 3
· 4 - 5
● 6 - 8
● 9 - 13

PROPOSED DISTRIBUTION OF HOSPITAL C.C.U.'S BY NUMBER OF BEDS

undercover agents would not have used such an overt origin as DIA. By 1973, Mercready had developed a project at DIA that required software for managing a database of attributes of the countries of the world, integrated with the Laboratory's display programs. In an era when some anti-war activists picketed university labs with military contracts—and one lab in Wisconsin was bombed—universities did not want direct contracts with military agencies. Harvard also had a policy that no personnel would do secret work. Yet, the specific offering of the Harvard mapping software was unique, justifying a sole-source contract without a bidding process. To assuage the various sensitivities and requirements, the prime contract was passed through Kindler Associates, a consulting firm set up in Harvard Square for this purpose. Kindler handled some of the copious paperwork and did everything that required a security clearance. The Lab staff working on the project were not required to have a security clearance, and the results of the project were openly described in the newsletter *Context* and in *Red Book,* the project portfolio.[9] The figure given for the first year of the contract was $150,000, which went a long way to plug the deficit in the Laboratory's budget. The openness of the Harvard connection led to one curious visit from a Bulgarian scientist who asked sharp questions about our software, accompanied by an interpreter who looked even more sharply at our unsecured shambles with stacks of computer output. This visit may have been totally innocent, despite the paranoia of the Cold War era, but it gave a whiff of the world of international espionage.

For the DIA requirements, an attribute management package was built with an implementation of Berry's "geographical matrix" of places, themes, and times. This project, in requiring an integration of all the display programs, highlighted how incompatible they all were. The resulting package, called the Program-Model Integrator (PMI), was pretty much a gigantic "kludge" (a technical term for a construction of less-than-appealing esthetics). The integration was done by instituting a common user interface, but the needs of each program were so specific that in most cases, it simply passed commands through in the terms used by each program manual. The user interface was a first attempt to move away from fixed fields on cards toward a language of keywords. All this work helped rebuild a critical mass of programmers. The Kindler/DIA contract also subsidized cartographic database development using the CIA's public domain World Data Banks. The project required many levels of reporting and paperwork far beyond the typical requirements of a university project. A good amount of the funds covered direct expenses of travel and deliverables. Trips by Laboratory programmers to DIA at Arlington Hall outside Washington, D.C. made it clear that access to secure computers was much more restricted than in the civilian sector. The presence of long-haired, bearded Harvard staff aroused substantial suspicion in the buzz-cut, pocket-protector world of data processing at Arlington Hall. In spy novels, these agencies may sound like an organized hive of purposeful activity, but the pace was actually very slow, hampered by low staff morale due to strict compartmentalization. When the operators mounted the wrong tape, they would deny that an insecure person had actually received output listing the strength of Soviet tank regiments, but they would quickly slip the output into the burn bag.

Some may point their finger at this project as a sign that the Laboratory was tainted by working for the military during an unpopular war in Southeast Asia.[10] There is no denying that the contract existed, but the ethics of the situation require some additional consideration. Did the Laboratory become a support for the whole agenda of Henry Kissinger's foreign policy? Perhaps, but was the effect significantly more than simply paying federal income tax? Did the capability to make a SYMVU of some attribute attached to the countries of the world raise the ability to sow death and destruction? Probably not. It would be more apt to describe the interaction as a matter of convenience for both sides. DIA put up with the Harvard subcontractor as a sole source for something that they wanted behind their green secrecy doors. Most likely the real requirements were not revealed. On the Harvard side, the contract provided funding to get over a dry spell. Working for the money may not offer the best of motives, but it is also not an uncommon one. The future software developments of the Laboratory were designed to avoid the inelegance of the PMI. There were many lessons learned on all sides.

A negative report

The administration of the Graduate School of Design took notice of the decline in Laboratory revenues as well as the lack of a director. Originally, the Laboratory had been attached to the Department of City and Regional Planning, but it had moved to report directly to the dean after a year or two. For a short period, the dean created a Center for Environmental Design Studies to reorganize research across the Graduate School of Design, but this unit failed to spark any interest or activity. The Laboratory was a small tub on its own bottom.

Dean Sert, an architect from the Gropius school who had overseen the process of creating the Laboratory, was replaced by Maurice Kilbridge, who had spent most of his career at the Harvard Business School. The coalition of architecture, landscape architecture, and planning was a whole lot more fragile than it was in the functional modernist era of Walter Gropius, whose Bauhaus presence had dominated the design school from the 1930s into the 1960s. Architects worldwide were passing into post-modernism, with a return of decoration and facades. The planners at Harvard had taken a distinctly economic turn. Neither discipline was particularly attuned to the spatial analysis and mapping tools of the Laboratory.

In early 1974, Kilbridge appointed a committee to examine the Laboratory and to make recommendations about its future. This committee included five faculty members drawn from each department in the Graduate School of Design. Robert Shafer, a planner, was chair. Carl Steinitz represented Landscape Architecture; Daniel Schodek, a structural engineer, represented the technical side of Architecture; Lozano, an architect with some links to the Laboratory, and Konrad Kalba from the design traditions of the Gropius era, rounded out the five. In addition, there were three outside members: James McKenny from Harvard Business School; Joseph Wyatt, director of the Computing Center; and Nicholas Negroponte, an architect who had moved toward computers as director of the Media Lab at MIT. The committee issued its report in May 1974; it consisted of six sparse pages of text with a three-page table evaluating three potential lines of action.

This faculty committee considered the primary function of the Graduate School of Design to be instructional. They found that the Laboratory's presence in the City and Regional Planning Department had declined, that the Landscape Architecture Department was running its own computer support operation (David Sinton working with Carl Steinitz), and that Architecture had little need for computing. The section titled "Evaluation" gives the core of their argument:

> *Evaluation*
>
> The current LCGSA is not central to the operations of the GSD or any department. While the present service operations serve a large community of users outside the GSD, these operations are not needed inside the GSD. The clearest indication of its tangential role in the school was the statements [*sic*] by departmental representatives that their departments would not be interested in assuming any of the LCGSA's service function if the LCGSA were dissolved.
>
> The major reason for this situation is the lack of interest in LCGSA activities on the part of faculty members who are in the normal academic chain of promotion in their departments. And the record shows that LCGSA has made several efforts to become involved in the school's teaching programs. In order for a research and service organization to thrive within an educational institution like the GSD, members of the faculty must play a central and active role in that organization.
>
> The following are our specific findings:
>
> 1. Present LCGSA leadership does not hold faculty appointments in the normal chain of promotion in one or more departments.

2. The LCGSA's focus has been too narrow. Recent LCGSA research has largely ignored the "Spatial Analysis" portion of its name. Its research has largely been descriptive, not analytic. Moreover, the focus of its research has not been on problems of physical design or on larger scale spatial analysis, which are active departmental concerns at the GSD.
3. Too much effort has been expended in servicing the outside world. This has been of benefit, but at a high opportunity cost.
4. The market for current LCGSA programs appears likely to decline in the immediate future because external organizations are rapidly acquiring in-house facilities and expertise.
5. Because of the gap between faculty and the LCGSA, the LCGSA has difficulty in contributing to the education programs of the school. These teaching programs are our primary concern.
6. In recent years LCGSA has been on shaky financial grounds, requiring school subsidy. However, in the present year, it is likely to be financially self-sufficient.[11]

Much of the evaluation was quite accurate. Yes, the acting director of the Laboratory had just an affiliate appointment in the City and Regional Planning Department, not a tenure track professorship. Howard Fisher did organize faculty connections to each department, and some of them (notably Steinitz) turned into permanent long-term roles. But once established, these faculty did not maintain a connection to the Laboratory. Item #2 about spatial analysis is quite revealing, since spatial analysis means different things to different disciplines. The Laboratory had been an outpost of geographers, and no one on the committee came from that background. Indeed, the Laboratory had concentrated on maps rather than more detailed building sites (apart from the work on space allocation inside buildings; see chapter 4). Was the work descriptive? Perhaps the Girl Scout Council contract was not high science, but it hardly defined the direction of the Laboratory. The division between descriptive and analytic becomes rather complicated when designing software and data structures for representation. In retrospect, it seems incredible that a review committee in 1974 could miss the eventual explosion of demand for computer software (item #4). The idea that user organizations would do it all in-house is quite mystifying. Bottom line: the Harvard faculty wanted a Laboratory that served internal requirements, and not one oriented to the outside.

The committee presented three recommendations: two extremes followed by a middle course. The first called for immediate dissolution, the second for a strengthening of the Laboratory (using resources not to come from existing programs), and the third for a restructuring of the Lab into a support center in computing and video media for the academic departments.

To some extent, the faculty wanted the Laboratory for Computer Technology that Fisher had promised as the result of the Ford Foundation grant. The addition of video shows the wave of popularity caused by the luggable video camera and reel-to-reel video production work. The Laboratory had invested substantial effort in video productions for instruction in architecture and correspondence courses for software distribution. Yet, video was not going to be the savior of the Laboratory.

Disregarding much of the text of the report, Dean Kilbridge opted for the second recommendation—strengthening the Laboratory by appointing a new director, a credentialed research scholar with a full faculty appointment. Finding a permanent director had been a concern for a number of years. It took Kilbridge another year to hire the right director. The dean's decision did not assuage the concerns of the faculty. In seven years time, much of this report would come back to the surface, but in the meantime the Laboratory had an opportunity to rebuild its program.

The question of leadership

When Warntz left, Allan Schmidt, who had been associate director, was appointed as "acting director." Schmidt, who had a master's degree in city planning from the University of Illinois but no PhD, had taught courses in planning at Harvard without getting an appointment on the faculty. In academic life, the adjective "acting" usually implies temporary appointments for perhaps a year. This arrangement lasted for five years, with much uncertainty over each annual reappointment.

Everyone who worked at the Laboratory appreciated Schmidt's gentle style. He was a wonderful listener, and could calm even the wildest of egos. He encouraged the young programming staff to take responsibility. He did not manage through tight budgets and specific deadlines for deliverables. This was not the kind of leader that the faculty committee wanted.

FISHER'S CANDIDATE

In spring 1971, before Warntz had formally departed, Howard Fisher had tried to organize a replacement. Fisher's candidate was Jack Dangermond. At this point, Dangermond had only about two years of experience running a small nonprofit operation, Environmental Systems Research Institute, in California. He had two master's degrees, the first from the University of Minnesota in urban planning, and the second from Harvard was described in his curriculum vitae of 1971 as having an "emphasis in systems for geographic information" with no mention that it was a master's in landscape architecture.

In a letter dated May 11, 1971, before being offered the job, Dangermond signaled reluctance. "I would like first to make a name for myself on my own," he wrote to Fisher. Fisher pushed hard, and Dangermond nevertheless came to Cambridge for an interview. Dangermond remained reluctant, and in a May 17 letter, Fisher applied more pressure. "You are only 26 years old now, or about to be this July, and by the time you are 30 or 31 you could have built a pre-eminent world reputation," Fisher wrote.[12]

Dangermond ultimately declined the offer. His letter of June 7, 1971 to Fisher makes it clear: "As you described the Lab's job is potentially a fantastic opportunity for myself, but I sincerely feel that it would not be as personally satisfying as remaining at E.S.R.I. with the freedom that I presently enjoy." The growth of the software industry was hard to predict, yet Dangermond had a clearer vision of the future than the Harvard faculty demonstrated three years later in their 1974 report. The trajectory of ESRI and the Laboratory remained interlinked over the next decades.

Playing "what if?" allows uninhibited flights of imagination. If Dangermond's energy had been applied to the Laboratory, the development of GIS and automated cartography might have been different. Still, it is not clear that a director of the Laboratory could be successful without a strong academic reputation and the support of the faculty. Dangermond decided not to embrace Fisher's dream, since he had dreams of his own.

TOM PEUCKER: A POTENTIAL CANDIDATE

Tom Peucker had spent a semester in 1969 at Harvard, the same year that Dangermond had spent at the Laboratory while also working on his second master's degree. Peucker was on leave from his academic job at the recently founded Simon Fraser University in British Columbia. The continuous semester system at SFU allowed Peucker two consecutive semesters at Harvard while still fulfilling his required two semesters per year by teaching in the summers. Peucker had participated in the research in the Laboratory with an independent perspective, more as visiting scholar than as staff member. Following his stay at the Laboratory, he had also made extended visits to the University of Maryland and the image processing group of Azriel Rosenfeld, as well as Horwood's group at the University of Washington. Peucker retained connections with the Laboratory, such as teaching a summer short course on automated cartography at Harvard in 1972 and 1973.

Both Peucker and Schmidt were invited to a NATO workshop on automation in cartography held in England in the spring of 1973. In the private conversations that make such events more valuable than the official proceedings, Peucker confided that he was applying for a prestigious professorship in Germany. Schmidt wanted Peucker to become a candidate for director of the Laboratory. As a kind of trial period and a chance to work out the offer with the dean, Schmidt arranged to have Peucker spend the academic year 1973–1974 at the Laboratory as Visiting Scholar.[13] This visit was quite fruitful on a research front (see chapter 7), but the dean did not appoint Peucker to the directorship. Instead, he created the review committee and set his sights on a more established scholar. Peucker went back to Simon Fraser, taking with him some of the programming talent from the Laboratory (Jim Little) and Landscape Architecture (Robert Fowler). Peucker's team at Simon Fraser, including the students David Douglas, Randolph Franklin, and David Mark, conducted ground-breaking research on the treatment of surfaces over the next few years.

BRIAN BERRY ARRIVES

In the period between 1966 (when he visited Harvard for Fisher's luncheon talks; see chapter 1) and 1975, Brian Berry had developed from young Turk to established scholar and member of the National Academy of Sciences. His quantitative geography of cities had mobilized a veritable procession of doctoral students and had influenced the training of urban planners. Meanwhile, the University of Chicago was moving to abolish its geography department. Berry was on the market.

Dean Kilbridge was looking—and not just for a director of the Laboratory; he wanted to provide leadership for the doctoral program in planning. This degree program was attached to the Graduate School of Arts and Sciences since Harvard University did not think that there were enough professors with doctoral degrees or an adequate program of academic research in many of the professional schools such as the Graduate School of Design. Berry was eventually appointed the Williams Professor of City and Regional Planning in July 1976. He was also given the role as director of the Laboratory. Berry quickly ratified the current structure of the Laboratory by naming Schmidt as "executive director."

Berry brought great prestige to Harvard, and considerable analytical acuity, but he did not need to lead the Laboratory in a new direction of research. By the time he arrived, the directions of a new Laboratory were established. Kilbridge had acted to strengthen the Laboratory, though not exactly as the faculty had desired. The tub had found a new bottom. Research and development for external outlets took precedence over the instruction. The questions raised by the Shafer committee were set aside, for a while.

NOTES

1. A version of the cycle of credit can be found in Bruno Latour and Steve Woolgar, *Laboratory life: The construction of scientific facts,* 2nd ed. (Princeton, N.J.: Princeton University Press, 1986).

2. Howard T. Fisher, *Mapping information, the graphic display of quantitative information* (Cambridge, Mass.: Abt Books, 1982). Howard Fisher, on a handwritten page (undated), considered a set of possible titles for the book, including "The mapping of unobservable or intangible surfaces," "The mapping of unseen surfaces," and "The mapping of Unseen Surfaces: Real and Imaginary" (HTF Papers, box 2, folder: The Book).

3. Office of Naval Research Contract 00014-67A-0298 lasted from 1967–1971; National Science Foundation grant GS-2833 lasted from 1970–1972.

4. Carl Steinitz, David Sinton, and Allan Schmidt, "A general system for environmental resource analysis," *Report to the Public Land Law Review Commission, Washington, D.C.* (Cambridge, Mass.: Steinitz Rogers Associates, Inc., 1970).

5. Carl Steinitz and Peter Rogers, A systems analysis model of urbanization and change: An experiment in interdisciplinary education (Cambridge, Mass.: MIT Press, 1970).

6. Ted Driscoll, "SOLARE: A computer program for automated terrain modeling," (Laboratory for Computer Graphics and Spatial Analysis, Harvard University, 1978).

7. John Bunyan, *The pilgrim's progress* (1678; reprint, London: Penguin Classics, 1965). Charles Maklin, *The Man of the world* (1792; reprint, Abacus ebooks, www.abacci.com/msreader/ebook.aspx?bookID=11585).

8. Geoffrey Dutton, *Point to point flow allocation model: User documentation,* (Laboratory for Computer Graphics and Spatial Analysis, Harvard University, 1977).

9. " . . . And another grant to modify Lab's programs," *Context,* no. 4 (June 1973), 5. Mark Kriger, "An interactive on-line resource allocation management system," in *Red Book,* VII.2–VII.6 (Laboratory for Computer Graphics and Spatial Analysis, Harvard University, 1974).

10. Among others, John Cloud, "American cartographic transformations during the cold war," *Cartography and Geographic Information Science* 29 (2002): 261–282; John Cloud, "Overlays of mystery: The curiously un-contested origins of analog map overlay (abstract)," in *Annual Meeting, Association of American Geographers* (Chicago, Ill.: Association of American Geographers, 2006).

11. Shafer committee report (HTF Papers, box 7, folder: Laboratory)

12. Letters between Fisher and Dangermond, May 11, May 17, June 7, 1971 (HTF Papers, box 6, folder: Dangermond).

13. Peucker did write a substantial plan for the Laboratory, including Thomas K. Peucker, "The future of the Laboratory for Computer Graphics and Spatial Analysis," internal proposal to Dean Kilbridge (1974).

SEVEN

On the Topological Path

Some of the most important changes start from quite modest origins. They also usually have multiple connections, each pointing back to even more shadowy origins. The story of the renewed Laboratory follows a set of distinct origins that contributed to a common result — topological data structures. Over the period 1972–1975, the Laboratory became one of the most persistent advocates of this approach to geographic information systems.

POLYVRT: a program to convert geographic base files

In July 1972, I joined the Laboratory as a programmer. While an undergraduate student at the University of Massachusetts–Amherst, I had overhauled CALFORM to permit more flexible shading. The distribution version of CALFORM was a merger of my UMass CDC 3600 version and the IBM 360 version (see chapter 5). While doing work for the state government on school segregation and busing in Boston, I had become familiar with the first versions of the DIME files developed by the U.S. Census Bureau (following the plans developed by the New Haven Census Use Study;[1] see chapter 1). These publicly available databases could provide detailed basemaps for thematic cartography of urban areas. The data structure of the DIME files made it difficult to use directly in the Laboratory display programs. Arriving at the Laboratory at the lowest point in staff numbers, I received Allan Schmidt's clearance to pursue a general purpose converter program. This package, soon named POLYVRT, was meant to provide easy access to publicly developed cartographic databases for users of Laboratory display packages. (The name had seven vowel-deficient letters, following the limitations of the CDC SCOPE operating system.) The mentality behind POLYVRT was summarized in a letter I wrote to the U.S. Geological Survey in 1976:[2] "There will never be a simple standard data format, only the ability to convert easily." The community spent many years in pursuit of a standard format before coming to the same conclusion.

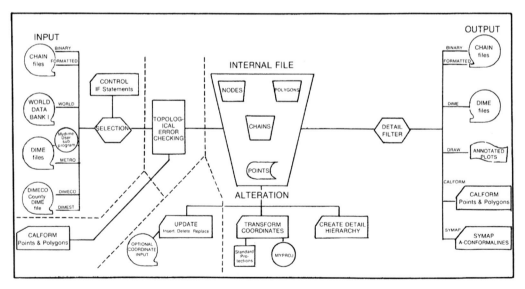

▲ POLYVRT system components. This program allowed input in a number of distinct formats and data structures. Certain manipulations were possible, including projections, generalization, and tedious manual editing. Output could be produced in a variety of formats for mapping programs. *(Source: LAB-LOG 1977, page 13, Harvard University Graduate School of Design)*

POLYVRT cut its teeth while serving to build the topological structure to upgrade the Central Intelligence Agency's World Data Bank I into a form usable for thematic cartography of the world. As I characterized it at AUTO-CARTO I in 1974, the CIA had adopted a data structure "unstructured as a plate of spaghetti."[3] To become useful for thematic mapping, each boundary line had to identify which countries were on either side of it. The topological coding was added manually, providing the base for world mapping required for the Kindler/DIA contract.

In addition to the World Data Bank, POLYVRT was designed to convert the major data sources available to U.S. users in 1972–1973. The U.S. Census Bureau sources, from the metropolitan DIME files at the street block level to the county DIME file at the national level, had a topological data structure.[4] POLYVRT followed this lead, using its own internal version of a data structure centered on polygons but based on "chains"—strings of segments that formed a boundary between two polygons. Adopting a topological data structure did not appear to be significant to the Shafer committee of faculty, but it became the basis for important developments in GIS software.

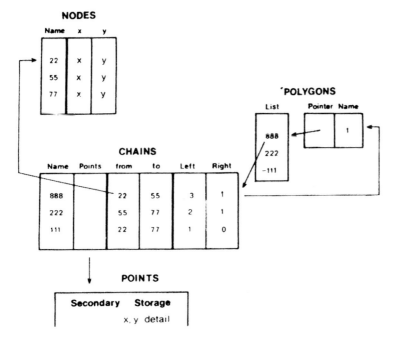

POLYVRT internal data structure. The central element was the "chain," a boundary segment between two nodes, separating two polygons. The cartographic detail to draw the chain was stored on a disk file. *(Source: Peucker and Chrisman 1975, figure 5)*

Taking a topological direction

In the academic year that Tom Peucker spent at the Laboratory (see chapter 6), he continued conceptual work on the topology of surfaces, a theme from Warntz's spatial analysis. Peucker and his team of students at Simon Fraser University were developing a topological data structure based on triangles eventually called triangular irregular network (TIN). He had found support for this work through the Office of Naval Research, the source of some of Warntz's support.

Peucker and I joined forces (respectively from three-dimensional and two-dimensional perspectives) to write a review article about data structures for cartography.[5] We submitted this text as a proposal to the National Science Foundation (NSF), Computer Science Division, listing Peucker as principal investigator, and me as coprincipal. This was a concrete sign that, on the date of submission in 1974, Peucker was being considered as potential director of the Laboratory. As the politics shifted and the dean appointed the Shafer committee, Peucker returned to his academic job at Simon Fraser. When NSF awarded the grant in 1975,[6] I was the only Harvard staff member named. As a then 24-year-old with just a bachelor's degree, I was not permitted to be the principal investigator because of NSF and Harvard policies. As a result, Allan Schmidt took on the role. Because it was not tied to specific deliverables and costly trips, the $230,000 provided by this grant had a much greater flexibility than the larger sum for the Kindler/DIA contract. The direction of the Laboratory took a path based on external considerations, in direct opposition to the recommendations of the Shafer committee.

GEOGRAF: JUMPING TO THE END-PRODUCT

In the 1974 proposal to NSF, and in the publications of the same year, GEOGRAF was introduced as a "system." Of course, proposals don't have to present finished work, and this system was just a sketchy diagram (see next page) in the proposal. LCGU, a key element of the relationships in the diagram, stood for "least common geographic unit"—an areal object that is the result of overlaying all the classes of polygons. (As I have to admit in retrospect, in mathematical terms, these are *greatest* common units, not least. As with many acronyms, words are stretched to obtain desired results. LCG really stood for Laboratory for Computer Graphics.) The ACR stood for an "attribute cross-reference," an unexplained nexus to interrelate all the various polygons that co-occurred at a given LCGU. The diagram was a slightly extended version of the POLYVRT data structure diagram which had been evolving since 1973 on the chalk board in Gund Hall 519, the back office where the staff congregated.

The main differences between GEOGRAF and POLYVRT involved adding multiple layers of polygons, all to be represented through a common base set of linear objects, called chains. The chain group was an intermediary that served the topological role of boundaries for a particular polygon set. Chain groups were also used for linear features (such as rivers or highways). My version of the diagram adds a pencil arrow connecting from nodes to chains, but the proposal actually sent to NSF does not show that arrow. The historical researcher has to be careful to make sure that evidence is not contaminated by later amendments. I am fairly sure that the pencil arrow was added in that time period, but I cannot remember when I added it. POLYVRT did not have a table of the chains around each node, and the original GEOGRAF copied that choice. In later discussions, I took the position that all topological relationships were worth storing, so I must have amended the diagram to fit my later opinion.

WHAT GEOGRAF WAS MEANT TO DO

GEOGRAF was designed as a universal storage system, a geographic database management facility without any connection to the limited world of database management in that era. The design criteria for relational database management had appeared as early as 1970, but it was a decade or more before anything remotely relational became a practical alternative. In 1974, a fixed-record mentality of business and accounting applications defined computing practices. Hierarchical models dominated what little there was of database management, with some network models that required specific preprocessing to generate "inverted" index access. In the scientific world, computation was central; databases were not in common use. To a large extent, GEOGRAF was an attempt to build all the functions of a database manager, as much as I understood those requirements at the time.

From the top level overview, GEOGRAF permitted collections of objects, grouped into classes. These objects would be nodes, chains, and polygons—whatever the topological model required. The software functions of GEOGRAF were specified in a nested scheme, with the operation of the storage system at a level beneath the specific application of the topological model. The storage system grouped some number of objects together into pages. If each object were its own record in a random access file, there would be too much overhead of unused file space, as well as too much time spent seeking data from the disk. The common solution at that time was pages of virtual memory. Pages for GEOGRAF would be fixed in length and big enough to handle

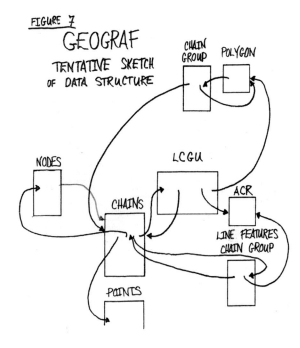

▲ Diagram of the fundamental object types in the topological data structure of GEOGRAF (1974). The POLYVRT data structure remains recognizable, with the addition of a layer of hierarchy to build multiple sets of polygons from one set of common basic areal units (LCGUs). At a particular polygon level, the "chain group" acts as the boundaries for those polygons. These groups are formed from the chains at the basic level. Linear features are also envisioned, simply as other chain groups without a polygon boundary function. *(Source: Hand-drawn diagram by Nick Chrisman occupied page 23 of NSF proposal, 1974)*[7]

a useful group of objects. The initial concept was based on a page size of 512 words (2K bytes in the IBM implementation). Objects in GEOGRAF were not simple, fixed-length records; they had to provide a variable length element. For a polygon, this was the list of chains around the outline. The points associated with a chain posed such distinct challenges (such as chains with more points than the page size would allow) that they required special point storage pages. Following the technique of POLYVRT, this variable length section was stored in a contiguous place in memory, packed in tightly with other variable length sections. This was efficient in terms of storage, but somewhat difficult to alter.

There were two methods to access objects—by name and by class. For the first, there were special "name pages" that provided a lookup function, storing the page location for a given identifier. This service used an interpretation of B-trees, taken from reading Donald Knuth's *Sorting and Searching,* a much-anticipated book that had appeared in 1973.[8] The B-tree requires a higher level of pages that indicate which range of identifiers appears on each name-page. Knuth's description showed that the overhead for this access method was quite limited. Parallel to the development at the Laboratory, others in the GIS field were also implementing this kind of access to objects in this period.[9] B-trees had captured the attention of the community.

The second access method provided a sequential access to all objects of a class, simulating a tape. This was done with a linked list of the pages for each object class. By having this kind of access, the system was still going to support programs that ran through all the data in whatever order it was presented, much like SYMAP.

The implementation of GEOGRAF fit closely into the network database technology of the period, best exemplified by the contemporaneous work of the CODASYL consortium.[10] The CODASYL group had advocated a programmer's approach to databases with specific relationships firmly wired with "inverted" access tables. The linkages were meant to operate through identifiers, not hardware addresses. Network databases could be quite fast at what they were designed to do. They did not support the use of any field as a key to relate to an unplanned other table; that was the core of Edgar Codd's relational model. (Codd, a researcher at IBM, had written his design criteria for relational database management in 1970,[11] but it was a decade or more before anything remotely relational became a practical alternative.)

This short introduction demonstrates that GEOGRAF was a tricky programming job with many unspecified details remaining to develop. The service routines were written, but debugging required some data to put into the system. Some higher-level programs would be required to access the data. Initially, an editing function was designed, but the full multilayer polygon hierarchies could not be built until a polygon overlay function could be written.

The proposal to NSF had given a loose sketch of a method to divide the overlay problem into reasonable units for computation. Using the approach to decomposing cartographic lines of the Douglas and Peucker line generalization algorithm[12] (written by David Douglas at Simon Fraser just before Peucker visited Harvard; implemented in POLYVRT), the proposal talked about dividing the database into those on the left or right of the band, then recursively applying the division until the computation was simple. In concept it might have seemed worth pursuing to those who reviewed the proposal, since it invoked solid computer science concepts such as recursion. However, the idea of dividing a complex mass of objects geometrically still required a lot of calculation. This algorithm was never even attempted at Harvard, though Peucker and Jim Little wrote a paper on the subject.[13] Although GEOGRAF (like Betamax) was presented as the wave of the future, an uneven infrastructure and events at the Laboratory conspired to make its implementation a low priority.

SELLING A VISION

While the functions of GEOGRAF were being programmed on paper, much of the effort went into a flurry of presentations. The Laboratory staff worked hard to convince the user community of the topological approach. This outreach effort began at a conference held during early December 1974 in Reston, Virginia. Titled "International Conference on Automation in Cartography," this event attracted about 400 people to the newly opened U.S. Geological Survey National Center. The shortened name, AUTO-CARTO I, stuck and created a series that lasted for over two decades. The organizers were Dean Edson and Warren Schmidt, both at the USGS, though Schmidt (no relation to Allan Schmidt) had just moved from the Central Intelligence Agency (CIA).

The conference turned into a running battle between the big systems of large users and the needs of smaller, more flexible applications. The conference began with a procession of large cartographic institutions that had been building hardware to input and output maps. The U.S. military at the Rome Air Development Center in New York, for example, had spent large sums constructing enormous machines to scan maps or to plot maps onto film a few meters by a few meters. There was a tension in the room as some asked for systems that would cost less than $100,000. The second day had sessions about software. The Laboratory took center stage, as Peucker and I appeared in a few successive sessions talking about topology, surfaces, and generalization. It was my first presentation at a professional conference, and I was excited and not a little nervous. Unlike most of the presenters, I had a written paper, carefully worded. I knew that I had a lot to say, and like many first-time presenters I did not want to wander far from my text. There was a noticeable chill in the room as I characterized World Data Bank II (developed by Warren Schmidt while at the CIA) as "unstructured as a plate of spaghetti."[14] My claim was that it was missing topology. The combination of our presentations made a strong case that some intelligence in data structures might be worth more than bigger machines. Of course, my opinions were not simply those of a 24-year-old junior programmer. Coming from Harvard, and supported by the more established Peucker, I had allies.

The Laboratory continued to make the case for topology on every possible occasion. In early March 1975, Allan Schmidt and I visited Dean Edson and Warren Schmidt at the USGS offices. Edson and Warren Schmidt revealed their plans for a digital cartographic database built from the topographic mapping series, and presented draft documents describing the project.[15] This process applied digital techniques to reproduce the cartographic output, not to produce the kind of data that would be of use to others. We wanted to convince them of the utility of topology, as a key to serving a user community. We fired back a letter the next week, and followed up with another trip to Reston. I was joined by Geoffrey Dutton and Denis White (just recently hired as a programmer) to mobilize a response. By April 11, 1975, we had worked out an agreement to present a three-day training and discussion session in early May.[16] Over a few weeks, there were at least four people working much more than full-time to create a session that explained the utility of topology. We had some internal allies working in the land-use project in the Geography Applications Group at USGS, which had adopted a topological data structure built by in-house programmers. However, these geographers were not in the Topographic Division (they would be merged into the National Mapping Division within a few years).

The core of the presentation was a diagram for a data model based on GEOGRAF, but with substantial amendments to address the specific content of topographic maps. It was labeled GEOGRAF 1.2, but called half-jokingly "Megalomane 1" by the Laboratory staff. Based on a model of integrated topology, one set of composite objects captured all the geometry with full topological consistency. These base entities were indexed into any number of thematic layers through the intermediary of chain groups. Since topographic maps portray a number of linear networks, the conceptual focus expanded past the purely areal overlay origins. Following the first figure reproduced here, we presented the user level view for political, survey, hydrography, transportation, and terrain thematic associations. The terrain diagram presented four distinct options, based on different data structures (contours, point samples, and TINs).

The Laboratory staff rushed to prepare three days of presentations and workshops in a motel down the road from Dulles International Airport. The large contingent from the USGS Topographic Division attended, though technically they didn't sponsor it (hence the meeting off-site). The effort invested at Harvard was about one person-year at normal speeds, covered by our NSF grant funds and other Laboratory sources. The USGS paid no more than a few air tickets.

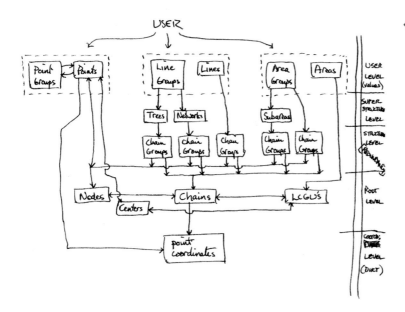

When Dean Edson announced the "Digital Line Graph" (DLG) project in September 1975 at AUTO-CARTO II,[17] it included explicit assimilation of topological principles. The data structure diagram used Laboratory terminology (chains, chain groups, etc.) that were changed in later documents. Edson thanked the Laboratory verbally in his presentation, but there is no reference to our efforts in his written paper in the proceedings. The production version of DLG files preserved a limited version of topology without the integrated character of GEOGRAF and Edson's presentation.

In this period, the Laboratory was making active efforts to do projects for federal agencies. One of the meetings with USGS was tied to a preliminary proposal to study digitizing for the Soil Conservation Service. There was also work on the Urban Atlas data for the U.S. Census Bureau. At AUTO-CARTO II, in September 1975, there was a prominent display of Laboratory software products. My paper[18] continued to sell the basic principles of GEOGRAF. In 1976 there were many groups around the world working on topology. The DIME technology had sparked similar developments in France, Sweden, and other countries. The Laboratory had consulting contracts with both the Tehran Development Council in Iran and Imelda Marcos's Human Settlements Commission for Metro Manila, Philippines. We would go anywhere to talk about the benefits of topological data structures, no matter how dubious the regime. A team of five presented a week-long training session in Manila in August 1976.

The Laboratory also had an opportunity to present its topological data structure ideas to the Defense Mapping Agency (DMA) through a contract in 1977-1978.[19] The integrated topology concept was largely absorbed by DMA. The heritage of GEOGRAF concepts is directly visible in military standards such as DIGEST (DIgital Geographic Information Exchange STandard) and the Vector Product Format (later VMap).[20] Other groups championed topological data structures in the same period, but the Laboratory's efforts enlarged our visibility in the research community.

Reality intrudes

The demands of specific applications have a way of countering theoretical suppositions. In the autumn of 1975, the Laboratory took on a contract with the U.S. Census Bureau, Geography Division. Although it was the originator of the topological concept in its DIME files, the Census Bureau had contracted with a vendor to digitize the maps of census tracts for each metropolitan area using a laser scanner. The files were used to produce a printed collection of brightly colored choropleth maps by census tract for each metropolitan area called the *Urban Atlas.* Unlike the current raster scanners that plow across a map in a single pass, the laser traced each polygon from a centroid. Starting from this central point, the laser swept out on an axis until it detected a line. It followed the line counter-clockwise around the polygon, always taking left turns at nodes, until it returned to the starting point. The result was meant to be a single polygon loop (what we now call a shapefile) for each polygon. Unfortunately, due to a lack of topological processing capability, some of the polygons were not correctly structured. The topological structure provided a way to verify the integrity of this resource. The Laboratory wanted to convert all the Urban Atlas data files to a topological structure. The Census Bureau, not totally convinced, permitted a pilot project to assess the process and the results.

URBAN ATLAS PROJECT

Denis White took charge of the Urban Atlas project with a selection of 10 polygon files to convert.[21] He had previously converted the file for Fresno, California, in a proof-of-concept pilot that had been used to attract the attention of Census Bureau staff. The Census Bureau had selected a few small cities (Altoona, Pennsylvania and Appleton, Wisconsin at the start of the alphabet, then they had included some of the largest metropolitan areas: Atlanta, Baltimore, Boston, Chicago, and Los Angeles).

The prototype had required programming to pull the polygons apart into segments, sort them on their midpoint, then attempt to match them with the other record for that segment on the adjacent polygon. With a few passes through POLYVRT to string the segments together, a chain file would result if the input was clean. The process worked entirely automatically for two of the small cities, Altoona, and Atlantic City, New Jersey. A few annoying little slivers appeared, and a few digitizing errors were detected. As city size increased, the POLYVRT storage had to be increased. We had created a .BIG version, and we went on through .BIGGER and .BIGGEST to .OINK, running at the largest amount of memory available on the Harvard–MIT IBM 370. POLYVRT's static storage system had difficulty shuffling the segments around to form them into coherent chains. The reason was that it

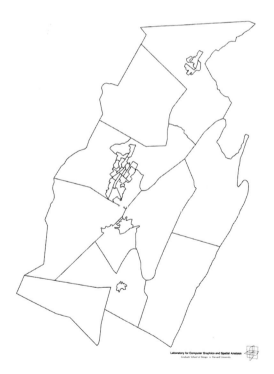

▲ 1970 Census tracts for Altoona, Pennsylvania as processed from the Urban Atlas file into a chain data structure. *(Source: Internal Report 75–6, page 23)*

had to move all the other points further on in the file when it had to add one point to a chain. Deletion was just as bad. The points were on an external disk file and the process got laborious. I, as the author of POLYVRT, was called in to try to tend to the beast.

Then we hit Chicago. Due to the highly orthogonal nature of Chicago tracts, the sorting process did not place the contiguous sides of a polygon in adjacent positions in the file. There were just too many ties. We tried all kinds of rotations, and finally one gave a bit better matching rate. Perhaps due to the reduced nature of the image scanned, the polygons did not line up as well as in other cities. There were 51 slivers that had to be manually corrected. This took about a week of batch jobs, error plots, attempted corrections, and late nights at the Computing Center. The errors in the file were laborious to correct with our limited interface. White and I dreaded Los Angeles, and started thinking of alternatives as the deadline for delivery approached rapidly.

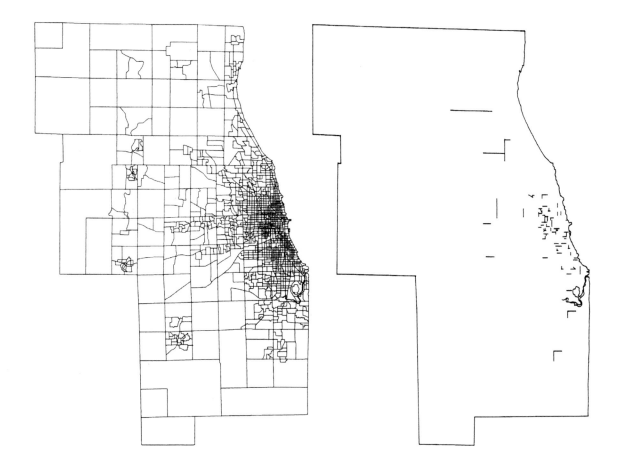

▲ 1970 Census tracts for Chicago urban area (left); sliver errors where tract boundaries did not match and had to be manually corrected (right). *(Source: Internal Report 75–6, pages 29–30)*

A DYNAMIC SOLUTION: CYCLONE

I whipped up a program originally called EATDIME that was intended to do a better job linking up the segments into chains. It had a dynamic data structure, in place of the static POLYVRT approach. An input segment was inserted based on the node identifiers at either end. If the node "cycled," meaning that the polygon identifiers matched in pairs (left and right) around the node, then the node could be treated and deleted. If a cycled node had just two segments, it was just a point along a chain, and the two segments could be strung together by hooking up the pointers. Once a chain reached a three (or higher) degree node at both ends, it was complete and could be written to the output. While this sounds a bit complicated, it ran reliably and fast almost as soon as it was written. Rather than spend another week pushing Los Angeles through the old process, the new program processed this largest file with no problem. There were still many serious errors to fix with our manual process, but the large file did not break the process.

The program was redubbed CYCLONE, since it cycled nodes and it was fast. This simple processor, with its radical shift to dynamic memory allocation, upset all of the presumptions of the GEOGRAF data structures. It opened the door for a much bigger development project.

NOTES

1. Donald F. Cooke and William H. Maxfield, "The development of a geographic base file and its uses for mapping," in *Proceedings, Fifth Annual Meeting* (Garden City, N.Y.:URISA, 1967); Donald F. Cooke, "Topology and TIGER: The Census Bureau's contribution," in *The history of geographic information systems: Perspectives from the pioneers,* ed. Timothy W. Foresman, 47–57 (Upper Saddle River, N.J.: Prentice Hall, 1998).

2. Nicholas R. Chrisman, "Comments on the draft GIRAS (LUDA) documentation of 24 March 1976," sent to James Anderson, Geography Applications Program, U.S. Geological Survey, May 19, 1976, 23.

3. Nicholas R. Chrisman, "The impact of data structure on geographic information processing," in *Proceedings, AUTO-CARTO I,* 167 (Reston, Va.: ACSM, 1974).

4. The Laboratory offered a service to produce base files of polygons for Laboratory software from these public sources (World Data Bank I and County DIME file) for a price of around $1 per polygon (minimum order 50 polygons). *Context,* no. 4 (1974), 4.

5. Thomas Peucker and Nicholas Chrisman, "Cartographic data structures," *The American Cartographer* 2 (1975): 55–69.

6. National Science Foundation grant MCS 74-14437-A01, 1974–1977. Original proposal: "Topological information systems for urban and environmental research," submitted January 1974.

7. Compared to the standards of the present day, such a hand-drawn diagram looks positively unprofessional. The rest of the proposal was 38 pages in double-spaced typescript with voluminous appendices. This was created during an era of greater flexibility and less expectation of typeset perfection in all documents. After all, it was an era before the office became computerized. Yes, we were the Laboratory for Computer Graphics, but we did not have anything remotely close to a drawing program on our computers yet, much less the interactive means to create illustrations.

8. Donald E. Knuth, *Sorting and searching,* vol. 3, *The art of computer programming* (Menlo Park, Calif.: Addison Wesley, 1973).

9. Marvin White, "The cost of topological file access," in *Harvard papers on geographic information systems,* vol. 6, ed. Geoffrey Dutton, 1–63 (Reading, Mass.: Addison Wesley, 1978).

10. COnference on DAta SYstems Languages.

11. E. F. Codd, "A relational model of data for large shared data banks," *Communications of the Association of Computing Machinery* 13 (1970): 378–387.

12. David H. Douglas and Thomas K. Peucker, "Algorithms for the reduction of the number of points required to represent a digitized line or its charicature," *The Canadian Cartographer* 10, no. 2 (1973): 110–122.

13. James J. Little and Thomas K. Peucker, "A recursive procedure for finding the intersection of two digital curves," *Computer Graphics and Image Processing* 10 (1979): 159–171.

14. Chrisman, "The impact of data structure on geographic information processing," 167.

15. Office of Research and Technical Standards, Branch of Cartography, "Digital cartographic data base description," draft document, February 1975.

16. Allan Schmidt (Harvard), letters to Warren Schmidt (USGS), dated March 13, March 26, April 4, and April 11, 1975.

17. Dean Edson, "Digital cartographic data base preliminary description," in *Proceedings, AUTO-CARTO II*, 523–538 (Reston, Va.: ACSM, 1975). Figure 7 on page 535 is a cleaned-up version of the GEOGRAF 1.2 diagram presented in May 1975.

18. Nicholas R. Chrisman, "Topological data structures for geographic representation," in *Proceedings, AUTO-CARTO II*, 346–351 (Reston, Va.: ACSM, 1975).

19. The Laboratory was subcontractor on Contract DAAK70-77-C-0265 from U.S. Army Topographic Laboratory, Fort Belvoir, Virginia, to The Analytical Sciences Corporation (TASC) in Reading, Massachusetts.

20. The team at ESRI that developed the Digital Chart of the World, and the format it used (then called the Vector Product Format), included some Laboratory alumni: Duane Niemeyer, Scott Morehouse, and Nick Chrisman as consultant on data structures.

21. Denis R. White and Allan Schmidt, "A report on the conversion of twelve Urban Atlas files to extended DIME files and their use in the preparation of base-map files for computer mapping," *Internal report 75-6* (Laboratory for Computer Graphics and Spatial Analysis, Harvard University, 1975).

EIGHT

ODYSSEY

While **SYMAP** attended the founding of the Laboratory, the most ambitious software product came in the second phase. The **ODYSSEY** system grew out of research on topological data structures and related applied projects. It came to occupy the efforts of an expanding staff as it was prepared for distribution in 1980–1981. **ODYSSEY** served as a prototype for the modern geographic information system.

ODYSSEY *emerges*

In a late-night session at the computer center in December 1975 as we waited for the final runs of the Urban Atlas project, Denis White and I got excited about the technique that we started to call "local processors." The new program CYCLONE (see chapter 7) had proven itself, and had made the Urban Atlas project a success. The key trick involved dynamic data structures, adapted to the specific problem at hand. Then, White figured out that a similar cycling program could assemble polygons to produce the polygon loop (shapefile) data structure that many graphics programs (such as SYMAP) demanded. He called this CYCLOPS. Somehow this got the two of us thinking about Homer's *Odyssey*, where the Cyclops lived close to a whirlpool. In the late-night ambience, it all seemed to make sense without any demonstrated proof.

What GEOGRAF needed was a reliable program to compute intersections, because the whole data structure depended on an integrated topology. From the experience with the static memory of POLYVRT during the Urban Atlas processing, GEOGRAF would evidently provide the wrong environment to mount this much more complex calculation. Extrapolating from CYCLONE's success, we hoped that the local processor approach would provide a way to keep the computation under control.[1] The next morning, we brought a diagram to the office to show to the rest of the staff. The system had the name ODYSSEY, a name selected without considering preexisting trademarks or whether we needed to dream up a dumb phrase that would turn into such an acronym. At the outset, the whole team agreed to avoid using any acronyms whatsoever in the names of programs or subroutines. We adopted a classical theme for the top level, and had subthemes from Norse or Greek myths, with occasional digressions to rhyming puns. The future module WHIRLPOOL played the key role of polygon overlay. At this stage there was a different program (called PASTA, sadly incompatible with the classical theme) to handle unlabeled input from digitizers. The package was completed with some display programs—taken all together, enough work for a few years of programming. Jim Dougenik shared our enthusiasm, and the Laboratory took a sharp turn away from the GEOGRAF database approach.

In contrast to the seemingly theoretical plans for GEOGRAF, ODYSSEY was at first immediately tangible. Local processing worked right away on data conversion problems for specific clients. In December 1975, ODYSSEY appeared as a collection of modules and processors, but not a unitary system under a single roof. Each processing function had to operate its own internal data structure, tuned to specific requirements. Information would be shared in the form of standardized sequential files. The coherence of the system came from the shared service modules and a common language interface.

The instant enthusiasm for ODYSSEY is apparent in how fast the Laboratory switched over to promoting a concept that was still being worked out. In January 1976, the month after the original evening in the Computing Center, the Laboratory submitted a twenty-six page description of ODYSSEY to Tektronix in an attempt to obtain support for development efforts. Tektronix was launching a desktop workstation product, the 4081, and we anticipated that our system could run on the small machines that would be emerging. The second paragraph of this document gives an idea of the projected clientele of the whole project: "It is anticipated that the ODYSSEY mapping system will solve, in a general fashion, many of the existing creation, maintenance, processing and display requirements of a large number of federal, urban, state and regional information planning agencies as well as satisfy land use and thematic mapping needs."[2]

There were two detailed diagrams showing the program modules in the system; the more complex one based on the conversion of data structures is included here. As with the GEOGRAF diagrams, it is a hand-drawn sketch. On the last page (26) there was a list of the programs with the percentage of completion in two columns: design and "program" (meaning coding, debugging, documentation, and everything else, presumably). CYCLONE merited 100 percent for design and 90 for program; after all it was working (although thorough documentation and user-proofing would probably take more time than the original programming burst). CYCLOPS was 90 percent designed, but only 10 percent programmed. The crucial WHIRLPOOL module was correctly shown as 10 percent designed, zero percent programmed. There was a module called ZEUS (identified as file manager and command language) that never was written. There was a lot of work ahead to make ODYSSEY a reality.

The importance of ODYSSEY was partially in what it did, but more critically in how it did it. For the essential function of planar enforcement that provided the overlay capability, the internal data structures were carefully constructed using the emerging literature on algorithmic complexity. Compared to the straightforward mathematical coding of SYMAP, ODYSSEY danced circles of dynamic data flow. These programming constructs were built on a series of service modules, intended to be reused across a collection of processors.

An elaborate diagram of the ODYSSEY ▶ processors, prepared within a month of the system's inception (dated January 1976). This diagram focuses on the conversions between data structures and does not show the display programs (they were on another diagram). The central data structure was the "chain," with planned connections to raster and shapefiles (here called "regions"). The circles labeled NAP, CAN, and CAP stand for files structured around topological relationships (respectively, Nodes Around Polygons, Chains Around Nodes, and Chains Around Polygons).

Of the programs specified in this diagram, only CELLMAP (a rasterizer) and RDCALF (the POLYVRT function to accept input from CALFORM) did not make it into the eventual distribution version of ODYSSEY in 1981.

(Source: The ODYSSEY Mapping System – An Introduction, January 1976, page 10)

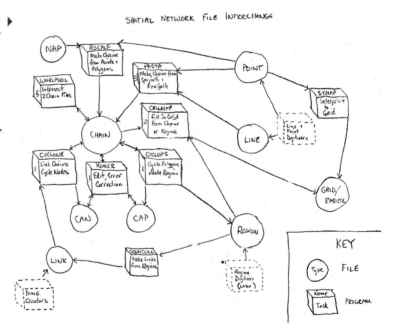

Tour of the competition: early GIS software

ODYSSEY was not produced in a vacuum; over the period of its gestation there were all kinds of developments around the world. While the literature of this period is certainly fugitive, the Commission on Geographical Data Sensing and Processing of the International Geographical Union provides sufficient documentation of the fitful development of GIS.[3] Resulting from a symposium convened by Roger Tomlinson in Ottawa during August 1972, there was a massive two-volume description of the state-of-the-art. Chapter 16 (on geographic information systems) was edited by Ray Boyle, the original designer of the first digitizing table. In it, each GIS was classified into one of five "families" based mostly on the basis of data structure. The label SYMAP was attached to the first family of relatively fine raster systems, even though the input to SYMAP itself fell more into the vector families four and five. The second family was for coarse cellular systems used in resource inventories of the era, such as LUNR (Land Use and Natural Resources inventory) developed for New York state with some input from the Steinitz group at the Laboratory. In this period a number of states developed natural resource inventories with square kilometer or square mile grid cells, similar to LUNR. The third group was organized around the urban content of census data. The topological structure of the U.S. Census Bureau DIME file was mentioned but not seen as something generic to apply outside the urban context. The fourth family used point data exclusively, and the fifth collected all forms of vector data structures, including MAP/MODEL and the Canada Geographic Information System (CGIS). While some of these distinctions persist, current functionality is divided on much different terms.

CGIS is widely considered the first of them all.[4] Its software was built by IBM Corporation under contract to the Canada Land Inventory (CLI), a continental scale effort to determine suitable land use. The maps for CLI were classified according to the approach to landscape evaluation proposed by Angus Hills (see chapter 3). While the report from the symposium classified CGIS along with the vector data structures, it had elements of raster processing designed around the recognition of lines from the simple photo-cell scanner used for input. This raster was used to calculate the overlay of two maps by simply writing each one to the raster and reconverting this composite input. CGIS had a reputation of creating lots of tiny sliver polygons. For whatever reason, IBM never sold a second copy of CGIS to another client. The system had substantial influence, but few direct descendents.

Around the same time as CGIS, MAP/MODEL was coded by Samuel Arms, a programmer with a regional government in Oregon.[5] His data structure used polygon loops similar to the SYMAP input. Analytically, MAP/MODEL went far beyond SYMAP. Common boundaries between adjacent polygons were detected and slivers controlled to some extent. The module to calculate polygon overlay compared every polygon in one set to all the polygons in the other set—what is called an N^2 algorithm, since the number of calculations is proportional to the square of the number of objects to process. By the 1970s, there were other software packages with essentially the same approach including ESRI's PIOS (Polygon Information Overlay System); Michael Goodchild's PLUS/X (Planning Land Use System eXtended); and the early MOSS (Map Overlay and Statistical System) from the U.S. Fish and Wildlife Service.[6] One such development was called the Natural Resource Information System. The U.S. Department of the Interior paid for two large commercial contractors, Boeing Computer Services and Raytheon Autometric, to develop the software. The version by Autometric was evaluated at the University of Wisconsin in 1976.[7] It ran for hours to calculate overlays with a few thousand points. The software still had a major logic flaw in tracing polygons from the linework, such that the area calculations were suspect in any case with inner rings (islands) or complex nodes.

To summarize all these early systems, the best evaluation of GIS software came a few years later. In 1980, in the process of evaluating bids for a natural resource system for the province of Saskatchewan, Roger Tomlinson, with his associates including Ray Boyle, concluded that there was no commercial system available that satisfied the needs.[8] It was this gap that the ODYSSEY team had embarked to fill.

SUPPORTING DYNAMIC MEMORY

The Laboratory distributed programs to university computer centers, government agencies, and a few large companies (mostly oil and forestry companies). There were multiple disparate computers and operating systems; just about the only unifying element was the FORTRAN compiler.[9] When ODYSSEY was started, the UNIX operating system (and its C language) was just a research project at Bell Labs. Early C implementations were also on 16-bit mini-computers that could not support floating point calculations on geographic coordinates. The choice of FORTRAN meant that the ODYSSEY team had to provide their own services that programmers now might take for granted. Virtually the only data structure supported by FORTRAN compilers was the array. Even more limiting, the size of the array had to be declared to the compiler and could not be altered at run time. There was one tiny loophole in what was called "blank" COMMON, a memory space that could be shared between subroutines but whose size did not need to be specified identically in all references. The provision of dynamic memory allocation shows how the ODYSSEY programmers built a set of services.

CYCLONE was transitional, still influenced by the array-based POLYVRT. In both programs there were separate, static arrays for nodes, chains, and polygons. While POLYVRT used its arrays sequentially without any dynamic component, CYCLONE chained together unused entries into a linked list. To create an object (node, chain, or point), it was unlinked from the free space and attached to their new topological relationships. A chain would control a linked list of points and pointers to the nodes at either end. When a node had "cycled," it was removed and references to it were unlinked (and marked as "complete"). When both nodes of a chain were marked complete, the chain was also removed, causing its dependent points to be freed up as well. Removal was done simply by linking the object back on the free space for the object class. This scheme worked well as long as the relative balance between the object classes could be predicted. Leonhard Euler's graph theory gives some guidance to the number of nodes and links in a graph, but the number of cartographic detail points along each boundary could fluctuate depending on measurement technology and scale of representation. Node degree is typically very close to three, though grid cities have some areas that approach four. For the Urban Atlas processing, the figures were reasonably stable.

In writing the polygon cycler, CYCLOPS,[10] Denis White adopted a more flexible solution. Instead of the distinct arrays for each object class, he put all of his data into one large space. He wrote a service module to manage the allocation and deallocation of objects in this space. Each unit of space was called a "nub," and the names of the functions all rhymed with nub.[11] (These names were part of a conscious strategy to eschew acronyms. Our joke was that the system was called NoAc for "no acronyms.") GRUB allocated a nub; SCRUB deleted it and returned it to free space. Each nub was a reserved space in "blank" COMMON, the one block of memory permitted to vary in size by the FORTRAN standard. For debugging, PUB dumped the memory to the printer (showing the batch style of our programming practice where huge piles of core dumps were the only way to track down a bug).

Dynamic memory allocation is pretty simple for fixed-length objects, but it gets more complicated for variable sized requests. NUBS implemented state-of-the-art programming techniques following Knuth and other resources of the period. The primary problem was termed "garbage collection." If you start with one big unallocated space, the first objects are placed by carving up the big space. If the program deallocates them in the exact reverse order, one might be able to restore the original big space. Dynamic operations are rarely so well behaved, since allocated objects get mixed up between blocks of free space. At some point, the remaining allocated objects must be moved into a compact position to restore a single remaining free space. The trick is to retain enough threads in the data structure to be able to rebuild the links to objects that have moved. NUBS became a service for all ODYSSEY programs, and each data structure had to be able to respond to the REDUB compactifier when it decided that free space was too fragmented or when it had to allocate some large object. In practice, this meant that all ODYSSEY data structures operated through indirect references, not direct memory pointers. This service is now hidden in object programming environments.

TALKING TO COMPUTERS: LINGUIST

Developing interactive programs had required new solutions to the user interface, replacing the rigid card-based controls of SYMAP (see chapter 5). The hardware of the time had limitations compared to current equipment. In 1975, and for at least dozen more years, a mouse was not an assumed appurtenance of a computer. The interaction followed the maxim: "In the beginning was the command line." The command line for ASPEX were keywords with parameters, such as "AZIMUTH=30; ALTITUDE=10." Like most programmers of the time, we hated spelling out commands and sought abbreviations. The keyword recognition for ASPEX used a tree data structure that would reject ambiguous commands, but accept any substring that was unambiguous. We built this tree data structure by hand, but began to think about more automated language definition. There were multiple proposals by Laboratory staff under the names SUGAR and TRELIS. As the process became more sophisticated, we added "verbs" to the keywords, creating a richer syntax. From the user perspective, these languages could be expressed in the railroad track diagrams that Niklaus Wirth had made popular.

From the programmer's perspective, the system became more automated, and table driven. Jim Dougenik and I ended up building a sophisticated language-specification module called GLIB that created language parsing tables based on a language description written in a Language Definition Language (LDL). Of course, we implemented this LDL as a GLIB dialect (in the Language Definition Language Language). The tricky problem with such bootstrapping is that the internals of the system are often one step behind, since the dialect for the new version has to be tested and implemented from the old platform. GLIB wrote out language tables as FORTRAN statements to be inserted in the target program. The packed numbers in the table were virtually undecipherable without a detailed understanding of the language data structure. Without GLIB, ODYSSEY programs would be impossible to maintain or extend. This linkage became important later on in the commercialization stage. In the target program, the GLIB tables were interpreted by the run-time module. Overall, the combination was called LINGUIST.[12]

8.5.7 ZOOM, SHIFT, and ROTATE

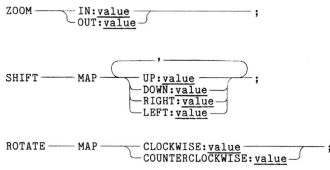

◀ Railroad track renditions of a portion of the PROTEUS language. The lines show how sentences can be constructed. In this case, a comma can be used to "SHIFT MAP UP:3, RIGHT:2;" without repeating the beginning of the sentence. These commands controlled the zoom and pan functions for the graphic display. *(Source: ODYSSEY Manual, volume 1, pages 8-44, 1981)*

Examples ZOOM IN:2;
          ZOOM OUT:1.5;
          SHIFT MAP LEFT:3;
          ROTATE MAP CLOCKWISE:30;

Syntactically, the recognition moved from keywords to whole sentences, with verbs, adjectives, and nouns. The tree-based recognition depended on the context, not the global lexicon. Thus "SET MAP WINDOW" could be rendered "SET MA W" if MAP and MINIMUM were the valid terms, but MAP would have to be spelled out if MAXIMUM was permitted after SET. WINDOW could be abbreviated W since there were probably few words associated with MAP. These sentences were described as a "finite state automaton," technically an LR(0) language (standing for left and right look-ahead zero). Writing lexical parsers was a common procedure; the UNIX toolkit acquired "Yet Another Compiler Compiler" (YACC) in this same period. GLIB went beyond YACC, though, in its semantic component. Most user command languages provide common functions of setting certain parameters, showing the current values, and then passing control to the program. LDL provided a mechanism to describe the kinds of parameters, including regular numeric fields, text strings, exclusive options specified by name, and nonexclusive flags to turn off and on. In the run time LINGUIST, new words could be added, for specific contexts, and values calculated based on the values of others (for instance "MAKE ZOOM FACTOR: MAP SCALE/3.2;"). Values could include arbitrarily complicated formulae including reference to external functions. There was a provision for branching (IF THEN ELSE) as well as procedures (in the form of command files).

```
(1,11 0)     OPEN       ASSIGN REG EACH:
(1,12 0)     CREATE     ASSIGN REG EACH:
(1, 11 12)   SHOW       SHOW:
(1, 0)       RUN        NOOP PROGRESSING:
(1,0)        QUIT       NOOP PROGRESSING:
(11, 13 0)   INPUT      NULL:
(12, 13 0)   OUTPUT     NULL:
(13, 80 0)   FILENAME   BACK:
END
FILENAME     OPEN       STRING: INL,INFIL(8) /"INPUT.DAT"/
FILENAME     CREATE     STRING: IOUT,IOUFIL(8) /"OUTPUT.DAT"/
END
```

▲ Fragment of a fictional language definition, written in the Language Definition Language. The numbers in parentheses are the "states" in which the word could be uttered. After the colon is the semantic interpretation of the word. FORWARD and BACK link to the second portion (after END) where compound terms are defined.

In this example above, the entry state is 1, permitting the "verbs" OPEN, CREATE, SHOW, RUN, and QUIT. The last two create one-word sentences (they end in the terminal state zero). OPEN leads to state 11 that expects INPUT, while CREATE leads through state 12 to OUTPUT. Both of these then converge on the word FILENAME. SHOW permits both 11 and 12. FILENAME can accept a value (state 80) or the sentence terminates. The compound section defines OPEN FILENAME and OUTPUT FILENAME as two distinct storage spaces with their own default character strings. *(Source: Harvard University Graduate School of Design)*

As a basic principle, the programmer could remain isolated from the specific outward presentation of the language. As long as the parameters were set, the program behind didn't need to know that the user was working in French or English or even Russian. In some prototypes we built languages that had the adjectives before or after the noun, the verbs before or after the nouns. They could all produce the intended behavior from the unmodified program. One major goal of the language system was to make documentation easier. A consistent syntax would mean that a user did not need specific instruction for each new module. More importantly, a question mark could be used at any time to provide the responses that would be allowed to finish a sentence. Despite all this flexibility, the programming features of LINGUIST were not fully used in the ODYSSEY package as implemented.

SUPPORTING A SYSTEM

Through 1976 and 1977, the ODYSSEY system took shape. The team expanded from Denis White and me with the addition first of Jim Dougenik, a programmer who had joined the Laboratory directly from an undergraduate degree at Harvard in computer science. Randolph Franklin, who had worked for Tom Peucker at Simon Fraser, became a PhD student in computer science at Harvard and joined the Laboratory as a research assistant. Scott Morehouse also joined the team in summer 1977 from an undergraduate degree at Hampshire College in Massachusetts where he had written a thesis about cartographic data structures (hardly the most common topic of discourse at that institution). In this initial period, most decisions about ODYSSEY were collective, consensual, and fluid. We would spend hours talking about directions, solutions, and data structures. Responsibilities were allocated, and each person wrote their own code. Then we would spend hours in painfully collective debugging. Usually Dougenik would fire up the program of the moment, stuff in the biggest data stream we had available, and make it break. He operated on our large-screened Tektronix 4014 (see illustration on page 87), capable of displaying 120 lines of code on the storage screen, with his Coke can close to provide the caffeine required. Using the highly arcane interface on the PDP-10 called DDT (Dynamic Debugging Technique), he would search the entrails to determine what had gone wrong. We called these "finger-pointing sessions," since trouble typically would come down to a suspected problem in one person's area of responsibility. That person would examine the results, work back through the operations, and maybe clear his name or have to program the fix. The interactive environment made for rapid corrections and testing cycles.

Decisions made by the team were not permanent. A new concept could lead to complete redesign of even the most fundamental services. One day I remember describing this process as "Darwinian selection," meaning that we would test ideas, and the fittest would survive. That day, while I was espousing this model of software development, I was twirling a thick dowel, one of two that had been lying around the office to prop open the windows (or a roller for plotter paper; our collective memories diverge on the specific nature of the sticks). The rest of the team treated the whole thing as humorous, if not a little pretentious. The next morning the dowel was labeled the "Darwinian Selector," and another similar dowel the "Ontological Enforcer." I had not invented evolutionary programming in its modern sense; mostly the team had put me in my place for such grand theorizing. In 1978, Morehouse termed the management of the early phase of ODYSSEY as "enlightened anarchy." [13]

From the start, we were writing a system, not simply programs. We built modules to use in all the programs, not just solutions patched into one particular place. We argued about each one, and usually redesigned them a few times. Morehouse developed a graphics module that would isolate the device drivers from the calling program. Our graphics primitives were very simple: MOVE, DRAW, NEW PAGE, and not much more. Geoffrey Dutton added some public-domain character sets to draw text with strokes that we imported from Tom Waugh

Scott Morehouse (seated) and Nick Chrisman deep in ▶ discussion sometime during the ODYSSEY period. The maps on the wall were not all from computer sources.

(Photo by Laboratory staff; from the collection of Denis White, used with permission)

in Edinburgh, and Dougenik tried to access the hardware polygon-fill functions for some of the video devices. At the base, the system was designed for plotters and storage screens.

Using the principles of GEOGRAF, I built a simple file system that was called SOCKS.[14] The output function was ITAWAY and the input was ITTOME. (The popular culture of the late 1960s and early 1970s had the catch phrase "sock it to me." Even President Nixon went on TV's *Laugh-In* in 1968 to ask "Sock it to *me?*") Each object had a fixed part and a variable-length part, where the length was recorded in the fixed part. For portability, there was a character-formatted version, transparent to the calling program. In the binary form, the objects were packed onto pages of fixed length to minimize overhead. SOCKS made the software more modular, but it had the inconvenience of requiring prior knowledge of the parameters to be able to open an existing file.

The parameters for SOCKS led to the longest running argument among the team. White came in with a scheme that required a "globals" file as the descriptor for each data file.[15] He put the SOCKS parameters and a coordinate window together on a distinct descriptor file so that a program could draw the map on the screen without having to read through the file to figure out the map extent. This simple "SOCKS and box" content contended with those who would build a real metadata system through the globals system. White added a number of extensions in early 1977 to provide the ranges of all fields (useful for data structures), metadata on projections, labels for categories, and unlimited amounts of documentation text. Morehouse remained a partisan of the simplest globals possible. In 1979, Dougenik evolved more advanced schemes, eventually choosing a tree structure to allow expansion and modular implementation. I expanded the tree concept to the idea of a single master directory system that would contain the descriptions of all data for a project area, an idea that was left unimplemented. At each new version there would be grumbling that we had to migrate all our files one more time. We had converters that converted OLD to NEW, then NEW–NEWER then NEW–GNU then GNU–GNUER then GNUER–GNUEST. In its full form, a globals file had a place for almost everything now required in the FGDC (Federal Geographic Data Committee) metadata standard. There was a processing history field that was meant to be carried through from processor to processor. The coordinates could note units of measure, projection, and parameters, but this extended to all fields, including attributes. White had a scheme for the attribute-attribute that turned into a philosophical debate about how much of a rule-base ODYSSEY would have to incorporate. At one extreme, we wondered if we would disallow such clear violations as the addition of nominal variables, or to allow users to do anything they desired. Since we had no comprehensive scheme for all the kinds of attributes, we ended up with the permissive approach, perhaps reflecting our anarchic stance on system design.

Making it all work

While a lot of effort went into the service modules, the top-level programs also took shape at the same time. The development of ODYSSEY followed the schema of that first pencil diagram fairly closely. CYCLONE and CYCLOPS were seen as the front end; we knew we needed an editor and output facilities. But, above all else, the system had to overlay layers, lots of layers—big ones—faster and better than ever before. In implementing the overlay capability, we found that this processor absorbed some functions that we had planned as distinct programs. WHIRLPOOL took its place at the center of the system.

Development of software in this period of the Laboratory was not an isolated enterprise. As the Urban Atlas project had tested our POLYVRT approach to failure, the ODYSSEY team took on some projects with delivery dates that provided motivation for getting the code operational. Beginning in summer 1976, we developed a proposal to the Defense Mapping Agency (DMA) that had a conceptual part (an elaboration of the GEOGRAF

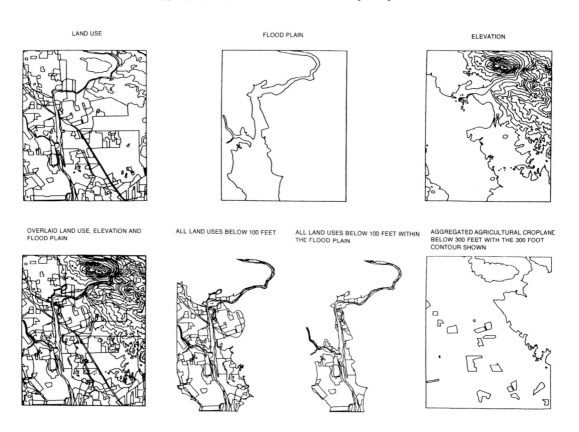

LAND USE FLOOD PLAIN ELEVATION

OVERLAID LAND USE, ELEVATION AND FLOOD PLAIN — ALL LAND USES BELOW 100 FEET — ALL LAND USES BELOW 100 FEET WITHIN THE FLOOD PLAIN — AGGREGATED AGRICULTURAL CROPLAND BELOW 300 FEET WITH THE 300 FOOT CONTOUR SHOWN

▲ *Top row:* the input layers for the test of polygon overlay. Land-use, floodplain, and elevation layers for a quarter-quadrangle, Healdsburg, California. *Bottom row:* analytical results of overlay and recombination of categories. Maps produced by the **program MAD.** *(Source: LAB-LOG 1978, page 19, Harvard University Graduate School of Design)*

integrated database design) and a practical demonstration that would show off ODYSSEY.[16] For this second component, we would take on a benchmark test that had been developed previously. The data involved contours, floodplain, and land use for the Healdsburg, California quadrangle. The test required overlay calculations, similar to those that took hours for the competitors examined by Tomlinson and Boyle[17] a few years later. We later found out that the systems tested to date had all failed. Work on this contract started in summer 1977 and continued into 1978. The programming development was stimulated by the challenge of actual applications, beyond the simplicity of known data. In retrospect, it seems somewhat foolhardy to take a contract for data processing before the capability existed.

WHIRLPOOL: THE MAIN PROCESSOR

Once the basic services were provided, the polygon overlay capability was the major concern—the acid test of vector GIS at the time. As it developed, this WHIRLPOOL processor ended up serving a variety of related functions that originally were expected to require distinct processors.

The competing programs to overlay maps in a vector mode used a brute force technique of comparing every polygon in one set to every polygon in the other. For example, the Laboratory had distributed a collection of algorithms in 1973, edited by David Douglas.[18] Randolph Franklin contributed ANOTB, an algorithm to overlay two polygons and produce any of the 16 possible resultant logical possibilities. The obvious programming solution was to embed this subroutine inside an iteration through two sets of polygons. This group of programs would talk about avoiding work through the use of a bounding box check, but in terms of computational complexity those checks still added up to the product of the number of polygons in the two sources (abbreviated to N^2 in programming jargon) . From the experience of the Urban Atlas files, we knew that sorting could help to produce a more limited neighborhood. While the Urban Atlas files were sorted using a system sort utility, this was possible because the processing worked by segment and was thus a fixed-length record. For WHIRLPOOL we wanted to work with variable-length records to handle chains with full cartographic detail. We also wanted to write a machine-independent system, not dependent on operating-systems services such as sorting. As we were beginning this work, we read the work of Warren Burton[19] and adopted monotonic sections of chains as the processing unit. The reason was that one monotonic section could only intersect another such section once. To avoid unneeded computation, it helps to know when to stop.

Example of creating monotonic sections ▶
from an input chain; one chain (with
nine points) breaks into three monotonic
sections. *(Source: from original illustration produced
by Nick Chrisman for presentation at 5th International
Symposium on Spatial Data Handling, 1992)*

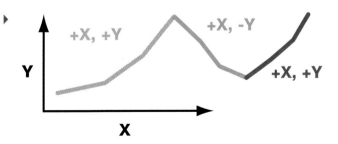

The sorting module PSYCHE (after a story from Greek mythology about tedious work of sorting seeds) served as front end of WHIRLPOOL. This module took over the NUBS memory and used it to full capacity to sort as many records as possible in memory, then to distribute the longest possible runs onto a series of scratch files. With some luck, a small input file would produce a single run. If it had to, PSYCHE used a polyphase merge to generate the final sorted output for any arbitrary amount of input. The overall algorithm came directly from Knuth's *The Art of Computer Programming*. This approach avoided specifying any limit on the size of files. The sorting module was used in various roles in the overall operation of WHIRLPOOL, but it was not, in itself, a particular innovation.

We were writing a research engine as much as distribution software. Dougenik knew our debugging needs, so he built the command language to facilitate debugging with the ability to step through the process and examine all memory structures at each stage. He also insisted on nearly compulsive statistics; everything was counted and standard deviations were recorded as well. For these figures we were able to see that the monotonic sections worked to reduce the number of objects, since even in parcel data or street networks there were enough curvilinear features to justify the overhead of the variable length objects.

not write a grand defense of raster-based analysis; he provided an overarching theory that accommodated both. My paper was about philosophy of science, not about programming choices.[21] The discussion found common ground and a way to work together.

More than anything else, this event signaled a change in generations. The invitations included many of the originators mentioned in chapter 1. Roger Tomlinson and Howard Fisher attended, along with representatives from Horwood's Urban Data Center and from the Experimental Cartography Unit in England. Professors Brian Berry, Duane Marble, and Waldo Tobler (three key players from quantitative geography at the University of Washington, introduced in chapter 1) were there, but the papers they discussed were presented by their students (Donna Peuquet and Stephen Guptill) and staff (myself included). At 27, I was far from the youngest person in the room. To some extent, we chose well in assembling a collection of people who proved central in the development of GIS, but also, as in many sociological settings, becoming a member of the network made future connections easier. It may be no accident that two of the lead designers of major commercial GIS software packages were in the room (Morehouse, who later went to ESRI and developed ARC/INFO, and Carl Reed, later designer of Genasys), but at the time we didn't know which of us would play that role and where the work would be done. From the Laboratory perspective, we wanted to highlight the ODYSSEY development, but the material available to write the papers in summer of 1977 was still preliminary. The descriptions of ODYSSEY, its data structures and algorithms, covered work in progress, not a completed package. These articles also demonstrate the approach to authorship at the Laboratory. Each member of the team wrote a paper—some of them a bit hastily—about some aspect of the system. We did not list all of the people involved in the work on that portion of the project. This often means that the publications of the Laboratory do not conform to the expectations of scientific teams to give credit to all members of the team in each publication. The presentations of the Laboratory must be taken as a whole, as a collective work.

One of the main outcomes of the Endicott House event was that it set a benchmark for a most successful discussion of the research agenda. Michael Goodchild and David Mark both attended and used Endicott House as their model for the "Specialist Meetings" that became a hallmark of the National Center for Geographic Information and Analysis (NCGIA) 11 years later.

Polygon overlay first has to compute the intersections of the line work, and then label the new lines with the proper parentage so that the new composite polygons could be related back to the input source polygons. In the first version we tried to operate these two operations in one pass through the sorted file. Dougenik constructed a dynamic data structure that would accommodate the chains (actually monotonic sections produced by the sorter) across a "band" (operated, in the ODYSSEY anti-acronym style based on allusions to all periods of history, by the "band director" routine SOUSA). We decided, for no particular reason, to run the preliminary sort process on the y-coordinates, specifically on the y-minimum of the section. The band is a region of the y-axis that is completely represented in memory at a particular moment. This is the zone where intersections can be determined. Dougenik could have simply checked each input chain against all the chains in memory. This would have ensured a drastic reduction compared to the competition, since the band would typically have the square root of the total number of objects resident ($R \approx N^{0.5}$). Our statistics demonstrated that this hypothesis was quite reasonable. The overall complexity would then be $N^{1.5}$, a distinct improvement over N^2.

But for Dougenik, this was not enough of a reduction. He implemented Warren Burton's line treatment technique in the first version, but it did not provide much advantage. Instead, he implemented a tree across the band using the *x*-minimum of each chain as the key. Using the programming literature available at the time, he used a height-balanced tree structure known as AVL.[22] AVL trees assure a $logR$ lookup time, but have weaknesses in that deletions are not strictly $logR$. R is the number of resident chains, approximately the square root of the overall number of total chains in the whole file ($N^{0.5}$).

To find the chains that might intersect, he could position a point in the tree using $logR$ comparisons, and extract the specific chains to intersect by tree traversal at no additional complexity. To use a tree structure for linear objects that take up some space along the line, he needed to extend the search on either side up to a fixed distance, and he needed to run a supplementary data structure for "long" chains that exceeded this length. Formally, these adjustments mean that the algorithm is technically $N^{1.5}$, but it operates much closer to $NlogN$ when tuned correctly. To give an idea of what this means, let's take a specific case of the overlay of 30,000 polygons against 30,000 other polygons (produced by a statewide map of groundwater contamination for Wisconsin processed in 1983). In the brute force technique, this would require 900 million comparisons. The simple band approach cuts this down to 19 million, but Dougenik's cross-band structure made only 2 million intersection checks. Put another way, it was 450 times faster than the prior programs on this size of dataset, and it got better with larger files. Dougenik's search data structures remained superior to the rest of the industry (by a factor of eight) for at least a decade or more.[23]

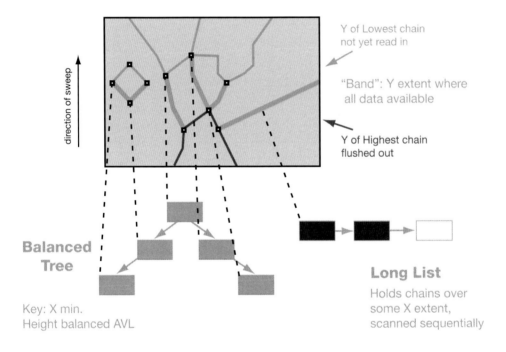

▲   Cross-band data structure, showing a map on top with the internal data structure below. On the map portion, the bolder tan lines are currently resident in memory. The lighter ones above are yet to enter, and the redder ones below have been flushed out.

(Source: Chrisman, Dougenik, and White 1992, figure 1; from Proceedings, 5th International Symposium on Spatial Data Handling, 1992)

As Michael Goodchild's contribution[24] at Endicott House so clearly demonstrated, the more highly detailed one's digital boundaries are, the more spurious (sliver) polygons will inevitably result from overlaying them (because of positional measurement errors, which may differ within and between layers). WHIRLPOOL's efficiency and speed unlocked a potential Pandora's box of bogus results that subsequent processing would need to winnow away. This prospect was not enticing, so the team decided to nip slivers in the bud by instituting a "fuzzy tolerance" to apply when intersections were detected.

These intersection calculations recognized any points within a specific tolerance, producing an enlarged menagerie of cases including fuzzy coincident points, and fuzzy and exact splits. David Douglas, in the 1974 paper, *"It makes me so CROSS,"*[25] described intersections in 64 cases; Dougenik expanded this to 91, using ternary logic (left, nearly equal, right) for each end of each segment. In the development of WHIRLPOOL the tolerance was a single figure that applied to all linework, but the research team knew that it would be a next step to allow different tolerances to different layers and even to specific features. For example, we wanted to make the parcels more accurate than the soils map. The team disbanded before those steps could be taken, but the code had hooks inside to accommodate it eventually.

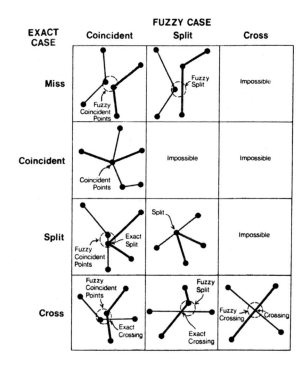

▲ Extended forms of intersection introduced by adding a fuzzy tolerance. Intersections calculated exactly may merge with other points through the action of the fuzzy tolerance.
(Source: Draft WHIRLPOOL Manual, 1979)

The first prototype of WHIRLPOOL included the polygon cycling component inside the same processor as the intersection calculations. The idea was to assemble the composite polygons and then write out the intersected chains with new polygon identification linked to both sources. The topological premises of polygon cycling proved to conflict with the geometric tactics of the intersection process. The cycling had to wait for all chains around a polygon to be finished, thus increasing the number of chains held in memory. Most importantly, the cycler had a hard time unlinking things when intersections divided polygons that appeared to be complete. The version of the code delivered to DMA in 1978 included this prototype WHIRLPOOL. It would perform overlays as long as the tolerance was not much larger than machine precision. Even as we delivered this code, we had discarded the approach and were evolving another solution.

The final WHIRLPOOL algorithm moved the polygon recognition to a later step where it would be operated based on geometric principles. Dougenik implemented a version of Rosenfeld's polygon detection algorithm[26] originally designed for raster imagery. In fact, this algorithm takes two passes. It works upward across the image (in our case, the vector boundaries) issuing new polygon identifiers when the boundaries create a new upward cusp. These are propagated along the lines to left and right as they move upward. If the polygon is convex, these two threads will meet at the top of the polygon, and everything will be correctly labeled. For concave polygons, there may be multiple identifiers issued that are found to be equivalent at downward cusps. WHIRLPOOL implemented this algorithm with two passes to keep memory requirements low. The last step was simply a renaming process to convert the temporary polygon labels to the final compressed set.

By deferring the polygon steps until later, the intersection processor was freed of substantial overhead. The output processing switched over to use nodes, rather than polygons. This processing ensured that the tolerance could be raised to perform serious changes to the input. Unlike some later software based on a greedy algorithm that permitted "fuzzy creep," the WHIRLPOOL process ensured that no point was ever moved more than once and never more than the tolerance.[27] This was ensured by a complex collection of data structures to implement the search for adjacent points within a tolerance, assembled into "clusters." While Dougenik reconfigured the intersection process (under the name HADES), I developed CIRCE (named after the enchantress who turned Odysseus's crew into pigs). The maze of data structures in CIRCE all come from Knuth's book, each one selected for a distinct role in searching. There was a binary search heap to provide the lowest cluster, the next candidate for output processing. There was a hash table to implement a spatial search in an integer "box" space. Since the hash table was almost entirely empty, the hash was a fast solution. The rest of it was a set of linked lists to assemble all the chain ends (called members) in each box that formed a cluster. When the cluster was finished, a procedure decided if the cluster could be turned into a single node, or if it needed multiple nodes. Input points were moved (once) onto the output nodes after all the intersections were processed. In this step some polygons would be vanished as lines became congruent. Only one line was output. If a whole polygon was inside the tolerance, it would vanish into the node, as a topological black hole. The big test occurred when we set the tolerance

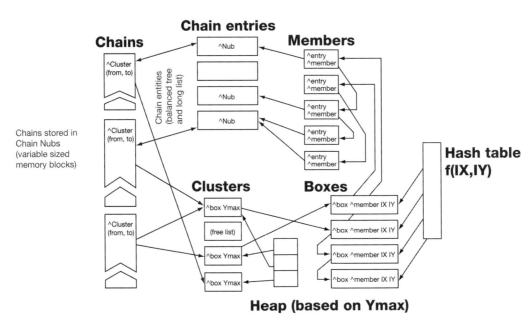

▲ Diagram of the CIRCE data structures. Like most ODYSSEY structures, the linkages run in a circle with various entrances provided by search algorithms. One could link from a specific chain to its cluster, then to the boxes that made up the cluster, then to the member entries that dealt with the points on the ends of chains, back to the chain entry. These chain entries were managed by HADES as a part of its cross-band searching structures. *(Source: Chrisman, Dougenik, and White 1992, figure 5; from Proceedings, 5th International Symposium on Spatial Data Handling, 1992)*

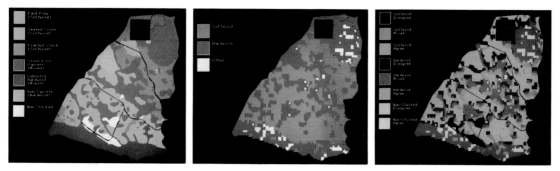

▲   On the left, a forest inventory map provided by the St. Regis Paper Company. In the center, LANDSAT classified land cover (distinguishing hardwood, shown as orange, from softwood, shown as green) converted to vector format. The map on the right shows the differences detected in the classification of the two sources. Agreements are indicated by lighter colors, with the major disagreements in darker browns and blues. This overlay was used to debug the fuzzy tolerance algorithm of WHIRLPOOL. Maps produced by POLYPS on the AED 512 terminal and Dunn camera. *(Source: LAB-LOG 1980, color insert, Harvard University Graduate School of Design)*

on our test file of the states of the United States to 10,000 kilometers (larger than the whole coverage). HADES duly found all the intersections and flagged them as being inside the tolerance. CIRCE assembled all the points into one big cluster and vanished the whole map into a black hole. The output was null, as it should have been. We cheered at the foolishness of making a whole map vanish.

In 1979, we took on a demonstration project for NASA that involved the LARS group (Laboratory for Application in Remote Sensing) at Purdue University and the St. Regis Paper Company. The idea was that our polygon overlay could determine changes in the vector forest inventories of the forest products company using raster remote sensing sources. The area covered in the test was in southern Georgia. It was in processing the overlay of vectorized Landsat data on top of the vector forest inventory that we worked the last bugs out of the full version of WHIRLPOOL.

WHIRLPOOL, as we had implemented it, relied on the geometry to create the set of polygons it discovered. Thus, a program originally intended for polygon overlay was quickly adapted to the problem of processing unlabeled digitizer input. Most users of a broad range of current GIS software products do not know that the functions called CLEAN (or BUILD) actually invoke the same processor as a polygon overlay. All these procedures require a tolerance, and produce a clean topology from the geometric data.

Equally, one of the input streams could be a point file. The polygon processing would embed each point within the appropriate polygon. These points could be used to label digitized linework (spaghetti) with polygon attributes (meatballs). In WHIRLPOOL, all of these different functions were handled in one small section of code that simply decided what to do with the various attributes. A few lines of code in the polygon naming phase were the only differences.

The output from overlay was more than the new chain file for the composite linework. There was a cross-reference file that linked the output polygons to the parent polygons from both sources. This file was organized as a rudimentary relational table, even though ODYSSEY did not have a relational database manager. Columns from the input data tables could be joined onto the cross-reference file as a service, or other ODYSSEY programs could perform this join later. The CALYPSO processor was specifically designed to provide areal interpolation—an estimate of an attribute based on the proportion of area from the component parts, weighted by area or some other attribute.

Embedded in code: the CIRCE heap

In chapter 2, the sorting routine demonstrated the lack of sophistication of the programming in SYMAP. The sorting was a simple bubble sort that made N^2 comparisons. In ODYSSEY, the data structures were better tuned and based on the algorithms known at the time. Since the data structures were quite complex, it is hard to show the code. Equally, the use of FORTRAN obscures what is going on. Yet, it makes sense to show one simple routine. HEPADD (we had run out of classical allusions at this depth) served to add a record (KREC) to the heap. This structure is stored in the NUBS space (declared as ISP and RSP, respectively, for integers and reals) at offset KHEAP. The algorithm consists of putting the new record at the end of the heap. If it is the only item, you are done. Otherwise, it is compared with the entries located at half the index (a binary tree stored in a compact space); if it is lower, the two are swapped. The total process takes at most $logH$ steps where H is the number of items in the heap. This heap only assures the item at the bottom is the lowest—not a complete sort, but that was not needed for CIRCE. It simply took off the lowest items, one at a time.

```
      SUBROUTINE HEPADD(KHEAP,KREC)
C-------------------------------------------------------------------------
      COMMON  ISP(1)                                    NUBS: one big storage space,
      DIMENSION RSP(1)                                  used for both integers and reals.
      COMMON /UNITS/ IOCMD,IOMSG,QPANIC
      LOGICAL QPANIC
      EQUIVALENCE (ISP(1),RSP(1))
      KEYLOC=ISP(KHEAP+2)                               Overhead for heap: first 4 words
      NHEAP=ISP(KHEAP+3)
      KBACK=ISP(KHEAP+4)
      KHEAP2=KHEAP+4
      NHEAP=NHEAP+1
      IF (NHEAP .GT. ISP(KHEAP+1)-3) GO TO 810          Check for overflowing space
      INDEX=KHEAP2+NHEAP                                Place KREC at far end of heap
      ISP(INDEX)=KREC
      INDEX=KREC+KBACK
      ISP(INDEX)=NHEAP
      IR=NHEAP                                          Initialize IR to last entry
   10 IF (IR .EQ. 1) GO TO 20                           Once IR gets to first entry, done.
      JR=IR/2                                           Set comparison to half of IR
      INDEX=KHEAP2+IR
      JNDEX=KHEAP2+JR
      I=ISP(INDEX)                                      Heap contains pointers
      J=ISP(JNDEX)                                      KEYLOC: offset for comparison
      INDEX2=I+KEYLOC
      JNDEX2=J+KEYLOC
      IF (RSP(INDEX2) .GE. RSP(JNDEX2)) GO TO 20        If item is greater, done
      ISP(INDEX)=J                                      Otherwise, exchange entries
      ISP(JNDEX)=I
C           FLIPPING ENTRIES, ALSO CHANGE BACKPOINTER
      INDEX2=I+KBACK
      JNDEX2=J+KBACK                                    and their backpointers
      ISP(INDEX2)=JR
      ISP(JNDEX2)=IR
      IR=JR                                             Now continue at new location
      GO TO 10
   20 ISP(KHEAP+3)=NHEAP                                When done, save new length
      RETURN
  810 WRITE(IOMSG,6810)
 6810 FORMAT(46H ERROR - INSUFFICIENT MEMORY IN HEAP STRUCTURE)
      QPANIC=.TRUE.                                     QPANIC signals an error
      RETURN
      END
```

(Source: Harvard University Graduate School of Design)

THE OTHER PROGRAMS AND MODULES

ODYSSEY grew to include what we decided to be a full range of services, a little closed system that could manage geographic information processing. We called it a "geographic information processing system," since we knew it did not have the database management system that we had foreseen as GEOGRAF. ODYSSEY had a changing list of programs, but in 1979 the basic modules were in place.

Diagram of the input and output of the ▶ ODYSSSEY system. Input sources are shown with hollow circles; output with solid circles. Values files are symbolized by "v," and cross-reference files (that provided the translation between different naming systems or between overlay parentage) are shown as "CR." The system was divided into four groups of processors, each with a few distinct programs. *(Source: "ODYSSEY System Summary," April 1983, page 3, figure 1)*

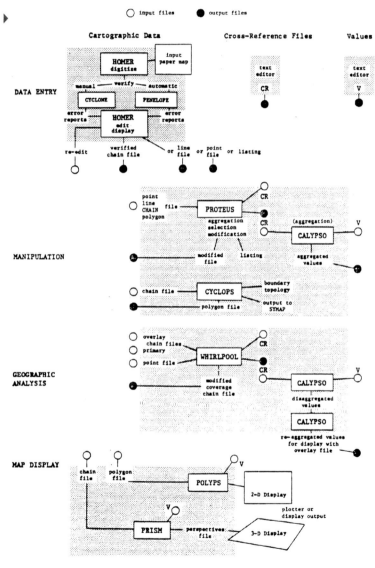

The editor program was called HOMER, the author of the original *Odyssey*. This program started life as FRED, since it was too simple to take the name of the renowned poet. With the addition of a cartographic processing module called ELF to provide projections and the Douglas-Peucker generalization routine, we settled for upgrading the name. HOMER could produce simple graphics and interface to digitizing tables. For marketing purposes, the version of WHIRLPOOL used to clean up input data was given the name PENELOPE, though it was essentially the same program with a different language dialect. PROTEUS emerged for another packaging of ELF with the ability to handle attribute files. PROTEUS could aggregate polygons by resetting the polygon identifiers to some attribute field (called "drop-line" in other software). In later stages, an additional program was added to perform attribute calculations. CALYPSO, another personage in the *Odyssey*, allowed weighted aggregation and disaggregation, based on the cross-reference files generated by WHIRLPOOL. The two first programs, CYCLONE and CYCLOPS, retained their place as converters in the system.

ODYSSEY had two display programs: POLYPS, for two-dimensional choropleth maps, and PRISM, for raising polygons in three-dimensional views. Randolph Franklin wrote the original PRISM, and used that work as the base for his PhD thesis. Scott Morehouse was responsible for POLYPS, a package for choropleth mapping with lots of graphic options, such as nominal, ordinal, and ratio legends. The origin of the name POLYPS is rather obscure, but it was not an acronym in any case.

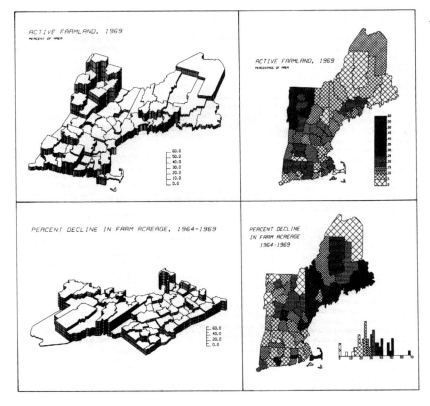

◀ Two attributes for the counties of New England displayed by PRISM on left and POLYPS on right. Both PRISMs use a continuous height legend and the heights of the polygons are proportional to the value. Top POLYPS uses a ratio legend (also called a "thermometer key") for the shading classes. Bottom uses a histogram of the distribution of the attribute.

(Source: Context 10, page 12, Harvard University Graduate School of Design)

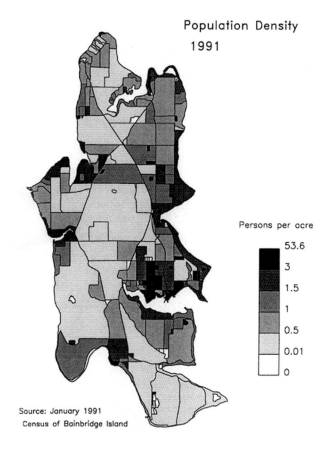

Population Density
1991

Persons per acre

53.6
3
1.5
1
0.5
0.01
0

Source: January 1991
Census of Bainbridge Island

POLYPS output using the "interval" key (ranges ▶
of the classes are indicated by labeling the breaks
between classes). This map was produced by
POLYPS using a PostScript driver added to
ODYSSEY with the appearance of laser printers
in the mid-1980s. The font system was not
converted to use native PostScript. Census blocks
for Bainbridge Island, Washington, 1991 special
census tabulation. *(Map by Nick Chrisman)*

While PRISM worked directly from the common chain file data structure, POLYPS required CYCLOPS to generate a simpler polygon loop (shapefile) data structure. This permitted POLYPS to shade in a polygon at a time, and not get engaged in the larger data structure. This choice shows how each program sets its own scope of memory, and it foreshadows the later reappearance of shapefiles as the basic form of geographic data exchange, despite all the talk about the superiority of the topological format.

There were other programs written, such as a DIME interface (written by Anne Hunt White), and a prototype multilayer display module (called MAD, an anagram for the sponsor agency) produced for the DMA (Defense Mapping Agency) contract.[28] Building on the basic system services, ODYSSEY was open to extension at fairly modest cost. As the programming team completed their first version, the question became how to transfer the package to the user community.

Going commercial

There is a big leap required to get software ready for distribution. The Laboratory was well-aware of Fred Brooks' rule of thumb (in his book, *The Mythical Man-Month*[29]) that it took three times the effort to convert a program to a package, and three more times to convert it to a system. We thought we had taken pains to do the best we could, but there was a lot more to do. A number of staff were employed to write documentation, first for users, then also for programmers. As early as 1978, Morehouse issued a four-page position paper calling for stronger integration of ODYSSEY as a system,[30] as well as an end to the anarchic management style. The question was first under what setting the work would be done.

At the outset, the history of the Laboratory set the orientation. SYMAP and the other packages were distributed in the form of FORTRAN source code. We had one primary version (usually for IBM OS/360), and the user was expected to modify this for any local peculiarities. In the design of ODYSSEY, we took particular care to isolate all machine-dependencies and operating system interactions. The rule book of transportable FORTRAN became a guiding principle.

During this period, the legal status of software was being explored in all sectors (academic, government, and commercial). Originally, software had little value. Companies like IBM packaged their software with the hardware to try to sell more machines. This is when the terms "hard" and "soft" were put into use, implying that the hardware was the real stuff. The Laboratory did assert copyright for SYMAP, though we discovered in 1975 that no copy had been officially deposited to establish the claim. The process of claiming copyright changed, and, following advice from Harvard corporate lawyers, the Laboratory added a very concise license agreement as a requirement for software distribution. The program developers presumed that ODYSSEY would simply appear as another item in the catalog (called LAB-LOG since its inception).

Like software publishers before and since, the Laboratory announced ODYSSEY long before it was ready to distribute. The LAB-LOG dated July 1978 included a section describing ODYSSEY, with illustrations of the overlay results for the Healdsburg test data. The text gave the highly precise date of October 1, 1978 for the release of a first module for input and editing, with a promise of 1979 for another unspecified release. The 1980 LAB-LOG included a more detailed list of modules that corresponded to the programs as they emerged. The description used the present tense, as if the program could be ordered, but, in the back, the order form said "Write for separate catalog."

Over a period in 1978 and 1979, the Laboratory management, including Brian Berry as director and Allan Schmidt as executive director, came to the conclusion that ODYSSEY should be completed to higher standards than SYMAP. It would have professionally written user documentation, and complete programmer documentation. In short, it would be prepared for commercial distribution. The exact nature of the distribution was not decided, since they believed that a commercial placement would come after the package was properly prepared. In a series of staff meetings, the members of the ODYSSEY team considered this development. I decided to go to graduate school in Bristol, England, taking myself out of the software development team. Denis White decided to continue research work and pull out of the software team. Scott Morehouse took up the challenge of manager of the commercialization process. Jim Dougenik joined him on the team, along with some of the other programming staff (including Bruce Donald and some student assistants). Other programmers were hired to work on this phase, and the team established its own office in a separate building on Sumner Road, just behind Gund Hall. As with any software system, the documentation was the hardest part. A team of writers, editors, and graphics production staff focused on producing manuals for users[31] as well as internal documentation for programmers. A new focus on marketing the Laboratory's products began to emerge, adding to the increase in staff.

The commercialization process was more or less complete in 1981. But ODYSSEY had become more than just another package of software to make ready for distribution. The process of preparing it became a huge preoccupation of the Laboratory, and ODYSSEY's fate determined the future of the Laboratory.[32] But all this runs somewhat ahead of the story. The next chapter will cover the rest of the activity at the Laboratory during the period that ODYSSEY was being developed. Chapter 10 will bring all the threads together to continue the tale of commercialization.

NOTES

1. The concept of a "local processor" was proclaimed in a paper presented at some conferences in 1976; Nicholas R. Chrisman, "Local versus global: The scope of memory required for geographic information processing," *Internal report 76 14* (Laboratory for Computer Graphics and Spatial Analysis, Harvard University, 1976).

2. Eric Teicholz, Denis White, and Nicholas Chrisman, *The ODYSSEY mapping system: An introduction* (Laboratory for Computer Graphics and Spatial Analysis, Harvard University, 1976), 1.

3. Roger Tomlinson, ed. *Geographical data handling* (Ottawa: IGU Commission on Geographical Data Sensing and Processing, 1972).

4. Roger Tomlinson, "The application of electronic computing methods to the storage, compilation and assessment of mapped data" (PhD thesis, University of London, 1974); Roger Tomlinson, "The Canada Geographic Information System," in *The history of geographic information systems: Perspectives from the pioneers,* ed. Timothy W. Foresman, 21–32 (Upper Saddle River, N.J.: Prentice Hall, 1998).

5. Samuel Arms, "Computer mapping in selected geographic information systems," in *Proceedings, Sixth Annual Meeting,* 218–221 (Clayton, Mo.: URISA, 1968).

6. Hugh Calkins and Duane F. Marble, eds., *Computer software for spatial data handling,* vol. 1, *Full geographic information systems* (Ottawa: International Geographic Union, Commission on Geographical Data Sensing and Processing, 1980).

7. Peter Van Demark, "Results of test runs for the Department of Administration portion of the NRIS project," (University of Wisconsin Cartographic Laboratory, 1976).

8. Roger Tomlinson and A. Raymond Boyle, "The state of development of systems for handling natural resources inventory data," *Cartographica* 18, no. 4 (1981): 92.

9. Nicholas R. Chrisman and R. Denis White, "Programming for transportability: A guide to machine-independent FORTRAN" (Laboratory of Computer Graphics and Spatial Analysis, Harvard University, 1976).

10. R. Denis White, "CYCLOPS conventions and assumptions," *Internal report 76-5* (Laboratory for Computer Graphics and Spatial Analysis, Harvard University, 1976).

11. Carl Eichenlaub and R. Denis White, "NUBS memory management module," *Internal report 77-4* (Laboratory for Computer Graphics and Spatial Analysis, Harvard University, 1977).

12. James A. Dougenik, "Development of a lexical and syntactic analyzer," *Internal report 76-13* (Laboratory for Computer Graphics and Spatial Analysis, Harvard University, 1976); Craig Latham, "LINGUIST," *Internal report 77-6* (Laboratory for Computer Graphics and Spatial Analysis, Harvard University, 1977); James Dougenik, "LINGUIST: A processor to generate interactive languages," in *Harvard papers on geographic information systems*, vol. 3, ed. Geoffrey Dutton (Reading, Mass.: Addison Wesley, 1978).

13. Scott Morehouse, "Software perspectives on ODYSSEY," internal memorandum, August 21, 1978, 2. It also says "Concepts are a nice currency to deal in, however they are easily counterfeit by fantasy." (page 2).

14. Nicholas R. Chrisman, "ODYSSEY SOCKS: Fixed-variable binary input-output," *Internal report 76-8* (Laboratory for Computer Graphics and Spatial Analysis, Harvard University, 1976).

15. R. Denis White, "ODYSSEY file formats," *Internal report 77-1* (Laboratory for Computer Graphics and Spatial Analysis, Harvard University, 1977).

16. The Laboratory was subcontractor on Contract DAAK70-77-C-0265 from U.S. Army Topographic Laboratory, Fort Belvoir, Virginia, to The Analytical Sciences Corporation (TASC) in Reading, Massachusetts.

17. Tomlinson and Boyle, "The state of development of systems for handling natural resources inventory data," 92.

18. W. Randolph Franklin, "ANOTB," in *Collected algorithms,* ed. David Douglas, III.16–III.35 (Laboratory for Computer Graphics and Spatial Analysis, Harvard University, 1976).

19. Warren Burton, "Representation of many-sided polygons and polygonal lines for rapid processing," *Communications, ACM* 20, no. 3 (1977): 166–171.

20. Geoffrey Dutton, ed. *Harvard papers on geographic information systems* (Reading, Mass.: Addison Wesley, 1978). (All articles indexed on ESRI Virtual Campus.) A complete list of all papers is on the CD accompanying this book.

21. David F. Sinton, "The inherent structure of information as a constraint to analysis: Mapped thematic data as a case study," in *Harvard papers on geographic information systems*, vol. 6, ed. Geoffrey Dutton (Reading, Mass.: Addison Wesley, 1978); Nicholas R. Chrisman, "Concepts of space as a guide to cartographic data structures," in *Harvard papers on geographic information systems,* vol. 6, ed. Geoffrey Dutton (Reading, Mass.: Addison Wesley, 1978).

22. AVL for the names of the two Russian authors (Georgii Adelson-Velskii and Evgenii Landis).

23. R. Denis White, "A design for polygon overlay," in *Harvard papers on geographic information systems*, vol. 6, ed. Geoffrey Dutton (Reading, Mass.: Addison Wesley, 1978); James Dougenik, "WHIRLPOOL: A geometric processor for polygon coverage data," in *Proceedings, AUTO-CARTO IV,* 304–311 (Washington, D.C.: ACSM, 1980); Nicholas R. Chrisman, James A. Dougenik, and Denis White, "Lessons for the design of polygon overlay processing from the ODYSSEY WHIRLPOOL algorithm," in *Proceedings, 5th International Symposium on Spatial Data Handling,* vol. 2, 401–410 (Charleston, S.C.: IGU, 1992).

24. Michael F. Goodchild, "Statistical aspects of the polygon overlay problem," in *Harvard papers on geographic information systems,* vol. 6, ed. Geoffrey Dutton (Reading, Mass.: Addison Wesley, 1978).

25. David H. Douglas, "It makes me so CROSS," in *Introductory readings in GIS,* eds. Donna J. Peuquet and Duane F. Marble, 303–307 (London: Taylor & Francis, 1990). Also distributed by the Laboratory in 1974.

26. Azriel Rosenfeld and A. Kak, *Digital picture processing* (New York: Academic Press, 1976).

27. Dougenik, "WHIRLPOOL: A geometric processor for polygon coverage data," 304–311; Nicholas R. Chrisman, "Epsilon filtering: A technique for automated scale changing," in *Proceedings, Annual Meeting,* 322–341 (Washington, D.C.: ACSM, 1983).

28. Michael P. Goldberg, Allan H. Schmidt, and Nicholas R. Chrisman, "Integration and analysis of multiple geographic data bases: An application of ODYSSEY," in *Harvard Library of Computer Graphics,* vol. 2, ed. Patricia Moore, 81-98 (Cambridge, Mass.: Laboratory for Computer Graphics and Spatial Analysis, Harvard University, 1979).

29. Frederick Brooks Jr., *The mythical man-month: Essays in software engineering* (Reading, Mass.: Addison Wesley, 1975).

30. Morehouse, "Software perspectives on ODYSSEY," 2; Geoffrey Dutton, "Navigating ODYSSEY," in *Harvard papers on geographic information systems,* vol. 2, ed. Geoffrey Dutton (Reading, Mass.: Addison Wesley, 1978).

31. Scott Morehouse and Martin Broekhuysen, *ODYSSEY user manual* (Cambridge, Mass.: Laboratory for Computer Graphics and Spatial Analysis, Harvard University, 1982).

32. Nicholas R. Chrisman, "The risks of software innovation: A case study of the Harvard Lab," *The American Cartographer* 15 (1988): 291–300.

NINE

Parallel Developments

While **ODYSSEY** took years to develop, it was not the only focus of interest. Some development dealt with the display of gridded data; some dealt with graphic interaction. The **ODYSSEY** toolkit also led to **BUILDER**, a tool for 3D architectural rendering. The Laboratory began to organize annual user conferences under the title "Harvard Computer Graphics Week," drawing hundreds of registrants. All these activities, combined with the **ODYSSEY** development, pushed the Laboratory to its high tide in terms of staff members.

A raster counter-current

POLYVRT, GEOGRAF, and ODYSSEY established the Laboratory as a proponent of vector technology and topological data structures. In the adjacent office along the corridor, the students working for Carl Steinitz and David Sinton labored away hand-coding grid data bases,[1] and writing tools for what was later called map algebra.[2] It would seem that the divisions were clearly drawn. In this period, Geoffrey Dutton issued an internal document titled "Minority report on gridded data.[3]" It was barely four pages of type-written text without illustrations, presenting a number of arguments for using rectangular arrays as a mechanism to display continuous surface data. This document appeared in 1976, giving a flavor of the discourse that filled the Laboratory. Though the verbal arguments were a part of it, the main forum was to produce the tangible evidence, visualizations, and software to manipulate them. Dutton did much of this experimentation, but others played a role over the next few years.

In many respects, this work connects directly to the surface analysis of William Warntz presented in chapter 4. Dutton had been Warntz's last research assistant at Harvard, and attuned to a view of spatial distributions that the vector approach would never handle with much sensitivity.

A MINORITY REPORT: DOT.MAP

The "Minority report" was written to defend or explain the software project that Dutton had begun. It was called DOT.MAP[4] (some of us pronounced the period, so it was "dot-dot-map"). This program announced its presence to the operators at the Computing Center by hammering the liquid ink pen up and down as it randomly peppered dots across the plotter paper. Unlike the smooth sweeps of vector drawings ("swoosh," "zip"), it sounded infernal ("gathunk, gathunk . . . "). The operators feared for their precious plotters, and it took substantial coaxing to get them to let some of them run to completion, often with significant attention to tending the delicate Leroy pen nibs.

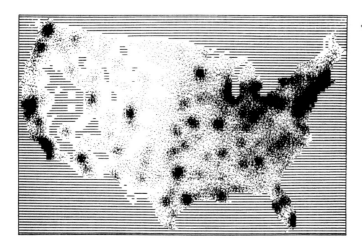

◀ 1970 U.S. population: 1 dot equals 5,000 persons. The area outside the United States and the area with less than 5,000 persons per cell are filled with horizontal lines. As in most dot maps, dots coalesce to form a solid shading. Produced by DOT.MAP with a pen plotter.

(Source: LAB-LOG 1978, page 37, Harvard University Graduate School of Design)

The program was originally designed to take the SYMAP output produced for SYMVU and to symbolize it with the classic "1 dot equals 500 cows" legend from hand-drawn thematic mapping. DOT.MAP found its real medium when the Laboratory took delivery of the Tektronix 4014 vector graphics terminal with the then huge (19-inch) green screen. This device had an addressable space of 4096 by 3000 or so, a resolution still hard to attain. As a storage screen, each phosphor dot could be illuminated without need for a refresh cycle or any memory to store the image. The spectacle of producing the images was absorbing (and, at 960 characters per second, tedious) in its own right.

The overall framework was that each cell in the datagrid translated to a little rectangle on the screen. The value of the surface could be rendered with the dots, or a swarm of other symbolisms, often in combination. For instance, contours could be traced through the display, along with inclined contours (contours produced by tilting the surface).[5] Properties of the surface, such as slope lines, could be calculated. Uncertainty in determining contours could be shown as hachured contour lines: thin where the slope was steep, thick where the slope was gentle. These produced a kind of fuzzy contouring. As the technology evolved away from the monochrome 4014, grayscale images were included.

Examples of the vector ▶
symbolism produced
by DOT.MAP: four
displays of terrain data
for Hanslollik Island
in the Virgin Islands.
Each map uses different
kinds of contours in
combination. Maps *a* and
c have inclined contours.
Maps *b* and *c* have regular
(horizontal) contours.
Map *d* has just fuzzy
contours. Horizontal
band shading has been
added to *a* and *b*. *(Source:
LAB-LOG 1978, page 17, Harvard
University Graduate School of
Design)*

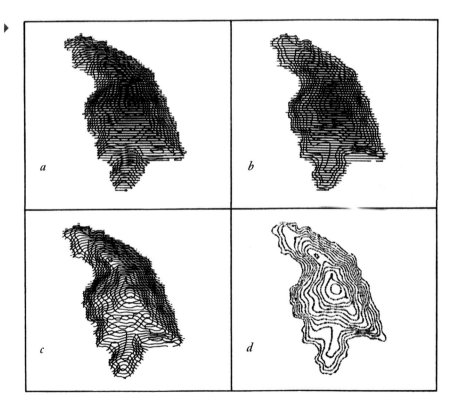

a

b

c

d

DOT.MAP evolved from its plotter version to an interactive program in the same era as INPOM (see chapter 5). It was controlled by keywords, with interactive prompting for numerical parameters. This made it difficult to maintain and to convert for different computer systems. DOT.MAP was offered for sale at the same prices as CALFORM ($900 commercial, $600 nonprofit) in 1978 with the promise that it would be replaced by a restructured program called MIRAGE. This program was planned to display multiple images (to allow simultaneous display of various measures of a surface for example), in 2D and 3D with transparency and anti-aliasing, and an advanced language based on the GLIB table-based parsers. Dutton presented DOT.MAP's capabilities and plans for MIRAGE at a computer graphics conference in 1977.[6] Like a desert mirage, this software never emerged to take tangible form. Perhaps the name fated it to join the ranks of software promised before their time, i.e. vaporware.

SEURAT: LAND ALIVE

Dutton applied a pointillist approach adapted from the nineteenth-century French expressionist, Georges Seurat, to terrain display.[7] This technique built upon the experience of DOT.MAP, recharged by the arrival of an AED 512 color display with the capacity for rendering a huge palette of millions of colors, with 256 colors displayed at any time. For each pixel in a terrain matrix, the SEURAT program produced a four-pixel square

---

A vision for imagery

Geoffrey Dutton articulated his reasons for seeing the world as surfaces in a few short paragraphs at the end of the "Minority report." It goes far beyond an argument over the technical choices of cartographic representation. While this may sound like the beauty queen's wish for world peace, it gives a sense of the vision that motivated some of the Laboratory staff (presented without editing from the 1976 original):

"I was first drawn to computer graphics as a medium to create images of the field (and its components) of human presence across the surface of the earth. Teilhard de Chardin, the mystic Jesuit anthropologist, called that field the "noosphere," the "thinking layer" of the earth. I, following Warntz, following Stewart, call that field "potential of population" because we can calculate it using a physical model, but also because the proximity to people in some deeply felt sense measures the potential for human achievement that exists anywhere. Perhaps, I maintain that if the thought of a field of consciousness can exist, that such a field either now exists or will exist, this represents an entity, a complete entity. We are all part of one consciousness, a complex entity which reflects the planet which bore it.

"To create visionary images of this and other stages of earth's evolution is an important task now at hand. In order for the people of the earth to free themselves, feed themselves, and fuel themselves, there must be widespread visions of a future more meaningful than the present, a vision of a process of integration. In time, individuals may literally achieve a consciousness extending across the planet. In that richness of existence, the present will be ever meaningful, for we will at last have transcended the little territories which have long constricted our awareness, and we can bask in the pulsating diversity of our opalescent sphere.

"Aren't images of that sort worth working for?"[8]

on the screen showing gradations of one of four hues: red for elevation, yellow for northwest illumination hillshading, and blue and green for slope and inverse slope. These properties were calculated from the terrain matrix, interwoven on the display screen.

This approach came about because of the limited number of colors available on early color displays. By halving the spatial resolution (displaying each pixel as four), the spectral palette was increased enormously. Each of the four components could have 64 gradations, while combining these into one pixel would not permit anything beyond a two-bit distinction on the four axes. The optical mixing of adjacent color dots demonstrates that principles from art can apply to the analytical field of thematic cartography.

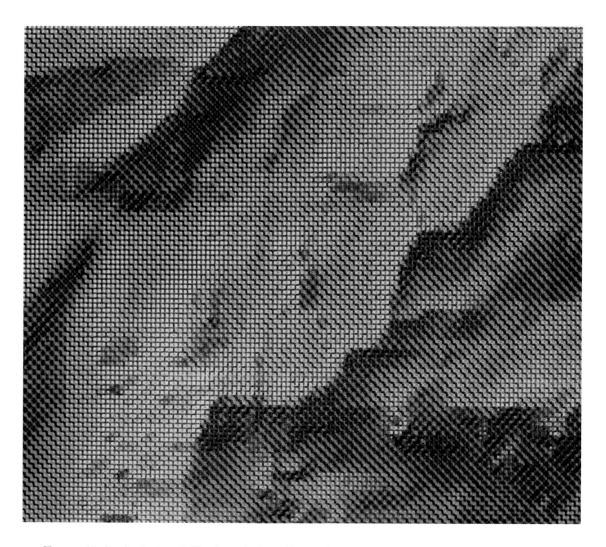

▲   Topographic data for the Dent de Morcles in the Swiss Alps, produced by the SEURAT program. Image from AED 512 produced on a Dunn camera, rescanned from published format. *(Source: Dutton 1982)*

Stretching the domain of maps

The Laboratory had begun with a commitment to improving graphic communication. Allan Schmidt's movie of Lansing, Michigan (see chapter 2) had demonstrated that the computer age could lead us toward dynamic maps. Every day at the Laboratory was a day for trying something new—for example, taking a simple list of election figures from the morning newspaper and visualizing the overnight vote results. A few of these mapping experiments carried out in the period from 1975–1982 give a flavor of the creative verve, as well as the obstacles to overcome in a period before digital graphics became a consumer product.

▲ The wall in Allan Schmidt's office accumulated examples of map experiments, project results, and images sent by colleagues around the world. This picture, taken to advertise the upcoming Harvard Computer Graphics Week in 1979, had Schmidt pointing at the color prints produced with Polaroid film from the Dunn camera. *(Source: Context 10, Spring 1979, page 6, Harvard University Graduate School of Design; photo by Bradford F. Herzog)*

AMERICAN GRAPH FLEETING

For the bicentennial issue of *National Geographic* in July, 1976, the Laboratory staff had produced three population surfaces to present the changes of population since 1790.[9] These three snapshots suggested a more complete animation. In 1979, Dutton made what may be the first thematic spatio-temporal hologram, apparently the only example of a holographic four-dimensional cartographic display.[10] Viewed by looking into a cylinder 16 inches in diameter, the hologram image illustrates changes in population for the United States over 181 years as it turns. The images appear to be a solid three-dimensional object inside the cylinder, in full stereoscopic presentation.

The hologram originated with a sequence of images showing the U.S. population by county from 1790–1970. Each annual surface is based on interpolation from the decennial census data, smoothed onto a grid of 82 by 127 cells. A preprocessing program, developed by Dutton with the assistance of Jim Dougenik, was required to take the census figures by county and cumulate them into the grid. Cells with fewer than 500 people (about two persons per square mile) are shown as blank, which places an emphasis on the westward expansion of the U.S. population. These data grids were then visualized using ASPEX (see chapter 5) to show them as three-dimensional images. The viewpoint starts over the Caribbean Sea and shifts two degrees with each year, rotating full circle as you move one turn around the image. The view also moves in a corkscrew upward from 30 degrees at the start to 60 at the end. The two-degree horizontal shift in viewpoint between images enhances stereoscopic depth.

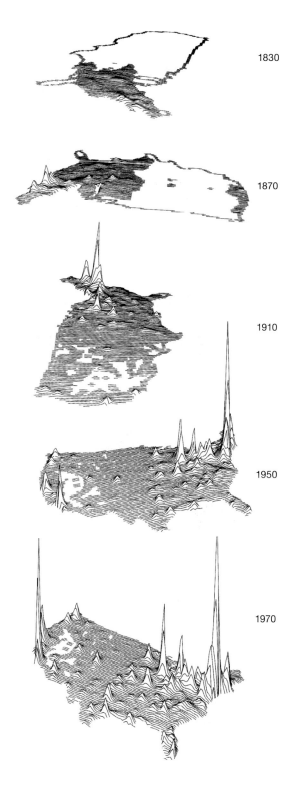

1830

1870

1910

1950

1970

Frames from the movie: each image presents the U.S. ▶ population in a given year, viewed from a specific azimuth and altitude. Played in sequence, this shows a rotation around the country as the surface changes. *(Source: Dutton 1979, American Graph Fleeting documentation)*

All of this seems easy enough for the modern computer user. After all, we have become used to having a "personal computer," with a reasonable resolution graphics screen and the ability to control the speed of presenting images. In short, we all have the ability to make our own movies. It was far from the case when Dutton took on this project. ASPEX was running interactively on the PDP-10 computer at Aiken Labs. Plotter commands were written onto a 9-track tape (a 10-inch wide reel of tape a half-inch wide). Dutton picked up the tape and took it to AVCO, a commercial computer operation located in Burlington, Massachusetts, where they offered plotting onto 35 mm unsprocketed film. As the holographic service bureau required 16 mm film, the 181 images had to be produced on paper, which were pin-registered and photographed onto 16 mm high-contrast film using an animation stand, five frames per image. With the titles and credits, the movie is 1,080 frames (the capacity of an 18-inch-diameter integral hologram), which when played through a projector takes only 45 seconds to run.[11]

The storyline

American Graph Fleeting tells a story of continental scale expansion of a population through fleeting imagery. Dutton grew up in an era when newsreels were run at the beginning of movies, and stentorian narrators intoned the *March of Time* that wrapped technology and history together to lead inevitably to suburban housing, cars with fins, and consumer nirvana. The text at the beginning of the film presented this story in careful hand-written calligraphy:

In 1790 the first census of the newly United States counted about four million citizens. Nearly all of these non-native Americans lived within 200 miles of the Atlantic Ocean, occupying only 240,000 square miles of the 48 states-to-be. The other ninety percent of the land was known mainly by rumor.

Inevitably the rumor spread, pursued by settlers, and the Republic surged westward. In a century's time sixty million people had engulfed the frontier, pushed by population pressure and pulled by the land's promise. Then, with little territory left for expansion, population growth focussed inward, signaling the Age of Cities.

The drama of America's expansion and urbanization is at best dimly portrayed in the statistical snapshots of the census; but graphically assembled in space as maps and viewed as a process in time, even simple statistics of human habitation can come to life. To this end population data for U.S. counties have been assembled and interpolated in space and time to produce 181 maps of American population densities, one for each year from 1790 to 1970.

The only features on these maps are those of population itself, depicted as a surface, a data terrain. In these demographic landscapes the height of the surface represents density of population in that place, and the volume enclosed between the surface and its base plane is proportional to the size of the total population.

The features of these surfaces are easily apprehended. Where the terrain rises, population densities increase; where it ends, wilderness begins. Its valleys show where inhospitable locales have limited human occupation of the land; its summits locate urban centers, at first barely distinguishable, but dominating the peoplescape as the twentieth century unfolds.

During the eighteen decades depicted, inhabited territory grew tenfold in extent, the population increased fifty-fold and the number of people dwelling in cities multiplied by more than seven hundred. This growth is shown in one-year steps, with the viewpoint steadily shifting around the compass, starting and ending over the Caribbean Sea.

The movie was converted into a hologram on a special optical bench at the Holographic Film Company in New York City. The master films were exposed frame-by-frame by shining a split laser beam through each frame, constructing an interference pattern on the master film A positive print of the hologram was then wrapped in a 16-inch plexiglass cylinder with a polarizing filter inside that to make the back wall appear black and opaque. Illuminated with light from the same angle as the laser, the hologram image was visible.

Exposing an integral hologram from the movie ▶
film. Diagram shows how the laser shown
through the 16 mm film image interferes with the
reference beam to expose the holographic film.

(Source: Dutton 1979, American Graph Fleeting documentation)

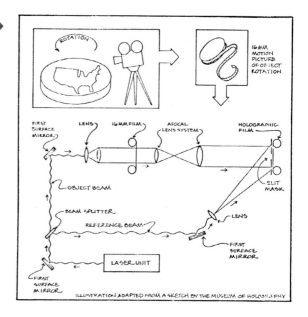

Geoffrey Dutton viewing the ▶
American Graph Fleeting hologram
at the Laboratory. The hologram
took center stage at the Harvard
Computer Graphics Week in 1979.

*(Source: Context 10, Spring 1979, page 14, Harvard
University Graduate School of Design)*

AIR: Animated Information Retrieval

One afternoon, while flying from Washington, D.C. to Boston through the busy Northeast Corridor, Dutton noticed a number of other airplanes pass by, and it started him wondering how dense the air traffic in America might be. During the following month or two, he produced a program to portray a day in the life of commercial aviation. For data, he obtained a tape of schedules for flights between the 35 largest cities in the United States from the Official Airlines Guide for May 1980 (about 7,000 flights in all). Each airport was given a location on a basemap colored to show the time zones. The animation ran on a Tektronix 4027,[12] using the native programming language embedded in the device to manage the movement of icons to represent flights between city pairs. As the day progressed, the time zone backdrop changed color. The user could make animation update the location of aircraft in flight as often as desired, but if the interval was less than about 15 minutes, the device could not update its display in real time.

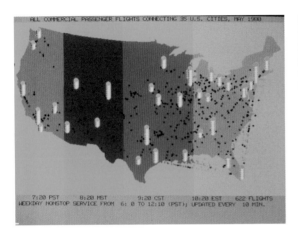
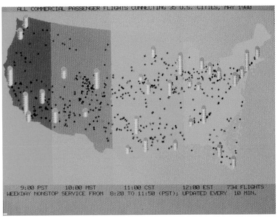
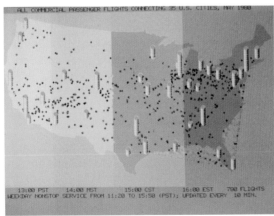
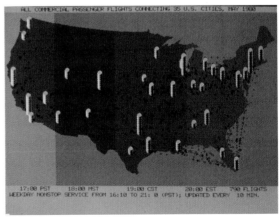

▲   Snapshots from the AIR animation at various times. Imaged on the Lab's Dunn camera from the Tektronix 4027, from RGB signals that were projected one at a time from a monochrome CRT onto 35 mm Ektachrome film through appropriately colored rotating gels. The slideshow was presented at Harvard Computer Graphics Week in 1981 and in the lobby of the Harvard Graduate School of Design in 1982. *(Source: slideshow version of AIR, scanned from originals, courtesy of Geoffrey Dutton)*

CARTOGRAMS

A cartogram distorts space to display a thematic attribute; in the most common form of cartogram, a set of polygons is resized so that each polygon has an area proportional to some thematic value. Cartograms of population or electoral strength are the most common examples. Waldo Tobler's experiments with cartograms were a part of automated cartography that he described in his luncheon seminar in May 1966, and in his later contacts with the Laboratory.[13] I thought that I could improve on Tobler's algorithm using the topology of polygon boundaries. In my first meeting with Tobler at AUTO-CARTO 1, I promptly told him that I thought his approach was wrong. He used a grid-cell approximation of the population surface to approximate the distortion iteratively. I pointed out that his calculation lost too much population out to sea. Mostly, I objected to the less-than-perfect fit even after a hundred iterations. I held out for a vector solution. This has led to a long-term discussion about the purpose and calculation of cartograms that still continues. In 1977, Jim Dougenik took up the challenge of coding the topological approach, and found that it led to troubles when the distortion field was not smooth. He produced a new algorithm based on the distance decay of the distortion field (a heritage of the gravity models of the Warntz approach to surfaces). Duane Niemeyer produced a poster for Harvard Computer Graphics Week 1980.[14]

% Of Popular Vote For Kennedy — 1960 Presidential Election

Two maps showing the percentage of popular ▶ vote in the 1960 U.S. presidential election by state. The top gives the impression that Nixon (the red colored states) won the election. The bottom, a cartogram produced using Jim Dougenik's algorithm, adjusts the area of each state to be proportional to the electoral vote. This cartogram achieved a high level of fit after only eight iterations, a vindication in the argument with Waldo Tobler. Because it uses centroids, it works better for convex polygons, as in the center of the country. Peninsulas, islands, and other concavities such as Cape Cod and Long Island unfortunately tend to disappear.

(Source: Context 1982-83, page 8, Harvard University Graduate School of Design)

% Of Popular Vote For Kennedy — 1960 Presidential Election

Collaborating with artists and designers

The Laboratory in this period employed people from a scattering of disciplines. For the most part they were planners and geographers who had come in contact with computers, or computer people who had come in contact with maps and graphics. Of course, this little community was far from isolated. On the Harvard campus, there were many opportunities for discussion, including monthly meetings of people interested in "form," the self-styled "Philomorphs," an eclectic club of eccentrics that included Michael Woldenberg, with his hierarchy of branching systems; Cyril Smith, a metallurgist and crystallographer from MIT; Arthur Loeb, a founding father of what he called "Design Science;" and Stephen Jay Gould, the evolutionary theorist who was working then on the morphology of snails on tropical islands and in the Burgess Shale, the legendary fossil find in the Canadian Rockies. The monthly meetings were usually hosted by Loeb in Sever Hall or the Carpenter Center, not far from the Laboratory. Dennis Dreher (pages 156–157) was invited on one occasion to present his kinetic geometric wire sculptures. This intellectual community encouraged the Laboratory staff to greater imagination about spatial analysis.

In this world, the Laboratory held its own as a place where technical ideas could be seen as creative alongside the purest art, and the results of cold technology subject to the same critical and esthetic eye. Pop culture heroes such as Buckminster Fuller came through on tour, nodding as the screens filled with green drawings. Benoit Mandelbrot, whose book on fractals captured the attention of the scientific community, came to work with Dutton on images of surfaces. Yet, the discipline of cartography sets its own rules, and the art and science of making maps is often more mundane than artistic. The Laboratory's collaboration with artists and designers had a number of specific outputs mostly related to the toolkit an artist uses.

Digital Etch-a-Sketch: ARTIST

In 1976, Manuel Felguerez, an established abstract artist in Mexico, won a Guggenheim Fellowship with the intention of spending a year at Harvard. Among other things, he had the idea that a computer might allow him a new kind of control over drawings. While he talked to high-level people at Harvard in design and art, and obtained his grant, none of these high-level administrators alerted the Laboratory staff until he was about to arrive. Not wanting to disappoint the visitor, Geoffrey Dutton was delegated to mount a simple drawing package.

All we had for graphics at this time was the big green-screened Tektronix 4014. It had glorious resolution, but the storage screen had the huge inconvenience of remembering everything. Messages written by the program, and commands entered by the user, would clutter up the graphics screen. The only option was to erase the whole thing and redraw everything. There was no mouse, no little arrow moving across the screen, just a lame set of thumbwheels for both x and y that maneuvered crosshairs in both directions. These lines were shown at a lower intensity so that they did not stick on the screen display. Dutton wrote a program with one-character commands so that the prompt and

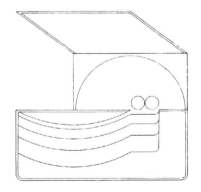

▲ Sketch produced by Manuel Felguerez in 1976 using the ARTIST program on the Tektronix 4014. *(Source: Context 8, May 1976, page 15, Harvard University Graduate School of Design)*

response could be performed in silent mode. The user had to touch a "−" to draw a line to the indicated point, or the space bar to simply move there. Pressing the "/" key erased the display and redrew the contents without the clutter. The program acted as a pantograph, storing a sequence of move and draw commands, but these primitives could be bundled up into objects. The objects could then be called back at a different scale and orientation, be assembled into groups, and include one another. Objects could be saved as files for later use and modification. The program ARTIST was up and running in very short order.

The Mexican artist made a few drawings with ARTIST, but mostly it became a graphic illustration vehicle for documenting programs. Dutton generated a tutorial for DOT.MAP and SEURAT using this interface. Being single characters, the commands were pretty cryptic, and not everyone could keep all 30 commands in their mind. The development of desktop illustration software required a different technology for user interaction. Nonetheless, 10 years were to elapse before the first of these, MacDraw, would be available for use on personal computers.

Hierarchy of squares output from ▶
ARTIST, with five smaller sized squares
centered on four corners and center of
the larger square. While inspired by
fractal concepts, this demonstrates
the ability to invoke a geometric form
(here a square) in different sizes and
orientations. *(Source: Context 8, May 1976, page 6,
Harvard University Graduate School of Design)*

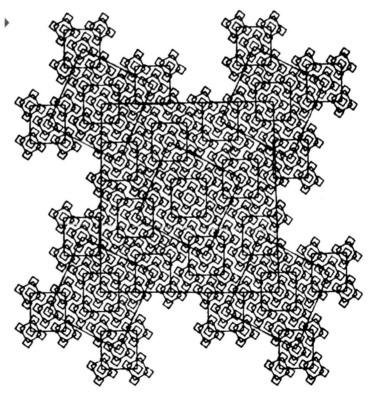

ARCHITECTURAL RENDERING: BUILDER

As part of the Graduate School of Design, the Laboratory had sporadic contacts with design disciplines (primarily architecture) that worked with built objects rather than with maps. The OTOTROL program in the first years of the Laboratory (see chapter 5), and much of what followed, produced wireframe drawings that were far from realistic. Hidden line calculations were easier for coherent (single-valued) surfaces in programs like SYMVU. Architectural applications require arbitrary objects positioned in 3D space in complex arrangements, making the hidden surfaces harder to derive. A few prototype programs were developed,[15] but not distributed to users.

In 1981, after a period of less emphasis on architectural applications, Bruce Donald created BUILDER to manage complex three-dimensional objects generated as extrusions of planar forms. A base polygon was given as a two-dimensional form, then extended through the third dimension to end up on a (perhaps different) polygonal form. In simplest form, if applied to a map of building footprints, they could all be extruded to their roof height, assuming flat roofs. Any three-dimensional shape could be produced, though it might take a few separate extrusions to model a complex roof gable structure. The extrusions did not have to be vertical. A beam could be created in cross-section and extruded horizontally; walls and floors could be extruded as very thin polygons.

BUILDER calculated hidden lines from any vantage point (even within the rooms of buildings). It also shaded surfaces according to assumptions about illumination, but it did not do the computationally intense ray-casting that is now a part of realistic scene generation. BUILDER was programmed using the ODYSSEY toolkit for memory management and particularly the language system. It was the best example of the use of the programming language side of LINGUIST (nested functions, conditional execution, and extensible terminology).

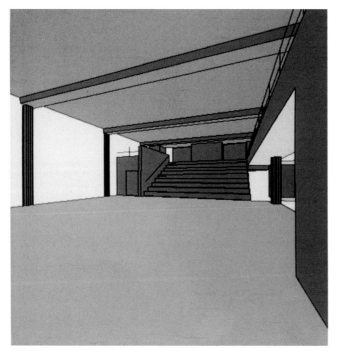

◀ **View inside Piper Auditorium at Harvard Graduate School of Design produced by BUILDER.** *(Source: Context 1982·83, page 10, Harvard University Graduate School of Design; image below © Bruce R. Donald. Reprinted with permission from* A Familiar Space in Two Dimensions *[Piper Auditorium CAD Study] by Bruce Donald and Paul Stevenson, 1982)*

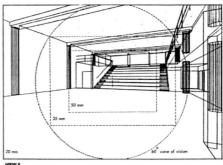

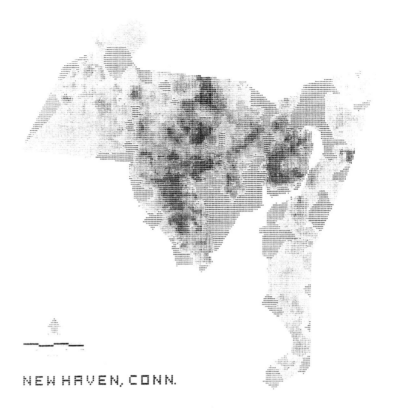

Colored SYMAP output produced by ▶
passing the paper through the printer
three times with different colored
printer ribbons. Population density
by census blocks from the 1967 test
census in New Haven, Connecticut.

*(Source: original map produced by Donald Cooke and
William Maxfield, 1967; used with permission)*

NEW HAVEN, CONN.

BURSTING WITH COLOR

Everyone at the Laboratory had an opinion about color. We were constrained so firmly by the limitations of black-and-white printers and plotters, and we longed for ways to produce zippier color images. Back in the earliest days of 1967, Donald Cooke had worked out a technique to run the paper three times through the printer with changed carbon paper to produce a color map of New Haven. Howard Fisher wrote Cooke a rather discouraging letter:

"As to your colored maps, if you invented that system, I can only commend your great ingenuity. As an example of creative problem solving, I was particularly impressed when I first saw some samples of your work. However, my own feeling is that color is not worth the extra effort—assuming that the very best use can be made of black and white output." [16]

Color hardware eventually improved, and the Laboratory staff made various efforts to figure out how to put them to use. The first day our Tektronix 4027 arrived (around 1979), Dutton worked hard at the color wheel to select a subtly green background with bright green text, as close to the Tektronix 4014 as he could get. Howard Fisher had studied with Professor Arthur Pope, and built a version of Pope's color solid and Munsell's space for classroom use.[17] Denis White worked to reconstruct the CIE color space on the AED terminal, as a way to figure out the capabilities of the equipment.

Our work with color included a collaboration with a visual artist from Maine, Dennis Dreher, and his artist spouse, Gemma Morrill. The Laboratory invited the two as artists-in-residence. Their main commission was to develop depictions of color spaces, working with Fisher on the Pope solid, and on a massive matrix of painted wooden balls. Dreher had the idea of creating an inverted perspective so that you could show the full range of tertiary colors in a color space, as a cubic 3D array viewed from the vanishing point. Dreher had worked out his own geometric approach to the construction. Randolph Franklin figured out a way to render this by tricking his VIEWPLOT program to draw the most-hidden lines, rather than the ones that would be visible in a normal view.

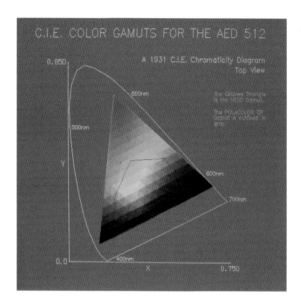

◀ A slice of the CIE color space produced on the AED 512 color terminal by Denis White. *(Source: Collection of Denis White, used with permission)*

◀ A 6×6×6 matrix of cubes, viewed down the main diagonal, with the farthest (smallest) object shown "in front" (inverted perspective). Drawn by VIEWPLOT; Randolph Franklin, programmer. Based on a concept for inverted perspective developed by Dennis Dreher and executed in his painting of a three-axes color cube, now in the collection of Allan Schmidt. *(Source: Context 9, January 1978, page 6, Harvard University Graduate School of Design)*

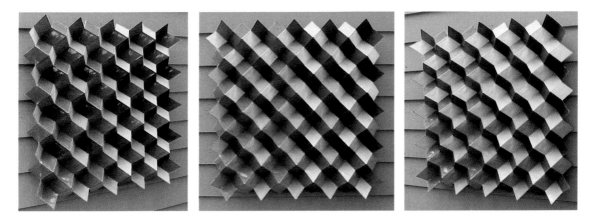

▲ Sculpture by Dennis Dreher based on the display technique in the SEURAT program. *(Photo courtesy of Geoffrey Dutton. Used with permission of the artist.)*

Dreher painted a number of color mixture demonstrations, including a sculptural version of Dutton's SEURAT system of four-color shading woven from strips of colored paper. This was a case where the artist followed the computer program.

In other cases, the programmer followed the artist. One painting by Dreher, showing the mixture of three pigments in a triangular format, was reproduced by me as a way to demonstrate a screening technique for silk screens (and similar technology) where you wish to avoid dot overlap. The share of three pigments changed a floating point in the center of a triangular mesh, and the colored zones shrunk back from the edges to leave a black background around the dots to control intensity. The triangular mesh flipped back and forth so that adjacent triangles had the same color along the shared face. The resulting quadrilaterals were the objects plotted. Because none of the quadrilateral "dots" overlapped, color separations could be generated that could be printed using brighter opaque inks (additive RGB colors) rather than the transparent pigments used in printing conventional CMYK color separations. Dreher and the staff reasoned that the precision and intensity of colors produced by such a system would improve on the muddiness of then-current ink jets, but the devices to support it did not yet exist. Later, in 1986, Dreher and Dutton collaborated on a revised version linked to the early PostScript laser printers; for various reasons the concept did not find favor in the graphics industry and was not further pursued.

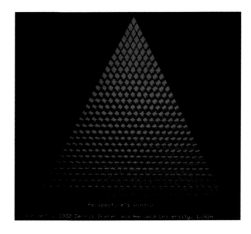

▲ A triangular diagram of color mixing; concept by Dennis Dreher 1973, executed in 1980 by Nick Chrisman on AED 512 terminal using quadrilateral shading software. *(Used with permission)*

Harvard Computer Graphics Week

The 1977 symposium at Endicott House catered to the research community, but the Laboratory also reached out to the broader user community. There were six annual Harvard Computer Graphics Weeks held in mid-summer at the Hyatt Regency Hotel on the banks of the Charles River. These events drew three hundred or five hundred people with as many as 35 sessions crammed into five days. These events followed on a long line stretching back to the 1967 conference, but with a much increased public. In the early 1970s, there had been an annual one-week seminar on computer mapping. Those events had attracted perhaps 30 participants. With the Harvard Computer Graphics Week series, the one-room events evolved into dozens of parallel sessions and a large audience.

Some sessions dealt with the core geographic information interests of Laboratory software, but there were also some general computer graphics sessions. Many of the applications were quite similar to those at current user-oriented conferences, with strong showings from local government, environmental planning, transportation, and similar fields. Instead of minimal question-and-answer sessions after each paper, the speakers sat at "roundtables" scattered around the hall, providing a less threatening and more productive atmosphere for discussion after each session. The conference papers appeared in 19 volumes of the red-covered series *Harvard Library of Computer Graphics.*[18]

These conferences were not your typical academic affairs. Certain speakers were attracted by having their expenses covered. Some were paid for giving workshops. The Hyatt put on sumptuous lunches at the penthouse level overlooking the Charles Basin. There were cruises on Boston Harbor. But most of all there were the bags and T-shirts. The bags were canvas, of a quality that has allowed them to survive 25 years of constant use in the family of any participant who lugged them home filled with copies of the conference papers.

These events attracted substantial media coverage, including short segments on the local television news coverage. In 1980, one television reporter looked surprised as Eric Teicholz talked about the coming generation of personal computers. She asked if he really meant that there would be a computer in every home; his response was: "Sooner than you think."

Harvard Computer Graphics Week was a hybrid between a scientific conference and a trade show. In these early days of the field, research mixed closely with practice. At the 1979 event, for example, the presenters were called "faculty," and included 33 from industry, 26 from government, and 25 from academic institutions. The industry component was from decision-making ranks, not just technical-level staff, with 14 using the title of "president" or "vice-president." By the 1981 event, 16 of the 34 exhibitors were from industry. The Laboratory contracted with a conference management firm to stage the event, while holding on to the selection of papers and the production of the proceedings. The editorial function allowed the Laboratory to build up a publications and graphics unit that employed five people by 1981. Overall, the Laboratory made a tidy sum from the first few years. By 1982, the Graduate School of Design wanted more control over these events, as well as a slice of the revenue. The focus shifted, and attendance dropped off. This transition is a small piece in the larger story of radical restructuring of the Laboratory.

NOTES

1. The project on "Managing Suburban Growth" was funded by the National Science Foundation from 1972–1976; Carl Steinitz et al., "Managing Suburban Growth: A modeling approach," (Landscape Architecture Research Office, Harvard University, 1976); see also chapter 3 of this book.

2. Map algebra emerged from the grid analysis programs traced in chapter 3. Dana Tomlin had written analytical (neighborhood) functions for IMGRID before leaving Harvard for Yale. The term "map algebra" took public form in his paper presented in 1983 (proceedings not published until 1985). C. Dana Tomlin, "A map algebra," in *Harvard Computer Graphics Conference,* vol. 2, 1–46 (Cambridge, Mass.: Graduate School of Design, Harvard University, 1985).

3. Geoffrey Dutton, "Minority report on gridded data," *Internal report 76-11* (Laboratory for Computer Graphics and Spatial Analysis, Harvard University, 1976).

4. Geoffrey Dutton, "DOT.MAP user's reference manual, version 3.0" (Laboratory for Computer Graphics and Spatial Analysis, Harvard University, 1978).

5. Previous programs at the Laboratory had calculated contours, including OBLIX. Peucker had discussed the construction of Tanaka's inclined contours with computers. Adrian Thomas, "OBLIX: A two and three dimensional mapping program for use with line plotters," in *Red Book,* V.50-V.52 (Cambridge, Mass.: Laboratory for Computer Graphics and Spatial Analysis, Harvard University, 1970); Thomas K. Peucker, Mark Tichenor, and Wolf-Keiter Rase, "The computer version of three relief representations," in *Red Book,* VI.93–VI.94 (Cambridge, Mass.: Laboratory for Computer Graphics and Spatial Analysis, Harvard University, 1971); K. Tanaka, "The relief contour method of representing topography on maps," *Geographical Review* 40 (1950): 444–456.

6. Geoffrey Dutton, "An extensible approach to imagery of gridded data," SIGGRAPH 77 (San Jose: Association for Computing Machinery, 1977), volume 2, 159–169.

7. Geoffrey Dutton, "Land alive," *Perspectives in Computing* 2 (1982): 26–39.

8. Dutton, "Minority report on gridded data," 3–4.

9. Three SYMVU surfaces appeared in the July 1976 issue of *National Geographic* in rather oblique perspective.

10. Geoffrey Dutton, "American Graph Fleeting: A computer-holographic map animation," (Laboratory for Computer Graphics and Spatial Analysis, Harvard University, 1979). The movie used to generate the hologram was also called *Manifested Destiny.*

11. This movie is available on the CD that accompanies this book. The credits for this production include programming: James Dougenik, Geoffrey Dutton, and James Little; film animation: Jody Culkin; calligraphy and design: Bruce Kennett; holography: The Holographic Film Company; and direction: Geoffrey Dutton.

12. The Tektronix 4027 terminal displayed 16 colors from a palette of thousands of colors. It had a built-in BASIC interpreter that permitted small programs to run locally. It took vector commands similar to the storage terminals like the Tektronix 4014 terminal, and converted them to raster locally.

13. Tobler had originally described cartograms in his doctoral thesis: Waldo Tobler, "Map transformations of geographic space," (PhD dissertation, University of Washington, 1961). The paper I had read in 1974 included new results; Tobler sent me his documentation later, starting a correspondence on the subject that continues. Waldo Tobler, "A continuous transformation useful in districting," *Annals, New York Academy of Sciences* 225 (1973): 215–220. Waldo Tobler, "Cartogram programs" (University of Michigan, Department of Geography, 1974).

14. Published later: James A. Dougenik, Nicholas R. Chrisman, and Duane R. Niemeyer, "An algorithm to construct continuous area cartograms," *Professional Geographer* 37 (1985): 75–81.

15. These new programs included VIEWPLOT, by Randolph Franklin.

16. Howard Fisher, letter to Donald Cooke, 29 April 1968 (HTF Papers, box 15, folder: New Haven Census Use Study).

17. Howard Fisher donated these models of the color solids to the Fogg Art Museum toward the end of his career. They are now in the special collection of the Loeb Library. Howard Fisher and James Carpenter, *Color in art* (Cambridge, Mass.: Fogg Museum, Harvard University, 1974).

18. Patricia Moore, ed. *Harvard Library of Computer Graphics,* 19 volumes (Cambridge, Mass.: Laboratory for Computer Graphics and Spatial Analysis, Harvard University, 1978–1981).

TEN

Crisis of Direction

The long expansion of the Laboratory came to a sudden end in 1981. Plans to commercialize the ODYSSEY package had increased expenditures, but the commercial placement of the software became highly problematic. The Harvard administration, for years distant from the operations of the Laboratory, became a direct force in setting directions that required drastic reduction in staff.

Choosing a future

At each conference he organized, Allan Schmidt would hold a final session under some title related to "future directions."[1] Often the participants who had detailed ideas of current technology would stumble in trying to predict the future. While others remained tied to the hardware of computer graphics, and glimpses of software, Schmidt's grand vision placed databases much more at the center of the picture. His view of the future in a 1979 article includes insights about consumer access to geographic services that took two more decades to become attainable for the wide public. His term for the technology of the future, "Mapavision," did not catch on, but all of its features are recognizable.

"Recent breakthroughs at Harvard University in the development of cartographic data structures will eventually produce a situation in which society will witness the evolution of Everyman's map: the ability of the average citizen to produce a computer generated map of virtually any subject, for any location, for any time. . . . The potential of use and misuse of the emerging technology is truly staggering. . . .

"Personal uses of computing will undoubtedly include the ability to generate computer maps using a new technology known as Mapavision. Mundane applications will include preparation of route maps at home or en route for the journey to work, play, shopping, picking up the kids, etc., taking into account existing traffic conditions and a minimum travel path (especially for those families with many children!). Shopping for a particular product will be facilitated by preparation of a map showing the locations of all stores having that product in stock. Vacation trips can be planned and updated during the trip to take into account weather, road conditions, changing interests of the travelers (including those kids), and accommodations available. Cross country travelers will have the novel opportunity of not being able to get lost due to the constant availability of a map on their TV screen which pinpoints their current location. Of greatest importance, however, will be everyone's ability and right as a free citizen to display information related to recent and forthcoming public policy issues on the national, regional, and local level. . . .

"The medium of computer graphics may prove to be the messenger (if not the message) by which all people will most effectively benefit from the emergence of computer technology."[2]

Getting to such a grand vision was not direct or obvious. The programming staff was full of confidence that ODYSSEY set new standards in performance and software integration. Technically, the Laboratory was setting the state of the art. The Laboratory took strong action to lead the development of the geographic information sector. In 1978 and 1979, Harvard Computer Graphics Week attracted increasing crowds of potential users for more sophisticated systems. Money flowed freely, as the conference expanded. In parallel, there was a twice-monthly commercial *Harvard Newsletter on Computer Graphics,* produced by an external consultant.[3] In addition, a series of management-oriented training seminars attracted corporate managers at full commercial rates ($395 for one day; $495 for a two-day event). The seminars were held at the Harvard Faculty Club and throughout the country in a dozen different cities. In 1979, about half of the seminars were given by Laboratory staff, but as it evolved the Harvard presence diminished. The subject matter expanded to general information systems management.

Commercializing ODYSSEY

The increasing presence of the Laboratory in the commercial sector extended to software dissemination. The timing seemed right; ODYSSEY appeared to offer commercial potential. The budget for the basic operations of the Laboratory (outside of specific research grants and contracts) was based on projections of this revenue for the coming year. During the late 1970s, the trend had been ever upward. Revenue[4] for fiscal 1978 was just under $300,000. This expanded to $440,000 for the next year, and it doubled again for fiscal 1980 to well over a million dollars. Expenses also expanded, so that the Laboratory always showed a small deficit. Increasing revenue at this rate would look very promising to a venture capitalist, but not to a university administration. The difficulty was not so much the deficit as the increasingly commercial nature of the revenue. Harvard University had an overriding interest in retaining its status as a tax-exempt, nonprofit institution, and business income from the Laboratory's operations could not exceed a rather low threshold. Something had to be done to rectify the situation.

From one perspective, the Laboratory had as large a user base as many commercial enterprises of the period. The 1978 list of confirmed users of existing Laboratory software (mostly SYMAP) included 469 institutions in 26 countries.[5] Of these, the majority were universities and research centers (246). There were 139 governments, with about half at the city or county level. Commercial users added up to 84, in the resource, aerospace, and computer sectors. Some of these users were a single professor teaching a course on cartography, but others were spending large sums on geographic information. In 1979, the U.S. Forest Service, for instance, sent us a report[6] showing that they were spending over $400,000 (1979 dollars) maintaining their in-house GIS software, most of which was far below even the 1979 state of the art. Overall, the Coopers and Lybrand accounting firm estimated that the Laboratory held about a 2 percent market share of the whole computer graphics industry for 1980.[7]

The Laboratory had brought out a number of new products in the 1970s simply by adding them to the catalog. Sales costs were low, and the existing base would buy into the new products. ODYSSEY had been dangled in front of the clients for a few years as a future product. Yet, it was clear that ODYSSEY was much bigger than prior Laboratory additions. At the same time, technology was changing rapidly; many of the public agencies were moving away from the centralized computer service to set up dedicated minicomputers explicitly for geographic information work. At the first Harvard Computer Graphics Week, the redoubtable Grace Hopper, a stalwart and vocal veteran of computing in the U.S. Navy, railed against the paperwork required to purchase a computer through the U.S. government. She had started work on the very first electronic calculators and computers in the 1940s, and played a role in early computing languages in the 1950s. She saw the potential for cheap processing chips that would cost a lot less than the red tape to buy them. The purchasing process went through a complex dance of requests for proposals (RFPs), benchmarks, and bundled contracts. The hardware, software, and training were all meant to be included, and the marketplace was responding with "turnkey" systems. The late 1970s saw a number of startup companies building integrated hardware-software systems specifically for automated drafting and cartography. One of these was M&S Computing (later Intergraph), which hired David Sinton away from Harvard's Landscape Architecture Department around 1980. This computer graphics industry was expanding rapidly.

DIPPING A TOE IN THE MARKET

During 1978 and 1979, the Laboratory staff were on the verge of responding to some of the RFPs. The Tennessee Valley Authority (TVA), a federal government entity that manages hydroelectric production from a string of dams and also works on regional development, put out a huge RFP in 1979. In April, we received a 20-page document with the core geographic information processing requirements. In less than two weeks, I had produced a letter with a 12-page response, point by point. I cautioned them that their specification was not worded to ensure the technical character of a response. I was confident that ODYSSEY would be able to provide most of the required functions, but the list was long and detailed—much of it a wish list. In August, the full RFP arrived.[8] It was 164 pages long. Over Labor Day weekend, I wrote a 12-page analysis of the bidding criteria. I did not see how we could reply in the two-week period requested, or even by the extension to the end of September. I was particularly worried by the inconsistencies between the desires for regional analysis and the limited capabilities of available computer platforms. For example, they wanted to use floating point numbers, stored in 32 bits, to cover their 1,000-kilometer-wide region with a precision of one foot. The standard floating point just did not provide enough bits for this demand, yet some vendor was going to pretend it would be feasible. My overall evaluation was: "This still has the flavor of a search for a system to perform untold wonders."[9]

Later in 1979, Roger Tomlinson issued a call for interest in bidding on a project for the Saskatchewan Forest Inventory.[10] The preliminary specification of data handling requirements[11] was quite detailed—and certainly ambitious. The Laboratory staff were tempted to respond, and the manager of the software project, Scott Morehouse, flew to Saskatoon to attend a bidder's conference. The level of the Laboratory's commercial presence can be measured by the fact that Morehouse hitchhiked from the airport to the client's office in Prince Albert, in northern Saskatchewan, spending the night in a field along the road. The Laboratory did not bid on this system, but 10 companies did. Most submissions were a hundred pages or more. Five were taken through a four- or five-day benchmark. Tomlinson and his associates (notably Ray Boyle and Michael Goodchild) found no submission adequate. The overall complaint was slow response of the systems offered. The polygon overlay capability, for example, was only conducted on a small map with 22 new polygons to intersect into the existing inventory. Only one of the competing systems had software that could carry out this task, and it took six hours to complete. Normally such failures of the commercial sector would be kept highly confidential, but Tomlinson and Boyle published a summary paper in *Cartographica*. They concluded that the existing software "should be rethought and rewritten before anyone buys it."[12] That is exactly what happened, but it took a few years.

The GIS industry was on the edge of its creation. Everyone hoped it would be big; we just didn't know how big, or what would be involved in making it big.

The emerging market for GIS spurred the Laboratory to prepare ODYSSEY for distribution. It was apparent that the software would be revolutionary, if it could get to market quickly. The test of overlay calculations demanded for Saskatchewan was similar to the Healdsburg test that ODYSSEY had completed in a few minutes, not hours. That test was done with the prototype ODYSSEY in 1977–1978.[13] In the more demanding St. Regis Paper Company demonstration performed for NASA in 1979,[14] the new WHIRLPOOL produced an overlay with 250 polygons in four minutes of CPU time on our old PDP-10. But we all knew that commercial success was only partially related to technical excellence. We had to choose how ODYSSEY would be distributed.

The story of the commercial development of ODYSSEY is complicated. There were a number of distinct discussions and agreements. Some of these were kept confidential and are only apparent from passing mention in some other document. A number of separate tracks were active at the same time, as some players worked alone without communicating with the others. This account will cover the parts of the story that I can document.

In the winter of 1978–1979, Allan Schmidt had a series of discussions with industry contacts. The idea of a commercial spin-off company (called LCG Inc., internally) emerged.[15] It was proposed to have Harvard ownership. A proposal for venture capital from the Harvard Management Company (the corporate unit that manages the vast endowment of the university) was turned down. The person selected to be the chief executive officer of the company, Jack Sheets, and Schmidt continued to look for venture capital from IBM and a subsidiary of General Electric.[16] The deal with IBM included computer hardware that would have to be housed in a new wing of Gund Hall, a complex and expensive undertaking. At Harvard Computer Graphics Week in 1979, there were discussions with a software company, ISSCO.[17] By November 1979, a year later, the decision inside Harvard was still not complete.

The whole process of technology transfer from a university to the commercial sector had to be invented. There were very limited models at this date. Schmidt continued to seek advice in search of a commercial solution.[18] In late 1979, he hired a tax lawyer from Cleveland, Robert Blomberg. This expert in the tax status of universities produced a 63-page opinion.[19] Fundamentally, commercial income from software was judged incompatible with Harvard's nonprofit status. Blomberg proposed three nonprofit corporations, each owned by Harvard, to isolate separate types of income (from publications, software, and seminars). Schmidt also retained Coopers and Lybrand to audit the Laboratory in the context of building a business plan and market study. The drawback of the new company was the need for venture capital. Licensing the software to an existing company offered what seemed a faster route to commercial success and a positive revenue stream. Sheets, Schmidt, and Denis White met with ISSCO (Integrated Software Systems Corporation), a computer graphics firm, in February 1980. They made an agreement in principle to license the software to ISSCO in return of 50 percent of the gross revenue. The correspondence with ISSCO[20] shows that this step was still connected to the idea of founding LCG Inc., but it became an alternative due to simpler legal hurdles.

Meanwhile, the recently formed Harvard Committee on Patents and Copyrights was pulling together the university's response. In April 1980, Stephen Atkinson produced a 22-page report[21] suggesting that the best approach was to hand over the whole of the Laboratory's intellectual property to a single for-profit company (an expanded LCG Inc.) with minority Harvard participation. He counseled against the ISSCO deal. He also reiterated the firm policy that the Harvard name could not be used for commercial purposes. Atkinson's closely argued case was not convincing to the Harvard administration. In this same period, a proposed Harvard spin-off in biotechnology was shelved due to criticism from the pharmaceutical sector. Derek Bok, president of Harvard at the time, spoke publicly against the conflict of interest inherent in spin-off corporations formed by faculty. The publicity of the biotech sector caused the Harvard administration to opt for a firm demarcation between Harvard and any commercial activity.[22]

If there could be no spin-off, the commercial activity had to be done entirely by the commercial sector. Through a decision process involving the Laboratory, the new dean of the Graduate School of Design, and the university, the agreement with ISSCO was confirmed, and announced in September 1980.[23] The arrangement required the code to be delivered on short schedules (two weeks for the first installment). Programmers were added to the core team that had been working on the commercialization push. Laboratory staff expenses expanded rapidly as testers explored all the options, technical writers constructed user manuals, and publications staff put them into printable form. The staff numbered around 45 at the peak of this expansion.

The Laboratory's expenditures for fiscal year 1981 were budgeted over $3 million.[24] These costs were meant to be covered by revenues from ISSCO, as well as the expanding revenues from the seminar series. On paper, the payback was meant to occur within one fiscal year, something few businesses would expect.

The relationship with ISSCO did not move ahead smoothly. The deliverables were tightly scheduled, and there were substantial misunderstandings about who would do which tasks in preparing the system for sale. The Lab's commercialization team had tested the software, removed many bugs, and written technical documentation and user manuals. Yet, the commercial sector demanded something different, usually simpler without the artistic expression. I remember a tense meeting with the ISSCO team as we tried to work out a viable agreement on deliverables. Jack Dangermond (at this time president of the then small firm ESRI) attended to help negotiate between the sides.[25] Some snappy color ads trumpeting the Harvard software[26] appeared in various trade publications, probably without full approval from the university. The base license price was set at $20,000 for the basic ability to produce a thematic map, with a list of add-ons that brought the whole system to $60,000. In the software market of the time, some much simpler capabilities were being sold at such prices. But the marketing of geographic analysis was not entirely a matter of price when the RFP process required a one-hundred page response covering hardware and software.

Costs of packaging the software spiraled upward, with very little revenue apparent. A terrifying sucking sound was pulling the little tub into a vortex of missed expectations.

HARVARD GRAPHICS SOFTWARE

Percent first and second generation immigrants, 1970
Source: Bureau of the Census

Put Your Information In Perspective

Innovative Graphic Display

Harvard Graphics Software provides a fresh look at your data. Significant facts become immediately apparent. Maps may be produced for any geographic area—from nations to city blocks. Two and three dimensional maps in either black and white or color can be produced on your CRT or plotter. Using an easy to understand command language, Harvard Graphics Software is available for use on large scale or super-mini computers, with over 700 installations world wide.

A Geographic Information System

One part of Harvard Graphics Software is a series of four interactive computer programs which manage and display geographically based information. This program series is known as the Harvard Geographic Information System. The three dimensional plot shown above was produced by PRISMAP, one of

the four programs in the system. The Harvard Geographic Information System permits users to capture, record, manage, analyze and display any geographically referenced data. With black and white and color computer mapping capabilities it simplifies data reduction and interpretation. In addition it can merge two or more independent data files to allow for multi-dimensional geographic analysis. The Harvard Geographic Information System is distributed, installed and serviced with training provided by:

ISSCO
Integrated Software Systems Corporation
4186 Sorrento Valley Blvd., San Diego, CA 92121 (714) 452-0170
Ask for Bob Adams
In Washington, D.C. and New York contact:
Alan Paller
AUI Data Graphics
1701 K St., NW
Washington, D.C. 20006
D.C. Phone (202) 331-1800   N.Y. Phone (212) 567-7288
Reprinted from American Demographics magazine

◀ Advertisement for the ODYSSEY software produced by ISSCO in 1980. Printed in *American Demographics*, a trade journal for marketing professionals. The image had appeared on the cover of LAB-LOG in 1978. *(Source: offprint from American Demographics)*

THE DEAN TAKES CHARGE

Through most of the 1970s, the dean of the Graduate School of Design was Maurice Kilbridge, an academic planner who had made a career in the Harvard Business School. His term as dean finished in 1979. Gerald McCue, an architect, became dean in the 1979–1980 academic year, a time when decisions about commercialization were being discussed.

For Harvard, one of the unsettling issues for any commercial venture was the use of the Harvard name. Although President Derek Bok had signed a welcome letter for the packet handed out to each registrant at Graphics Week 1980, the administration was not happy with the use of the Harvard name, even for Harvard Computer Graphics Week. Seeing the ISSCO ads titled "Harvard Graphics Software" perturbed them. Then the administration noticed that the Laboratory letterhead had inserted a 3D space frame (the Laboratory's logo since 1968; see chapter 5) inside the university's traditional seal. The university's Office of Heraldry demurred that we had not received permission for such a modification. This was not a matter to be brushed aside in the traditions of an ancient institution. More importantly, the Harvard Business School got wind of the management seminar series, probably from the highly aggressive direct mail marketing. The Business School had its own series of management seminars covering much of the same topics about information systems. Business School officials were highly upset. If it had been a conflict between equals, perhaps some arrangement could have been reached. But the Business School was much more powerful and longer established. The Laboratory management seminar series was cancelled, leaving an additional gap in revenues.

The dean of the Graduate School of Design did not like losing out to the Business School. The mounting deficit looked like it would exceed a million dollars. What had been a rapidly expanding part of the design school—with a strong prospect of making money—was now a huge headache. As an additional irritant, the mapping and spatial analysis in ODYSSEY did not fit with the vision of design that Dean McCue wanted to build. The first set of discussions to forge a strategy to resolve the deficit occurred in private meetings with the director of the Laboratory, Brian Berry. There was no agreement, and Berry issued a one-line resignation as director on November 5, 1980.[27]

By summer 1981, Dean McCue took charge of the Laboratory's fate.[28] The contract with ISSCO was terminated, effective September 1981.[29] The budget would be pruned back drastically, by staff layoffs. Another commercial placement for ODYSSEY would be sought. A transitional budget was crafted that showed a slight surplus, but accounts receivable from the seminar series never materialized, and other revenue was below expectations.

Laboratory for Computer Graphics and Spatial Analysis
Graduate School of Design   Harvard University

 Harvard Laboratory for Computer Graphics and Spatial Analysis

▲   The Laboratory's logo was a "space frame," a wire-frame drawing of the intersection of three planes. This image was adopted in 1968 from the output of Eric Teicholz's program (see chapter 5, page 78). Around 1978, the Laboratory had started to use another logo on its letterhead, one that inserted this space frame into the generic seal of the university. *(Sources: Image on top from cover of LAB-LOG 1977; image on bottom from cover of LAB-LOG 1978, Harvard University Graduate School of Design)*

Departures

Departures of Laboratory staff punctuated the academic year 1981–1982, bringing a staff of over 40 down to about 10 by 1983. The first to resign was the director, Brian Berry, in the first skirmishes with the dean over the seminars and the direction of the Laboratory in the later fall of 1980. Berry retained his title of professor through the spring of 1981, but left Harvard in June 1981 to become dean of public affairs at Carnegie Mellon University. Berry's announced departure led to a complex story related to my continued employment. When I returned to Harvard in April 1981 from England, where I had been working on my doctoral dissertation, I was told that my paychecks had been stopped. (I was entirely funded during 1979–1981 by a National Science Foundation grant; Berry was principal investigator.) The associate dean, Kate Rooney, had decided that my absence had been intolerable; beyond that, my academic supervisor (Berry) was no longer present to protect me.[30] Since her attempt to terminate me happened after I had returned, the action backfired. The day that an expected paycheck did not materialize, I went without appointment to the associate dean's office. I made it clear that I was back at work at the Laboratory; her answers were evasive. Eventually I received notification from university officials that I had resigned,[31] and I promptly wrote back that I had not done so. These officials were not amused to find that the associate dean had no evidence of a resignation; she had simply reported my resignation to get me off the payroll. I was reinstated, with considerable apologies from the dean, the associate dean, as well as the university administration.[32] Some of the staff saw changes coming and made their own decisions to move on. By the summer, Scott Morehouse had decided to take on the job of lead programmer at ESRI in Redlands, California.

Dan Schodek, a structural engineer working in the Architecture Department, was appointed acting director of the Laboratory in July 1981. In early September (just after the Harvard Computer Graphics Week event), Allan Schmidt issued an ambiguous note[33] about exploring new opportunities through a leave of absence. The niceties were only paper-thin. Eric Teicholz, the associate director, resigned to go into the consulting sector. At a subsequent staff meeting, the message was unambiguous. Some of the programmers were given notice, notably Jim Dougenik and Tom DiGennaro, who both left to take programming jobs in the Boston area. The whole publications component of the Laboratory was fired, along with a majority of the support staff. Some of the employees found other jobs within the Graduate School of Design (for instance, Anne Hunt White worked as programmer for Kate Rooney's new Wang system for office automation). Some of the more research-oriented staff held on a bit longer, some leaving eventually to enroll in graduate school (for instance, Bruce Donald entered a PhD program at MIT).

I held out through the academic year, long enough to get my PhD completed, and to line up an academic job at the University of Wisconsin–Madison. Unlike my superiors, my letter of resignation[34] was three single-spaced pages addressed to Bok, the university president. I expressed the goals of Fisher and Warntz in founding the Laboratory, and my reasoning why Harvard should reestablish a geography department. I noted that at the University of Wisconsin I would have a wider range of colleagues in geodesy, cartography, remote sensing, and all the mapping sciences. I developed an argument that computers and programming were changing the role of research scholarship. The president responded within a week with a polite note[35] wishing me continued success. In my case, the leaving was not particularly painful.

The word about the Laboratory got out into the commercial sector, with a note about the "reining in" of the Laboratory staff by Harvard administrators.[36] Six of the remaining staff mounted a defense, saying that the research mission would be strengthened by the changes in orientation. Allan Schmidt added his own column, adopting much of the official line about the role of research.[37] This was a hard case to make, and most of those who signed the letter did not stay at the Laboratory much longer. In August 1982, Schmidt's leave of absence turned into a dismissal. At this point, the professional staff of the Laboratory consisted of seven. They tried to develop greater links to the rest of the Graduate School of Design, but when their research proposals were not funded, three more (Geoffrey Dutton, Martin Broekhuysen, and Bruce Donald) were given notice in April 1984.[38] By the fall of 1984, there were five employees left, three of them part-time.

The gloom of diminished staff size was intertwined with the eternal optimism that some new grants would arrive to reverse the situation. The next chapter will describe this period of uncertainty and the gradual process by which the Laboratory eventually vanished.

NOTES

1. There was a "future directions" discussion at the Endicott House event. Eighteen short responses are in volume 1 of the proceedings. Schmidt chaired a plenary session titled "Future directions" in 1978 and 1979. It reappeared in 1981 as a concurrent session.

2. Allan H. Schmidt, "Future directions of computer graphics" *Context* 10 (1979): 16.

3. *Harvard Newsletter for Computer Graphics* was edited by Stanley Klein, who had a connection to the group that helped organize Harvard Computer Graphics Week. The newsletter appeared twice-monthly in 1979 and 1980, and had an annual subscription price of $125. It continued as the *Stan Klein Newsletter for Computer Graphics.*

4. Figures from Stephen Atkinson, memorandum to Henry Meadow, Harvard Committee on Patents and Copyrights, April 7, 1980. Atkinson cites an audit of Laboratory finances completed in March 1980 by Coopers and Lybrand. The Harvard fiscal year ran from 1 July to 30 June.

5. "Current Program Users," July 20, 1978, compiled by Barbara Chrisman and others.

6. U.S. Forest Service, "Resource Information Display System Project—RIDS: Status of May 5, 1978" sent to Harvard by Thomas George, May 17, 1978.

7. The 2 percent figure comes from an estimate of the size of the computer graphics market in 1980 ($65 million) derived from a study by Frost and Sullivan in 1978, compared to the expected 1980 sales of the Laboratory ($1.7 million). (Atkinson memorandum, page 5, see note 4.)

8. Tennessee Valley Authority, Solicitation J4-604350, August 21, 1979

9. Nicholas Chrisman, "Review of TVA Solicitation," memorandum, August 31, 1979.

10. Roger Tomlinson, letter, November 15, 1979.

11. Tomlinson Associates, "Preliminary specification of computer assisted data handling requirements for the Saskatchewan Forest Inventory," November 1978.

12. Roger Tomlinson and A. Raymond Boyle, "The state of development of systems for handling natural resources inventory data," *Cartographica* 18, no. 4 (1981): 92.

13. The test was performed as subcontractor to The Analytical Sciences Corporation (TASC) under contract ETL-0144 with U.S. Army Topographic Engineering Laboratories. The results of this test were also presented at Harvard Computer Graphics Week 1978: Michael P. Goldberg, Allan H. Schmidt, and Nicholas Chrisman, "Integration and analysis of multiple geographic data bases: An application of ODYSSEY," in *Harvard Library of Computer Graphics,* vol. 2, ed. Patricia Moore, 81–98 (Cambridge, Mass.: Laboratory for Computer Graphics and Spatial Analysis, Harvard University, 1979).

14. The Laboratory was subcontractor to Purdue University (LARS, Laboratory for Applications in Remote Sensing) on a demonstration project funded by NASA. The project was meant to design a forest inventory system for St. Regis Paper Company. The results of the overlay demonstrated that the 80-meter resolution of Landsat was not adequate for forest inventory.

15. I had no access to the proposals related to LCG, Inc. This is inferred from the Atkinson memo (see note 4).

16. Allan H. Schmidt, "Laboratory goals, objectives and potential sources of development support," memorandum to Brian Berry, Dean Maurice Kilbridge, and Laboratory staff, September 26, 1978.

17. Nicholas Chrisman, memorandum, July 19, 1979, refers to meeting with ISSCO.

18. Allan Schmidt, personal communication, 2004.

19. Document not available, cited by Atkinson memorandum (see note 4).

20. Sunny Harris, Vice President of ISSCO, letter to Allan Schmidt, March 6, 1980. This letter proposed a perpetual license agreement. In a subsequent letter, May 12, 1980, ISSCO proposed prices and provided copies of the advertisements placed in *American Demographics.*

21. Atkinson memorandum, see note 4.

22. Derek Bok, quoted in "Harvard says no to role in company," *Harvard University Gazette,* November 21, 1980. Also, "Commerce within academia," *Boston Globe,* November 1, 1980.

23. Harvard press release, September 4, 1980; ISSCO press release, September 17, 1980, gives fourth quarter 1980 as the date for software release.

24. Atkinson memorandum, page 19; see note 4.

25. Private meeting during Harvard Computer Graphics Week, July 1980.

26. Two ads were run in *American Demographics,* a trade journal for marketing professionals. One (with a PRISM display showing percent immigrant by state) is illustrated; the other had a color choropleth map of United States by counties.

27. Brian Berry, memorandum to Laboratory staff, November 5, 1980. Contents: "This is to inform you that I resigned yesterday as Lab Director, effective immediately."

28. This direction is evident in the treatment of the Laboratory in Graduate School of Design, *Annual Report,* (Summer 1981), 9.

29. Dean McCue and Daniel Schodek, memorandum to Laboratory staff, July 22, 1980.

30. Allan Schmidt, memorandum to Kate Rooney, April 22, 1981; it did not change her actions.

31. Robert Shenton, Secretary to the University, memorandum, June 10, 1981.

32. Robert Shenton, letter to Nicholas Chrisman, August 21, 1981.

33. Allan Schmidt, memorandum to Laboratory staff, September 18, 1981.

34. Nicholas Chrisman, letter to Derek Bok and Gerald McCue, March 29, 1982.

35. Derek Bok, letter to Nicholas Chrisman, April 6, 1982.

36. *Computer Graphics News,* November 1981.

37. *Computer Graphics News,* March/April 1982, 4.

38. Geoffrey Dutton did not leave quietly. He wrote a five-page, single-spaced letter to Dean McCue (April 16, 1984) that began with the sentence: "This is not an easy letter for me to write, and it may be equally hard for you to read."

ELEVEN

A Modest Continuation

Following the crisis and departures, a more modest Laboratory continued for almost another 10 years. Daniel Schodek served the longest as director in the life of the organization. Over this period the staff levels remained low, and the research program became more closely aligned with the Graduate School of Design. Considering its modest size, the Laboratory continued to play a role in the expanding world of computer graphics and spatial analysis.

Searching for connections

By early 1982, the word from Dean McCue and the Harvard administration was clear: The Laboratory was to be a research entity, not a development center looking for commercial placement. In addition, the work of the Laboratory must connect to the instructional mission of the school. The period of independence was over, but the transition was not so easy.

Harvard Computer Graphics Week was held as planned in late July 1982, with a letter of welcome from Dean McCue. The registration amounted to 500 over the full five days, a robust increase from the 300 the year before. Registration cost $420, with all the luxury of the Hyatt Regency Hotel thrown in. Allan Schmidt (not yet dismissed) was still chairman of the event. Once it was over, he was let go. The papers from the conference were not printed in snappy red volumes as they had been at early conferences, but eventually appeared with a comb binding. This full-scale event covered its costs, but did not do much to reduce the yawning budget deficit. The next year, the event was retitled "Harvard Computer Graphics Conference 1983." Unlike the strong industry presence of prior years, the plenary speakers in 1983 were nearly all academics. The sessions were designed to conform to the academic program of the Graduate School of Design, with no mention of the emerging applications of GIS in marketing or even in managing a municipality. The conference ran three days, cost $600 to register for the shorter period, and attracted many fewer people. The comb-bound proceedings appeared two years later, a sign that Harvard had lost interest. This event lost a lot of money, and it was the end of the series.

The Laboratory had a number of products, beginning with ODYSSEY, but not limited to it. The staff did not know if it would be possible to work on software of any kind, even if it had direct connections to design disciplines. To implement the ODYSSEY system, the Laboratory had evolved a toolkit (including the LINGUIST user interface, the graphics drivers, the file handling system and everything else) to generate polished packages for distribution, not simple proof-of-concept work that could lead to academic publications. The result of the programming effort had been the program itself, after all. It was hard to turn the corner from producing software for distribution to producing publications for research journals.

More than anything, the real need was funding. This was the period of the first wave of "Reaganomics," when the federal establishment was under huge challenges to justify every expenditure, and research funding was particularly tightened. The Lab staff wrote proposals to the traditional sources (like the National Science Foundation), and even tried to generate interest in a follow-up study at the Ford Foundation.[1] The Laboratory research staff made a concerted effort to develop a new research direction that would be supported with significant funding. In 1984, an internal memorandum listed 22 potential research projects, a few with proposals submitted, but for many the status was simply a "gleam in the eye."[2] No big projects materialized to fix the hole in the budget. The other avenue was to attach the Laboratory to the instructional mission of the school, where the tuition fees paid the bills. The more senior staff were all issued the title "research associate" to replace titles based on programming skills ("systems analyst," and such). In addition, the senior staff were assigned to work with one of the academic programs under the title "lecturer."

LANDSCAPE ARCHITECTURE

At its start back in the 1960s, the Laboratory had close links with the Department of Landscape Architecture, but these had diminished through the split described in chapter 3. Beginning in 1981, Denis White had started to work for Carl Steinitz's studio titled "Major Landscape Change," with the title of "lecturer." Carl Steinitz had run this year-long course since 1967. The area of the study changed each year, and the methods continued to evolve from the base established by the major NSF-RANN project mentioned in chapter 6, and the Delmarva Project before it. Still, in 1981 the grid-cell database for each project was entered manually by the students in the fall term, then used in the spring semester for the planning process. There was no room for the vector approach of ODYSSEY as yet. The regions chosen for each studio were unlikely to have any consistent digital resource available, though that would eventually change as federal and local agencies began to digitize their maps. In 1982, Steinitz's studio concentrated on the Monadnock region of southern New Hampshire.

In 1982–1983, White had been working on a display program called IMAGO that permitted color mapping in an era when color was still highly experimental. The name of the program made a connection to the terrain visualization work of the Swiss cartographer Eduard Imhof, who was also editor of the journal *Imago Mundi*. IMAGO could add a relief shaded topographic backdrop to a color-coded land-use map.[3] As with the SEURAT program (see chapter 9), the color devices of the period limited the number of colors displayed. With some care in constructing the color table, a typical land-use map could be shown with hillshaded relief. The grid cell database generated by the students for the studio course in 1982 had 23 land-use categories, each shown with six darkness levels for the hillshading effect. These required 138 entries in the color table, allowing a little room for labeling the legend and showing the roads.

Such displays catapulted the studio course from the chunky gray output of the line printer into a palette of millions of colors. Applied to the student project data for the Monadnock region, the results were quite stunning on the screen (and rather difficult to reproduce on the printed page, particularly from the printed copies that survive from that era). This work connected with Steinitz's interest in visual analysis. White collaborated on an evaluation of viewshed software, and some proposals were submitted, but not funded.

◀ A land-use map for the Monadnock region of southern New Hampshire, draped over the terrain by adding a grayscaled relief shading layer. Map produced by Denis White using the AED 512 terminal and the Dunn camera. *(Source: White 1985, figure 5, reproduced with permission of American Congress on Surveying and Mapping (ACSM).)*

Some of the Laboratory staff gave courses on computer graphics and graphics programming. A limited role emerged for the Laboratory staff to lecture on fundamentals of geographic information systems. This material was considered technical, and not worthy of a full separate course for many years. Some publications emerged, but it was not enough to justify even the residual staff.

In the discipline of landscape architecture, Dana Tomlin's map algebra (with its firm origins in David Sinton's IMGRID) provided a framework for teaching about geographic information processing using a raster viewpoint. In 1983, Tomlin returned to Harvard following his PhD at Yale. Together with Denis White, there were plans to develop proposals on modeling forest fires, measures for landscape ecology, and energy efficiency.[4] None of these was funded. Later in this period, Kelly Chan produced a PhD dissertation while working at the Laboratory (with Steinitz, Tomlin, and White contributing in various roles) that joined the map algebra to the vector world, but the software of the era was not yet ready for such a grand realignment.[5]

URBAN DESIGN

The smallest program in the school was Urban Design; it contained the residual planning component of the school after the City and Regional Planning Department had moved off to the Kennedy School of Government back in the 1970s. In 1982, as a part of the attempt to realign the Laboratory with each unit in the design school, Edward Popko was given the title "Lecturer in Urban Design."

Popko participated in a series of contracts to plan low-income housing programs as an alternative to squatter settlements in countries like India, Colombia, and Ecuador. These passed through the Harvard Institute for International Development, not the Graduate School of Design, so the credit and overhead went elsewhere. His use of geographic information and models did not resonate with the design aesthetics more common in the Urban Design program.

In parallel with ODYSSEY (back in the period 1979–1981), there had been a lot of investment placed in developing a transportation modeling package based on TOPAZ, an optimal allocation package written in Australia. NETWORK was originally written by Helvio Mation,[6] a visiting student from Brazil, and revamped to use the ODYSSEY toolkit by John Fehr. This work was completed in 1981, but its application to urban design problems was not achieved. The analytical side of planning had moved over to the Kennedy School of Government. Data-heavy urban transportation models for whole metropolitan regions were far from the professional focus on individual buildings. In the planning discipline as a whole there was a retreat from the grand claims of urban models, so the timing was wrong. The Laboratory did try to generate some proposals in this direction in 1983, including a venture into expert systems (then quite prominent in artificial intelligence) submitted for foundation funding with the collaboration of Bruce Donald, then a graduate student at MIT.

On his arrival at the Laboratory in 1983, Mark Van Norman, a newly hired assistant professor in Architecture, put some effort into a grand plan of an Urban Database Consortium[7] involving a number of units from Harvard, MIT, and nearby foundations and agencies. This was an effort to capture the interest of municipalities in constructing urban information systems. Municipalities embarked on huge investments in reworking their information infrastructure for operational reasons during the 1980s, but the Harvard proposal did not attract the millions of dollars in funding required.

Edward Popko

Edward Popko got an early start on the cutting edge of design by publishing "Geodesics (Industrialization and technology course supplement)" in 1968 while at the School of Architecture, University of Detroit. Given a prominent place in the original *Whole Earth Catalog,* this manual gave practical advice on homemade domes that sprung up as a requisite part of the hippie lifestyle. Popko spent most of the 1970s at MIT, finishing a PhD in 1980 on policies for low-income housing in Colombia. During this time, he developed a connection to projects on urban development in developing countries. He combined his analytics with photography, including a photo-documentary on human shelter issues in squatter settlements.

On arrival at Harvard in 1980, Popko's program Key Word In Context (KWIC) was put on sale for $1,100. Not a cartographic program at all, it took a text file (a rather rare item in those days, prior to word processing) and produced a listing of all the contexts in which a given word appeared. The Laboratory used KWIC to generate additional access to the bibliography of all the papers in the Harvard Library of Computer Graphics. The last two volumes of this collection were the index to all the articles in them, and all the literature that they cited.[8] While at the Laboratory, Popko retained his fervor for PL/I (Programming Language One) and IBM operating systems. When he left the Laboratory in 1983, he moved to IBM as a GIS industry specialist.

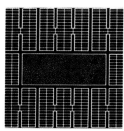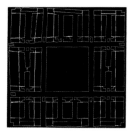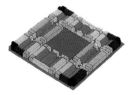

▲   Housing subdivision design. From left, first image shows a traditional subdivision plan. Second shows another plan, after manual digitizing. Third image shows the result after ODYSSEY cleaning and verification. Fourth shows a PRISM where heights and colors demonstrate the relative attractiveness of the lots. Produced by Edward Popko. *(Source: Context 1982·83, page 11, Harvard University Graduate School of Design)*

ARCHITECTURE

When the dean talked about the instructional role of the design school, he really meant architecture. McCue was an architect; Schodek, with more of a structural engineering background, taught in architecture. Clearly it was wise to find some connection to the kinds of work that would excite architects. Before Schodek became director of the Laboratory, he had collaborated with Laboratory staff to demonstrate the use of GIS for earthquake risk calculations for the city of Boston, a project supported by a grant from the National Science Foundation. This application highlighted the overlay capability of ODYSSEY, combining the shaking potential of the soil with the type of building technology by block. Schodek wanted to demonstrate that the soft landfills of Boston's Back Bay were particularly vulnerable to liquifaction following a repeat of the major earthquake experienced by the city in 1755. Combined with unreenforced row housing structures, the potential for damage is particularly large. By contrast, the wood-frame structures of triple-deckers could resist ground motion much better, and they tended to be located on the less vulnerable soils. Yet, the landscape scale of this work was from the mainstream concerns of the architecture discipline.

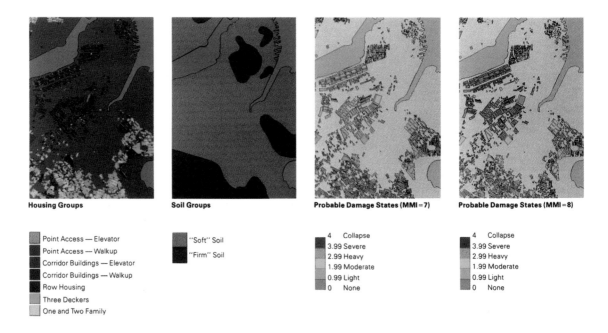

Housing Groups

- Point Access — Elevator
- Point Access — Walkup
- Corridor Buildings — Elevator
- Corridor Buildings — Walkup
- Row Housing
- Three Deckers
- One and Two Family

Soil Groups

- "Soft" Soil
- "Firm" Soil

Probable Damage States (MMI = 7)

- 4   Collapse
- 3.99 Severe
- 2.99 Heavy
- 1.99 Moderate
- 0.99 Light
- 0   None

Probable Damage States (MMI = 8)

- 4   Collapse
- 3.99 Severe
- 2.99 Heavy
- 1.99 Moderate
- 0.99 Light
- 0   None

▲   Analysis of earthquake risk for Boston, Massachusetts combining soil characteristics with building vulnerabilities. Probable extent of damage was estimated for earthquakes of Modified Mercali Intensity (MMI) of 7 and 8. Performed by Duane Niemeyer under the direction of Daniel Schodek, 1981. *(Source: Context 1982-83, page 9, Harvard University Graduate School of Design)*

BUILDER (mentioned in chapter 9) used the ODYSSEY toolkit to model objects in full three-dimensional space. It could produce reasonable renderings and all the flash of computer graphics. The problem was that the extrusion method required some sophistication to master. It used a programming-language interface, not a graphics workstation with dynamic response to WYSIWYG (What You See Is What You Get) tools. BUILDER was a tool written by a programmer in the era before the mouse attached itself to every computer. It did not find its way into the courses where cardboard models were the primary visualization tool.

The Laboratory made some attempt to provide programs to support drawing. Following in the steps of ARTIST (see chapter 9), from 1981, the program PICTURE (around 1985) used the LINGUIST language system to allow a student to learn how to build illustrations.[9] PICTURE permitted sequences of the commands MOVE and DRAW, extended with rectangles, circles, and polygons that could be shaded. Text could be displayed at a given position and orientation using stroked character fonts. A subsidiary program CHARM allowed entry of a new character font. The functionality of PICTURE foreshadows what emerged as industry standards a few years later in the programming language PostScript. PICTURE also signals a movement away from the FORTRAN that had unified all the programming efforts of the Laboratory. PICTURE was used to teach general courses on computer graphics in the Center for Lifelong Learning. In an era when making a computer draw a picture was considered a tricky feat, it encapsulated all the technical elements and permitted some control over the picture inside its very metric world. Later on, as the mouse emerged in 1985, PICTURE was replaced by a Pascal-only program called LABGRAF. It allowed click-and-drag to generate points, lines, rectangles, and polygons. The need for academic software to do these functions disappeared with the wide dissemination of MacPaint, MacDraw, and eventually other WYSIWYG drawing packages. Basic drawing functions were not enough reason to keep the Laboratory inside the Graduate School of Design.

All around the school, modernist functionalism was passé. Cornices and baroque details were back; the slabs of cardboard were amended with carvings of foam. Design was very political. And yet, designers were beginning to deal with computers. In 1983, Mark Van Norman was hired as assistant professor in architecture and given a role at the Laboratory. His PhD work had developed a tool for schematic design.[10] The prototype was called SPAM (an acronym for Schematic Phase Architectural Modeling, generated before he came in contact with the anti-acronym movement at the Laboratory), with a plan for a more developed version to be called SCHEMA (named more because it was a tool for schematic design, but perhaps with an acronym of little importance). With support from the National Endowment for the Humanities, Van Norman created this program to run on the early Macintosh. It allowed an architect to create a 3D arrangement of objects, then run various evaluations (cost, energy consumption, or whatever). SCHEMA was eventually distributed by the Laboratory at the cost of reproduction (calculated at $17.58, rounded up to $20). There was a long term interest in architectural software at Harvard, but it evolved away from the Laboratory. Eventually there were very close relationships with industry and software development far beyond that contemplated for ODYSSEY, but all this happened much later on.

Software reconsidered

In 1981 and 1982, Dean McCue wanted to stop all software distribution from the Laboratory. A few government users were intent on getting ODYSSEY operational without the commercial link, and a special deal allowed the New York City Planning Department and a few others to get the system directly from the Laboratory prior to the ISSCO deal. In April 1981, the dean hired Robert Hanson, a marketing specialist, to handle the transfer of ODYSSEY. Once the decision was made to terminate the ISSCO contract, there was a round of negotiations with other potential commercial outlets. In 1982, Synercom, a computer graphics hardware and software integrator firm, began to take interest, sending Timothy Nyerges, then a GIS software developer recently graduated from Ohio State University with a PhD, around to examine the goods closely. The agreement process was protracted, eventually leading to a result in 1984. Synercom, which sold complete hardware–software systems for computer-assisted drafting (CAD) clients like utility companies, agreed to market ODYSSEY as a part of its turnkey system. Its drawing systems were mostly used for engineering drafting—at the most literal level of mapping, and ODYSSEY offered the potential to expand into a true GIS. Synercom took all the Laboratory software in more of a cash-and-carry status, with little promise of support from Harvard. The expectations for revenue to Harvard were reduced, though still above what Synercom actually achieved. By the time that ODYSSEY appeared as a commercial product, other options were commercially available. The lead had been lost due to the uncertainties in coming to an agreement with Harvard.

In 1983, the Laboratory continued its flirtations with IBM. Dean McCue was open to proposals dealing with software development for instructional use, as long as someone would fund it. IBM appeared to be interested. Eventually IBM did provide funds for conversion of MAP to the IBM PC and the initial work on digitizing programs.

The prices Synercom charged for academic users led to restoring a distribution channel from the Laboratory—strictly for academic users. A catalog issued in 1985 as text pages with no sample graphics listed the long-term packages SYMAP, ASPEX, DOT.MAP (each at $400), and CALFORM (at $300). It is actually rather amazing that SYMAP, the old war-horse, continued to have sporadic sales through the 1980s. The basic architecture was 20 years old, and the last changes were made in 1975. Yet, the brand-name was established and academics continued to use it in courses long after other alternatives had appeared.

ODYSSEY REAPPEARS

In a reversal of policy, Harvard offered the full source code of ODYSSEY to university users. In 1983, the price was set at $10,000, generating some sales.[11] By 1985, Harvard dropped the price to $1,500[12] (a far cry from the $60,000 projected during the commercial phase just a few years earlier). The Laboratory continued distributing ODYSSEY at continually lowered prices (eventually $750) until 1988. By then even the lowered price did not make it attractive compared to the much more evolved commercial alternatives.

Distribution of ODYSSEY remained limited. At the Harvard Computer Graphics Conference in 1983, an ODYSSEY Interest Group was formed, with me as the chairman. Representatives of 13 users or potential users attended. No further meetings occurred. By 1988, Harvard had licensed the system to about 66 users, most of them universities. Distribution switched to the University of Washington, where I was located, in 1988. A small number of additional sales occurred, but interest declined and I found no time to upgrade the interface to modern expectations.

NEW PRODUCTS FOR NEW PLATFORMS

When Dana Tomlin returned to Harvard after his PhD in 1983, he brought with him a FORTRAN program that implemented his approach to raster processing, MAP or the Map Analysis Package (the culmination of the GRID and IMGRID developments mentioned in chapter 3). This version still ran on the mainframe and produced output on a line printer. Those constraints, stable since the era of SYMAP nearly 20 years before, were about to change radically. MAP had many versions, distributed by many institutions for wildly differing prices. After a conversion to the PC funded by IBM,[13] the Laboratory distributed MAP on two floppy disks for the IBM PC at the price of $20. Clearly, this provided the barest of cost-recovery and no income to support any maintenance or development. The freeware OSU-MAP for the PC, as well as the somewhat commercial MAPII for the Macintosh II and many others, derived from this version of the code. The new platforms of personal computers posed new problems in dealing with the graphics interface. Each PC had a different graphics card that imposed different limitations on colors. It was a tough period to maintain interoperability.

As Denis White's survey of microcomputer applications in 1985 showed,[14] the software of the era lacked many functions that were considered standard on larger computers. Some packages had no digitizing function, and some that did forced the user to align the map parallel to the x-axis. The programmer had left out the ability to rotate the coordinates. White, along with Jon Corson-Rikert, started work on a digitizing program, originally called TRACE.[15]

By 1986, the American Farmland Trust (AFT) became interested in making tools available to landscape planners and environmental managers in rural settings. They also had specific projects in mind dealing with disappearing farmland and environmental analysis that required GIS capabilities. By this time, ODYSSEY required repackaging for a new generation of computers called workstations (microcomputers more expensive than the early PCs). AFT saw ODYSSEY as a vector complement to the public-domain GRASS, a raster package funded by the U.S. Army Corps of Engineers. AFT funded a conversion of ODYSSEY to the UNIX world. Still, both ODYSSEY and GRASS lacked an interactive digitizing capability. Under the title of GRASSLANDS, AFT contracted with the Laboratory for development of an interactive digitizing package, extending work that Denis White had started on the IBM PC. The resulting software, called ROOTS, was available in 1988 to run on the Macintosh Plus, or a

UNIX workstation. Having a whole megabyte of memory seemed an enormous expansion, permitting random access to a whole map in place of the memory-conscious local processing of ODYSSEY. The PC version lagged behind due to the technical difficulties of the memory model of the early PCs. ROOTS was an elegant package that provided a WYSIWYG interface written using the rudimentary open source toolkit of the time.[16] ROOTS calculated the topology of digitized lines as they were entered. Lines were snapped to end exactly on established nodes. Elements of a map, such as a node or a chain, could be moved with various rubber sheet options that maintained the topology of the map. ROOTS provided a strong suite of assistance to the digitizing process far beyond what the commercial software of the era provided. In later work that extended past the formal end of the Laboratory, ROOTS evolved into PALMS as it was supported by a grant related to community improvements in Jordan. It is fitting that the last major program product of the Laboratory involved a dynamic calculation of the topological relationships, long such a hallmark of the Laboratory's niche in the academic community.

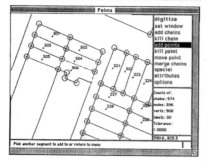

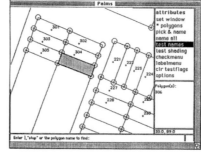

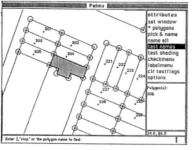

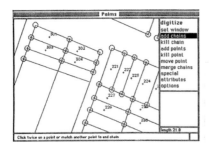

◀ The ROOTS and PALMS interface had hierarchical menus and a zoomable graphics window. Digitizing input was integrated in real time and shown on the screen. Topological errors could be flagged and corrected using a range of tools. This illustration shows four steps in editing a boundary between two parcels. Programming by Jon Corson-Rikert and Kelly Chan. *(Source: PALMS Program Description, 1990, figure 7, page 7)*

Dissolution

From 1985–1988, Denis White held the title of associate director of the Laboratory, reporting to Daniel Schodek, still the director. In this period, the staff of the Laboratory was just two or three people, with some students attached part-time. White managed the administrative side of the Laboratory, conducted research, and continued connections with the instructional program. Contracts supplemented the small income from the old software offerings. In 1988, White left Harvard to work for the Environmental Protection Agency research laboratory in Corvallis, Oregon.

The academic world, like most organizational life, prefers to make bold announcements of new beginnings. When an entity is closed, it usually happens quietly. In June 1991, the Laboratory for Computer Graphics and Spatial Analysis formally ceased operation. Stephen Ervin, the incoming director of computer services for the Graduate School of Design, decided to break with the old name and call his unit "Computer Resources." In many respects, this is what Howard Fisher had envisioned when proposing the Laboratory to the Ford Foundation. The services offered to students and faculty by Ervin's new unit far exceeded Fisher's dreams for delivering computer graphics to the design professions.[17] Computing was no longer a specialist function on the cutting edge of high-tech.

Harvard chose its strategic directions. Research on geographic information systems did not find an academic home as such in the long-term structure of Harvard University. The centers of research moved elsewhere, and development of software moved into a firmly commercial setting.

Eventually, Harvard found a value in geographic analysis, and a new center was created there in 2006. It represents a new tub, venturing off in new directions. The times have changed. Making a map with a computer is no longer a great accomplishment. Despite the differences, the story of the Laboratory for Computer Graphics and Spatial Analysis may help the new creation, and others like it, to encourage innovation and find new allies.

NOTES

1. Geoffrey Dutton, "The Harvard Laboratory for Computer Graphics and Spatial Analysis: A retrospective", Grant proposal, submitted to the Ford Foundation, September 30, 1982. (The term retrospective sends the message that the Laboratory was over.) In 1984, Schodek, Van Norman, and Donald submitted a proposal to the National Science Foundation for interactive structural system specification.

2. "Research Proposal Summary," June 1, 1984.

3. R. Denis White, "Relief modulated thematic mapping by computer," *The American Cartographer* 12, no. 1 (1985): 62–68.

4. "Research Proposal Summary," June 1, 1984.

5. Kelly Chan, "Evaluating descriptive models for prescriptive inference" (PhD dissertation, Harvard University, 1988); Kelly K. L. Chan and R. Denis White, "Map algebra: An object oriented implementation," in *Proceedings, International GIS Symposium,* vol. 2, 15–18 (Alexandria, Va.: Association of American Geographers, 1987).

6. Helvio Mation, "An application of computer graphics to network analysis," in *Harvard Library of Computer Graphics,* vol. 8, ed. Patricia A. Moore, 197–216 (Cambridge, Mass.: Laboratory for Computer Graphics and Spatial Analysis, Harvard University, 1980).

7. Mark Van Norman, Urban Database Consortium proposal, draft July 1984.

8. Patricia Moore, ed. *Harvard Library of Computer Graphics,* vol. 19, parts I and II (Cambridge, Mass.: Harvard Laboratory for Computer Graphics and Spatial Analysis, Harvard University, 1981).

9. R. Denis White, "A graphics system for instruction in computer graphics," in *Proceedings, Harvard Computer Graphics Week 1982* (Cambridge, Mass.: Graduate School of Design, Harvard University, 1982).

10. Mark Van Norman, "Computer aided database management and performance prediction for schematic design" (PhD dissertation, University of California, Berkeley, 1985). Van Norman's supervisor was Professor Horst Rittel. Mark Van Norman, "A digital modelshop: The role of metaphor in a CADD user interface," *Design Computing* 1 (1986): 95–122.

11. Announcement of release, The ODYSSEY System, April 1983.

12. LAB-LOG/SOFTWARE, May 1985 edition.

13. C. Dana Tomlin, "The IBM-PC version of the Map Analysis Package," *Internal report LCGSA-85-16* (Laboratory for Computer Graphics and Spatial Analysis, Harvard University, 1986).

14. R. Denis White, "Geographic information systems on microcomputers," *Internal report LCGSA-85-11* (Laboratory for Computer Graphics and Spatial Analysis, Harvard University, 1985).

15. Jonathan Corson-Rikert and R. Denis White, "The TRACE program for map digitizing," *Internal report LCGSA-85-18* (Laboratory for Computer Graphics and Spatial Analysis, Harvard University, 1985).

16. R. Denis White, Jonathan Corson-Rikert, and Margaret Maizel, "WYSIWYG digitizing: Real time geometric correction and topological encoding," in *Proceedings, AUTO-CARTO 8,* 739–743 (Baltimore, Md.: American Congress on Surveying and Mapping, 1987).

17. Paul Cote, "Three-tiered approach for GIS support at the Design School," in *ESRI Educational Users Group* (San Diego, Calif: ESRI, 2004).

TWELVE

Enduring Traces

The Laboratory for Computer Graphics and Spatial Analysis leaves traces in the current practice of GIS. Some are particular techniques of analysis embedded in software, while others are more diffuse. The people who passed through the Laboratory—those who made up the functioning of the place—continued their explorations in new settings. Would all of this have happened anyway, at some other, less special place? Perhaps, but hardly in exactly the same way.

Evaluation of Howard Fisher's vision

In September 1965, Howard Fisher submitted his proposal to the Ford Foundation. It described a four-and-a-half-year plan to operate a Laboratory for Computer Graphics inside the City and Regional Planning Department. The Laboratory he founded, over its 26-year lifespan, fulfilled the goals of Fisher's vision in nearly every respect. The prior chapters recount successes and disappointments over the course of a quarter-century, but most of the original goals were greatly surpassed.

In its most important essentials, Fisher's vision was borne out. Computers did bring changes all across society. The design professions did have much greater access to "factual information." Cities, and other governments up the hierarchy, did begin to use computers in a wide range of applications. Fisher's contemporaries, such as Edgar Horwood and Roger Tomlinson, used different mechanisms to disseminate their new developments to the world of practice. Horwood expected to operate an urban data processing center, a service to perform the computation for a wide range of users. Tomlinson planned a centralized information system (his Canadian Geographic Information System, or CGIS), reliant on specialized hardware and services. The software was necessary to support the operation, but CGIS was seen as a service center. Horwood's software did not circulate; neither did CGIS. Fisher, by contrast, designed a software package for broad use on the kind of equipment in regular use.[1] Hundreds of copies of SYMAP and successor packages went into university, government, and industry offices. Software for sale became a hallmark of the Laboratory, leading directly to conflict with the administration in the early 1980s.[2]

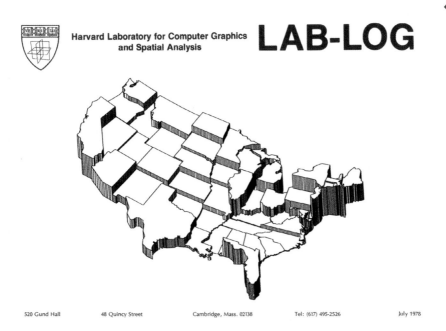

Harvard Laboratory for Computer Graphics and Spatial Analysis

LAB-LOG

520 Gund Hall   48 Quincy Street   Cambridge, Mass. 02138   Tel: (617) 495-2526   July 1978

◀ Front cover of the 1978 version of LAB-LOG, the Laboratory's catalog. This issue was 36 pages long with order forms in the back for publications and software.

(Source: LAB-LOG 1978, Harvard University Graduate School of Design)

What endures?

Proposals are rarely published, and for good reason. Prose that attempts to convince a funding agency makes all kinds of rash assertions about the future. Publications at the ends of grants have to be much more restrained, and consistent with the academic standards concerning reproducible results. With a 40-year distance from the founding of the Laboratory (and 15 years since its closure), enough time has elapsed to pick out some of the elements that endure.

The software distributed by the Laboratory became obsolete long ago. No self-respecting programmer would expect to get away with a user interface that required a "5" in column five to invoke a particular option. Of course, the whole technology of punched cards that created such an interface has completely vanished. Even the command line advances of LINGUIST are of little use in the expectations of modern interfaces. Similarly, the data formats developed for SYMAP and ODYSSEY would not be accepted in any current package. The media on which the Laboratory's software was recorded (for many years the reel-to-reel, 9-track magnetic tape) have disappeared, along with the operating systems on which the code depended. If we are looking for traces of the Laboratory, they will not come in direct form of the original products.

Harvard, like most institutions of the era, tied itself in knots trying to figure out how to protect the intellectual property in software. While Harvard made claims of copyright and licensed the code, the long-term result was produced by disseminating the packages. Hundreds of users—practicing professionals and, more importantly, students—were exposed to certain ways of addressing geographic information. SYMAP, unlike much of the other software in the 1960s, separated the basemap from the attributes to be shown on a particular thematic map. This feature later became so universal it barely registers notice. Certainly some later designer would have come up with the same division, but copying the SYMAP approach was easier than developing it on one's own. In addition, the division of objects into the dimensional classes of points, lines, and areas became a core concept in later developments. Of course, plane geometry had used these divisions for millennia, so it seems obvious in retrospect. This is a difficulty in looking backward—the particular historical choices can appear inexorable, as the uncertainties get forgotten.

Some of the traces are much more specific. While Fisher's attempt to rewrite cartographic terminology did not take root, some terminology from the Laboratory passed into the technical jargon of the discipline. Terms such as "cartographic spaghetti" were almost inadvertent at the time, but they filled a need and their colorful allusions attracted the ears of listeners. William Warntz's approach to surfaces led directly to the later development of triangular irregular networks (TINs), one of the main alternatives for terrain representation. The other alternatives (such as the digital elevation matrix) had much greater support from production agencies, but the TIN concept has endured because it provides a cleaner representation of surface properties. In parallel, Warntz's studies of least cost paths over complex surfaces sparked tools that have migrated from version to version as software has evolved.[3]

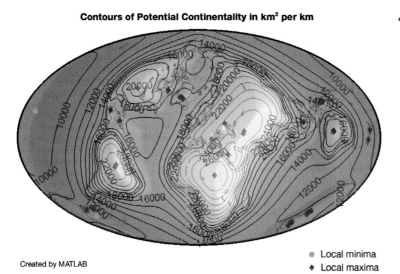

Contours of Potential Continentality in km² per km

Created by MATLAB

● Local minima
◆ Local maxima

Surface of continentality. A revised calculation of the surface of continentality, using the MATLAB numerical calculation toolkit. In calculations of potential surfaces the units are expressed as mass divided by distance, so for continentality the mass is the area of the continent (km squared). This produces a surface with a scale in meters, measuring the relative accessibility to land mass. The topology of the surface follows the one calculated by Warntz (see page 61). *(Image produced by and courtesy of Geoffrey Dutton)*

The most important question concerns the prototype GIS package, ODYSSEY. In many ways, this development was a poison pill. The Laboratory staked its future on continuing to disseminate software at the cutting edge, competing with all comers. The commercial sector in the late 1970s was quite weak, as Tomlinson and Boyle[4] attested in their evaluation for Saskatchewan (see chapter 8). The complexities of getting ODYSSEY to market may have signaled that the commercial sector had to become the main focus for development. Many of the ODYSSEY concepts were directly embedded in the first generation of GIS tools, including some that were rather specialized such as overlay with a fuzzy tolerance. The ODYSSEY separation of topological testing into a distinct phase (now called CLEAN in at least one major package) has survived even in an era when computation made it possible to calculate the topology on the fly as in ROOTS and a later generation of software. Thus, though ODYSSEY disappeared, it set a standard that others had to exceed. It placed the emphasis on topological data structures for a certain formative period, long enough to distinguish GIS from computer-aided drafting software.

People

The most enduring traces are those marked by the continued activity of the people who passed through the Laboratory. There were over 130 employees of the Laboratory, in various standings within the institution. Only a few have died, notably the first two directors. Many others continue to influence the practice of GIS and related fields, directly or indirectly.

Some of the Laboratory staff took the academic track, continuing through to PhDs. To use an example close at hand, I put my PhD to use to teach in departments titled landscape architecture, geography, and *sciences géomatiques*. A majority of former staff who obtained doctoral degrees ended up in computer science, not geography or planning. Only a few of the computer scientists are still working with geographic data or visualization (notably Jim Little, now at the University of British Columbia, and Randolph Franklin, at Rensselaer Polytechnic Institute). Not all those with doctoral degrees stayed in the academic sector, of course. The commercial software sector offered alternatives for a number of the Laboratory staff (with or without a PhD).

In the commercial arena, the founding presidents of three prominent GIS software companies (Jack Dangermond, of ESRI; Howard Slavin, of Caliper; and Lawrie Jordan, of ERDAS) worked for the Laboratory or were students in related programs. The rather cordial relationship between ERDAS and ESRI over a long period may have developed anyway, but the mutual connections to Harvard certainly played a role. The connections are closer than just sharing a common graduate school. Scott Morehouse left a role as manager of the ODYSSEY project to become the lead software designer at ESRI, bringing substantial experience that helped ESRI become a major player in the GIS software world. ARC/INFO 1.0 was not a copy of ODYSSEY, though some might think that was the case. Of course, the original version of ARC had a number of sequential processors that sorted the data much in the way that ODYSSEY processors did. Equally, the evidence of crucial differences is readily apparent. ARC/INFO made the crucial step of tying itself to a relational database management package, something that the Harvard team shied away from. Also, ARC was in other ways less sophisticated; the WHIRLPOOL overlay program had a cluster analysis capability to avoid the behavior called "fuzzy creep" in the early ARC.[5] Hugh Keegan and Duane Niemeyer also play senior roles at ESRI. The influence on the commercial sector does not stop with ESRI, either. The internal reports from the GEOGRAF and ODYSSEY development influenced software designers, and provided some common framework of where the problems were. At Intergraph, David Sinton was the project manager for one of the major attempts in the early 1980s to develop topological object-oriented software to confront the challenge from the then upstart ESRI. The software that resulted, called TIGRIS (designed by John Herring), bears a stronger resemblance to GEOGRAF than to ODYSSEY. The competing system at Intergraph (originally called MGE) is the basis of their current software offering.

▲ Reunion of Laboratory staff members in August 2004 in San Diego to honor Allan Schmidt for his Lifetime Achievement Award from ESRI. *Front row, from left:* Jim Little, Scott Morehouse, Mark Van Norman, Denis White, Anne Hunt White, Randolph Franklin, Bruce Rowland. *Standing behind, from left:* Hugh Keegan, Eric Teicholz, Allan Schmidt, Nick Chrisman, Kathy Kiernan, Geoffrey Dutton, Tom Poiker, Dennis Dreher, Jon Corson-Rikert, Duane Niemeyer. Note the Laboratory T-shirts (from 1976, 1979, and 1980) still in wearable shape. *(Photo: ESRI Graphics)*

This entire history of the Laboratory is actually only an introduction to a more productive period that followed. The world of GIS opened up at more or less the point that the Laboratory withdrew from the main arena. The people who had the honor and privilege to pass through the Laboratory were well-positioned to take up leadership roles as the field expanded in academic and commercial settings. The important era of implementation that followed presented great challenges, and even greater successes.

In a less direct way, the Laboratory demonstrated that it was possible to make a difference in the world of geographic analysis using computer tools. Beyond the Laboratory staff, there were many more hundreds, even thousands, who were influenced by learning cartography with a computer tool, or who attended a conference hosted by the Laboratory. For a long period, the Laboratory was a place to visit or consult if you wanted to learn more about geographic information. The network is vast and, of course, quite diffuse.

Analytical postscript

I delivered this story of the Harvard Laboratory for Computer Graphics and Spatial Analysis as a narrative without a lot of interpretation. Of course, this narrative is filtered through my particular role and memory. I have passed the draft to many of my colleagues from the Laboratory. They have spent long hours reviewing the text and providing important corrections. When in doubt, I relied on the written evidence I had from the period, not our failing memories. One of the main lessons in the academic study of science and technology is that a search for an objective account is more or less illusory. Every story is written from a point of view. The best I can do is to remain overt about mine. Readers have to play their own role in the process, since the technology becomes what users make of the legacy from the past. The importance of the developments at the Harvard Laboratory is not yet determined.

At the end of this account, I find many connections to common themes in studies of science and technology. The history of the Laboratory can be told to emphasize the big forces—the structures of organizations, the collision of big ideas—or it can be turned around into a story of specific persons, presented as visionaries or key leaders. Other accounts in the history of technology vacillate between these extremes. In 1987, I wrote a forceful structuralist paper,[6] arguing that the surrounding culture provides the framework in which a GIS must be developed. William Craig, an academic active in urban GIS, recently recanted some of his emphasis on organizations with a paper about white knights of spatial data infrastructure[7]—an argument that specific individuals mattered more than large forces. The reader can interpret the Laboratory either way, starting with the earliest days. Howard Fisher certainly played a key role of leadership; his personal choice of Harvard, however, appears to have elements of both personal and institutional logic involved. Fisher worked hard to construct a network of allies, to position the Laboratory as the obligatory point of passage to obtain knowledge about computer cartography.[8] In my reflection, both the large structural forces and the individual agency of each actor play a role. Others may want to see key ideas as the real story, evoking a truth that mortals can only see as shadows on the wall. At different times in the development of the Laboratory, one or the other might seem more crucial, but opposite interpretations are not far away.

At the center of this narrative, ODYSSEY demonstrates how a technical object becomes an actor in the network. This software creation did not stay put where it originators wanted it to stay; it took on its own role in a network of commercial potential and administrative nightmares. Of course, ODYSSEY is the product of big trends in software and the society at large, but always rooted in specific people living in particular places. The concept of an external, immortal realm of ideas seems very hard to apply to the complex interconnections of technological development and science. This brings to mind the analytical work of Bruno Latour on technoscience.[9] ODYSSEY lived and died by mobilizing a network of supporters, as well as a network of antagonists. The interplay of these forces was not a Greek tragedy with a fate predetermined. As Latour recounts in his dissection of a failed Paris subway transit system, for a technology to succeed, people must fall in love with it. In the final analysis, many fell in love with the Laboratory. They dedicated their lives and their intellectual energy to the place for years. As with many love stories, hearts were broken, promises not kept. Yet, the work at the Laboratory was not in vain. Many elements of the modern GIS emerged in this very special place. The human value nurtured by the Laboratory remains, a triumph of the best of the human spirit.

NOTES

1. I have developed my approach to this topic over a long period; see Nicholas R. Chrisman, "Academic origins of GIS," in *The history of geographic information systems: Perspectives from the pioneers,* ed. Timothy Foresman, 33–43 (Upper Saddle River, N.J.: Prentice Hall, 1998); Nicholas R. Chrisman, "Communities of scholars: Places of leverage in the history of automated cartography," *Cartography and Geographic Information Science* 32, no. 4 (2005): 425–433. The more conventional origins story can be found in Roger Tomlinson, "The Canada Geographic Information System," in *The history of geographic information systems: Perspectives from the pioneers,* ed. Timothy W. Foresman, 21–32 (Upper Saddle River, N.J.: Prentice Hall, 1998).

2. I wrote about this stage in the Laboratory's history earlier: Nicholas R. Chrisman, "The risks of software innovation: A case study of the Harvard Lab," *The American Cartographer* 15 (1988): 291–300. This book provides a more considered analysis with greater access to documents from various parties.

3. For a longer treatment of least-cost path calculations (and the importance of William Warntz) see David H. Douglas, *Least cost path in GIS,* Research Note 61 (Department of Geography, University of Ottawa, 1993).

4. Roger Tomlinson and A. Raymond Boyle, "The state of development of systems for handling natural resources inventory data," *Cartographica* 18, no. 4 (1981): 65–95.

5. As witness to the differences, I have had a long-term argument about the treatment of fuzzy intersections with ESRI programmers, starting with Armando Guevara. WHIRLPOOL avoided the problem termed "fuzzy creep" by waiting for all intersections to be detected before making any changes to the coordinates. WHIRLPOOL had its own bugs; sometimes it assigned lines to nodes in a way that violated topological constraints. Days of debugging did not locate the bug, though tiny changes of the tolerance could make it disappear in any particular case. Nicholas R. Chrisman, "Epsilon filtering: A technique for automated scale changing," in *Proceedings, ACSM Annual Meeting,* 322–341 (Washington, D.C.: ACSM, 1983); Nicholas R. Chrisman, James A. Dougenik, and Denis White, "Lessons for the design of polygon overlay processing from the ODYSSEY WHIRLPOOL algorithm," in *Proceedings, 5th International Symposium on Spatial Data Handling,* vol. 2, 401–410 (Charleston, S.C.: IGU, 1992).

6. Nicholas R. Chrisman, "Design of information systems based on social and cultural goals," *Photogrammetric Engineering and Remote Sensing* 53 (1987): 1367–1370.

7. William J. Craig, "White knights of spatial data infrastructure: The role and motivation of key individuals," *Urban and Regional Information Systems Association Journal 16,* no. 2 (2005): 5–13. This viewpoint was previously articulated by David Rhind, "Personality as a factor in the development of a discipline: The example of computer-assisted cartography," *The American Cartographer* 15, no. 3 (1988): 277–290.

8. The term "obligatory point of passage" comes from Michel Callon and others in what is termed "Actor-Network Theory." Michel Callon, ed., *La science et ses réseaux: Genèse et circulation des faits scientifiques* (Paris: La Découverte, 1989).

9. For Latour's approach to science and technology see Bruno Latour, *Pandora's hope* (Cambridge, Mass.: Harvard University Press, 1999); Bruno Latour, *We never were modern* (Cambridge, Mass.: Harvard University Press, 1993). The Paris subway system was called *Aramis,* after one of the musketeers: Bruno Latour, *Aramis or the love of technology* (Cambridge, Mass.: Harvard University Press, 1996).

Acknowledgments

Throughout the process of writing this book I have been sustained by the active support of many people. I intend to thank them all, though any list will leave out some of the indirect support that counts for so much.

For the period prior to 1972, I am indebted to those who worked at the Lab during that time; they helped to keep me on track. Allan Schmidt has supported my efforts with the kind encouragement that was the hallmark of his role in directing the Lab; he also kept an important archive of useful documents that helped me reconstruct the Lab's earliest period as well as the tangle of administrative nightmares that contributed to its eventual demise. Kathy Kiernan offered snapshots of memorable Lab parties as well as her memories of programming details. Geoff Dutton offered boxes of materials, a nuanced appreciation of Bill Warntz, and consistent advice on intellectual continuity throughout the narrative. Eric Teicholz also kept boxes of materials along with movies and other memorabilia. Tom Poiker spent many hours retelling stories and helping me get the feeling of the period, not just the details. Carl Steinitz provided open access to an impressively organized archive of his full career at Harvard as well as careful criticism of some chapters. Mike Woldenberg, Geoff Dutton, and Michael Goodchild corrected my wavering memory of the spatial analysis literature and the Warntz period. Jack Dangermond has offered his perspective on his part in these events along with his generous support for this book effort.

To deal with the period before the Laboratory, particularly the developments at the University of Washington, I have had active assistance from Bill Beyers, Dick Morrill, Ken Dueker, William Garrison, Waldo Tobler, and Brian Berry, as well as the documentary evidence from the late John Sherman.

The Harvard University Archives granted access to the collected papers of Howard Fisher, a collection that they characterized as both "voluminous" and "disorganized." I have examined each of the 34 boxes, but I did not read every scrap of draft or every letter. Herb Height (one of Fisher's assistants), and Morgan Fisher, a son, have assisted with additional material about Howard Fisher.

For the period from 1972 to 1982, when I was at the Lab, I have made sure to cross-check my memories with those of Allan Schmidt, Eric Teicholz, Geoff Dutton, Denis White, Anne Hunt White, Scott Morehouse, Tom Poiker, Hugh Keegan, Duane Neimeyer, Bruce Donald, Randolph Franklin, Helvio Mation, Jim Little, Mark Kriger, Michael Mainelli, Carolyn Weiss, and Dennis Dreher. Each of these people provided illustrations that first appeared on a poster exhibit at the ESRI User Conference in 2004 to celebrate the lifetime contributions of Allan Schmidt. Denis White and Geoff Dutton also provided reports, letters, and computer output to supplement the boxes of materials that I have moved across the continent and back. These two colleagues have continued to review the text through to final production.

For the period after 1982, I have relied on the files of Denis White, plus material and recollections from Jon Corson-Rikert, Mark Van Norman, Daniel Schodek, Steve Ervin, and others. The illustrations throughout the book are made possible by generous permission from the Graduate School of Design, Harvard University.

My personal trajectory following the Laboratory has allowed me to work with a community of graduate students. In writing this book, I have relied on discussions of method and theory with Francis Harvey, Barbara Poore, Ilya Zaslavsky, and Eugene Martin. Geof Bowker and Sergio Sismondo have provided assistance with social studies of technoscience. My interest in the process of change also reflects the work of my grandfather, Abbott P. Usher, and my mother, Miriam U. Chrisman. Her support has been quite crucial over the past two and a half years, periods of which have been more complicated than anyone could imagine.

This long list of collaborators does not absolve me of any responsibility. Any account is selective, emphasizing one particular perspective among other alternative interpretations. They all did their best to straighten me out, but I may have willfully avoided correction on some components. I also wish to acknowledge the support of the professional team at ESRI Press, who have combined their forces to make this not just a rapid process, but an enjoyable one. The editorial process began with strong encouragement from Christian Harder and the exacting editorial assistance of Michael Karman. Judy Hawkins took over management of the project in the middle period when an author wonders if a book will ever result from all the details. Editor David Boyles has provided a lightning rod for all the uncertainty and offered steady guidance toward the goal. Tiffany Wilkerson's copy editing helped hone the story, and Carmen Fye provided invaluable support in helping to gather copyright permissions. At key moments in the process, Shelly Sommer has provided assistance, most importantly in a final review of the manuscript. Also thanks to the Graphics group (including Tom Schwedler, Jay Merryweather, Ross Higgins, Betty Martinez, and Eric Laycock) who produced the video interviews and the rest of the attractive CD. The end result you see is not the product of the author as much as the magic of Jennifer Galloway, graphic designer, who has the dash to turn flat old graphics into a fresh story. The professionalism of this team has worked wonders.

Nick Chrisman came to the Laboratory for Computer Graphics and Spatial Analysis at Harvard University in 1972 from an undergraduate degree in geography at the University of Massachusetts–Amherst. While an undergraduate, he had obtained a copy of CALFORM, a program to produce choropleth maps on a pen plotter, from Harvard and converted it to operate on the UMass computer. He had digitized maps of census geography and produced thematic displays with CALFORM demonstrating the residential segregation of the city of Boston. Allan Schmidt, then acting director at the Harvard Lab, snatched him up before he could escape to graduate school.

Chrisman quickly became an ardent (often animated) advocate of topological data structures. He designed POLYVRT, a data conversion program, and joined with Denis White, Jim Dougenik, and Scott Morehouse to design ODYSSEY, a prototype vector GIS. Once the ODYSSEY prototype was complete, he went off to England to complete a PhD on error in GIS data. He took an academic job at the University of Wisconsin–Madison in 1982, then moved to the University of Washington in 1987. He has written a textbook on GIS (*Exploring Geographic Information Systems,* published by John Wiley & Sons, 1997 and 2002), and articles on topics ranging from the technological detail to the social context of GIS. In 2005, he became professor in geomatic sciences at Université Laval in Quebec City, Canada, and scientific director of the GEOIDE (Geomatics for Informed Decisions) Network. GEOIDE links over a hundred researchers across Canada working in a wide range of disciplines.

Abbate, Janet. 2000. *Inventing the Internet.* Cambridge, Mass.: MIT Press.

Arms, Samuel. 1968. Computer mapping in selected geographic information systems. In *Proceedings, Sixth Annual Meeting,* 218–221. Clayton, Mo.: URISA.

Barnes, Trevor J. 2001. Retheorizing economic geography: From the quantitative revolution to the "cultural turn." *Annals of the Association of American Geographers* 91:546–565.

Berry, Brian J. L., and Duane F. Marble. 1968. *Spatial analysis.* Englewood Cliffs, N.J.: Prentice Hall.

Berry, Brian J. L., Richard L. Morrill, and Waldo R. Tobler. 1964. Geographic ordering of information: New opportunities. *Professional Geographer* 16 (4): 39–43.

Brooks, Frederick P., Jr. 1975. *The mythical man-month: Essays in software engineering.* Reading, Mass.: Addison-Wesley.

Bunyan, John. 1965. *The pilgrim's progress.* London: Penguin Classics.

Burton, Warren. 1977. Representation of many-sided polygons and polygonal lines for rapid processing. *Communications, ACM* 20 (3): 166–171.

Butler, Kent S., William A. Gates, and Brent H. McCown. 1976. A resource management system, GRASP: Description of a land resource data base. *IES Report 88.* Institute for Environmental Studies, University of Wisconsin-Madison.

Calkins, Hugh, and Duane F. Marble, eds. 1980. *Full geographic information systems.* Vol. 1 of *Computer software for spatial data handling.* Ottawa: International Geographic Union, Commission on Geographical Data Sensing and Processing.

Callon, Michel, ed. 1989. *La science et ses réseaux: Genèse et circulation des faits scientifiques.* Paris: La Découverte.

Carson, Rachel. 1962. *Silent spring.* London: Penguin.

Cayley, Arthur. 1859. On contour and slope lines. *The London, Edinburgh, and Dublin Philosphical Magazine and Journal of Science* 18:264–268.

Chan, Kelly. 1988. Evaluating descriptive models for prescriptive inference. PhD diss., Harvard University.

Chan, Kelly K. L., and R. Denis White. 1987. Map algebra: An object oriented implementation. In *Proceedings, International GIS Symposium,* vol. 2, 15–18. Alexandria, Va.: Association of American Geographers.

Chrisman, N. R. 1974. The impact of data structure on geographic information processing. In *Proceedings, AUTO–CARTO I,* 165–177. Reston, Va.: ACSM.

———. 1975. Topological data structures for geographic representation. In *Proceedings, AUTO–CARTO II,* 346–351. Reston, Va.: ACSM.

———. 1976a. ODYSSEY SOCKS: Fixed-variable binary input-output. *Internal report 76-8.* Laboratory for Computer Graphics and Spatial Analysis, Harvard University.

———. 1976b. Local versus global: The scope of memory required for geographic information processing. *Internal report 76-14.* Laboratory for Computer Graphics and Spatial Analysis, Harvard University.

———. 1978. Concepts of space as a guide to cartographic data structures. In *Harvard papers on geographic information systems,* vol. 6, ed. Geoffrey Dutton. Reading, Mass.: Addison Wesley.

————. 1983. Epsilon filtering: A technique for automated scale changing. In *Proceedings, ACSM Annual Meeting*, 322–341. Washington, D.C.: ACSM.

————. 1987. Design of information systems based on social and cultural goals. *Photogrammetric Engineering and Remote Sensing* 53:1367–1370.

————. 1988. The risks of software innovation: A case study of the Harvard Lab. *The American Cartographer* 15:291–300.

————. 1997. John Sherman and the origin of GIS. *Cartographic Perspectives* 27:8–13.

————. 1998. Academic origins of GIS. In *The history of geographic information systems: Perspectives from the pioneers*, ed. Timothy Foresman, 33–43. Upper Saddle River, N.J.: Prentice Hall.

————. 2005. Communities of scholars: Places of leverage in the history of automated cartography. *Cartography and Geographic Information Science* 32 (4): 425–433.

Chrisman, N. R., James A. Dougenik, and Denis White. 1992. Lessons for the design of polygon overlay processing from the ODYSSEY WHIRLPOOL algorithm. In *Proceedings, 5th International Symposium on Spatial Data Handling*, vol. 2, 401–410. Charleston, S.C.: IGU.

Chrisman, N. R., and R. Denis White. 1976. Programming for transportability: A guide to machine-independent FORTRAN. Laboratory of Computer Graphics and Spatial Analysis, Harvard University.

Christian, C. S., and G. A. Stewart. 1968. Methodology of integrated surveys. In *Aerial Surveys and Integrated Studies*, 233–280. Toulouse, France: UNESCO.

Cloud, John. 2002. American cartographic transformations during the cold war. *Cartography and Geographic Information Science* 29:261–282.

————. 2006. Overlays of mystery: The curiously un-contested origins of analog map overlay (abstract). In *Annual meeting, Association of American Geographers*. Chicago, Ill.: Association of American Geographers.

Codd, E. F. 1970. A relational model of data for large shared data banks. *Communications of the Association of Computing Machinery* 13:378–387.

Cohen, Saul B. 1988. Reflections on the elimination of geography at Harvard, 1947–1951. *Annals of the Association of American Geographers* 78:148–151.

Cooke, Donald F. 1998. Topology and TIGER: The Census Bureau's contribution. In *The history of geographic information systems: Perspectives from the pioneers*, ed. Timothy W. Foresman, 47–57. Upper Saddle River, N.J.: Prentice Hall.

Cooke, Donald F., and William H. Maxfield. 1967. The development of a geographic base file and its uses for mapping. In *Proceedings, Fifth Annual Meeting*. Garden City, N.Y.: URISA.

Corson-Rikert, Jonathan, and Kelly Chan. 1990. PALMS program description. Laboratory for Computer Graphics and Spatial Analysis, Harvard University.

Corson-Rikert, Jonathan, and R. Denis White. 1985. The TRACE program for map digitizing. *Internal report LCGSA-85-18*. Laboratory for Computer Graphics and Spatial Analysis, Harvard University.

Cote, Paul. 2004. Three-tiered approach for GIS support at the Design School. In *ESRI Educational Users Group*. San Diego, Calif.: ESRI.

Craig, William J. 2005. White knights of spatial data infrastructure: The role and motivation of key individuals. *Urban and Regional Information Systems Association Journal* 16 (2):5–13.

Dacey, Michael F., and Duane F. Marble. 1965. Some comments on certain technical aspects of geographic information systems. *ONR Contract Nonr 1228(35), Task 389-142, Technical report 2*. Department of Geography, Northwestern University.

Dangermond, Paul Jack. 1970. California study. In *Computer mapping as an aid in air pollution studies*, vol. 2, report I, ed. John Goodrich. Cambridge, Mass.: Laboratory for Computer Graphics and Spatial Analysis, Harvard University.

Dougenik, James A. 1976. Development of a lexical and syntactic analyzer. *Internal report 76-13*. Laboratory for Computer Graphics and Spatial Analysis, Harvard University.

———. 1978. LINGUIST: A processor to generate interactive languages. In *Harvard papers on geographic information systems,* vol. 3, ed. Geoffrey Dutton. Reading, Mass.: Addison Wesley.

———. 1980. WHIRLPOOL: A geometric processor for polygon coverage data. In *Proceedings, AUTO-CARTO IV,* 304–311. Washington, D.C.: ACSM.

Dougenik, James A., and David Sheehan. 1976. *Symap user's manual.* Cambridge, Mass.: Laboratory for Computer Graphics and Spatial Analysis, Harvard University.

Dougenik, James A., Nicholas R. Chrisman, and Duane R. Niemeyer. 1985. An algorithm to construct continuous area cartograms. *Professional Geographer* 37:75–81.

Douglas, David H., ed. 1976. Collected algorithms. Laboratory for Computer Graphics and Spatial Analysis, Harvard University.

———. 1990. It makes me so CROSS. In *Introductory readings in GIS,* eds. Donna J. Peuquet and Duane F. Marble, 303–307. London: Taylor & Francis.

———. 1993. Least cost path in GIS. Research note 61. Department of Geography, University of Ottawa.

Douglas, David H., and Thomas K. Peucker. 1973. Algorithms for the reduction of the number of points required to represent a digitized line or its charicature. *The Canadian Cartographer* 10 (2):110–122.

Driscoll, Ted. 1978. SOLARE: A computer program for automated terrain modeling. Laboratory for Computer Graphics and Spatial Analysis, Harvard University.

Dueker, Kenneth. 2000. Edgar Horwood and URISA. In *Proceedings, URISA.* Orlando, Fla.: URISA.

Dutton, Geoffrey, ed. 1973. Size and shape in the growth of human communities. *Ekistics* vol. 36, no. 215.

———. 1976. Minority report on gridded data. *Internal report 76-11.* Laboratory for Computer Graphics and Spatial Analysis, Harvard University.

———. 1977a. Point to point flow allocation model: User documentation. Laboratory for Computer Graphics and Spatial Analysis, Harvard University.

———. 1977b. An extensible approach to imagery of gridded data. *Proceedings, SIGGRAPH 77,* 11 (2):159–169 San Jose, Calif.: Association for Computing Machinery.

———. 1978a. Navigating ODYSSEY. In *Harvard papers on geographic information systems,* vol. 2, ed. Geoffrey Dutton. Reading, Mass.: Addison Wesley.

———, ed. 1978b. *Harvard papers on geographic information systems.* Reading, Mass.: Addison Wesley.

———. 1978c. DOT.MAP user's reference manual, version 3.0. Laboratory for Computer Graphics and Spatial Analysis, Harvard University.

———. 1979. American Graph Fleeting: A computer-holographic map animation. Laboratory for Computer Graphics and Spatial Analysis, Harvard University.

———. 1982. Land alive. *Perspectives in Computing* 2:26–39.

Edson, Dean. 1975. Digital cartographic data base preliminary description. In *Proceedings, AUTO-CARTO II,* 523–538. Reston, Va.: ACSM.

Eichenlaub, Carl, and R. Denis White. 1977. NUBS memory management module. *Internal report 77-4.* Laboratory for Computer Graphics and Spatial Analysis, Harvard University.

Faust, Nickolas. 1998. Raster based GIS. In *The history of geographic information systems: Perspectives from the pioneers,* ed. Timothy W. Foresman, 59–72. Upper Saddle River, N.J.: Prentice-Hall.

Fisher, Howard T. 1982. *Mapping information, the graphic display of quantitative information.* Cambridge, Mass.: Abt Books.

Fisher, Howard, and James Carpenter. 1974. *Color in art.* Cambridge, Mass.: Fogg Museum, Harvard University.

Fowler, Robert, and James Little. 1979. Automated extraction of irregular network digital terrain models. In *Proceedings of an International Conference on Computer Graphics and Interactive Techniques.* Chicago: ACM-SIGGRAPH.

Franklin, W. Randolph. 1976. ANOTB. In *Collected algorithms,* ed. David Douglas, III.16–III.35. Cambridge, Mass.: Laboratory for Computer Graphics and Spatial Analysis, Harvard University.

Garrison, William L., R. Alexander, W. Bailey, M. F. Dacey, and D. F. Marble. 1965. Data system requirements for geographic research. In *Proceedings, Third Goddard Memorial Symposium,* 139–151. Washington, D.C.: American Astronautical Society.

Goldberg, Michael P., Allan H. Schmidt, and Nicholas R. Chrisman. 1979. Integration and analysis of multiple geographic data bases: An application of ODYSSEY. In *Harvard Library of Computer Graphics,* vol. 2, ed. Patricia Moore, 81–98. Cambridge, Mass.: Laboratory for Computer Graphics and Spatial Analysis, Harvard University.

Goodchild, Michael F. 1978. Statistical aspects of the polygon overlay problem. In *Harvard papers on geographic information systems,* vol. 6, ed. Geoffrey Dutton. Reading, Mass.: Addison Wesley.

Goodrich, John, ed. 1970. *Computer mapping as an aid in air pollution studies.* Cambridge, Mass.: Laboratory for Computer Graphics and Spatial Analysis, Harvard University.

Haggett, Peter. 1965. *Locational analysis in human geography.* London: Edward Arnold.

Haggett, Peter, and Richard J. Chorley. 1969. *Network analysis in geography.* London: Edward Arnold.

Hills, G. Angus. 1966. The classification and evaluation of land for multiple uses. *Forestry Chronicle* 42:1–25.

Hopkins, Lewis D. 1977. Methods of generating land suitability maps: A comparative evaluation. *American Institute of Planners Journal* 43:386–400.

Horwood, Edgar, Clark Rogers, Arnold R. M. Rom, Norma Olsonoski, William L. Clark, and Stevenson Weitz. 1963. Computer methods of graphing, data positioning and symbolic mapping: A manual for user professionals in urban analysis and related fields. Department of Civil Engineering, University of Washington.

Isard, Walter. 1956. *Location and space economy: A general theory relating to industrial location, market areas, land use, trade and urban structure.* Cambridge, Mass.: MIT Press.

Johnston, Ronald J. 1979. *Geography and geographers: Anglo-American human geography since 1945.* London: Edward Arnold.

Kinzy, Stephen. 1992. Horwood's short laws. *Urban and Regional Information Systems Association Journal* 4:85–86.

Knuth, Donald E. 1973. *Sorting and searching.* Menlo Park, Calif.: Addison Wesley.

Kriger, Mark. 1974. An interactive on-line resource allocation management system. In *Red Book,* VII.2–VII.6. Cambridge, Mass.: Laboratory for Computer Graphics and Spatial Analysis, Harvard University.

Landscape Architecture Research Office, Graduate School of Design, Harvard University. 1967. *Three approaches to environmental resource analysis.* Washington, D.C.: The Conservation Foundation.

Latham, Craig. 1977. LINGUIST. *Internal report 77-6.* Laboratory for Computer Graphics and Spatial Analysis, Harvard University.

Latour, Bruno. 1987. *Science in action.* Cambridge, Mass.: Harvard University Press.

———. 1993. *We never were modern.* Cambridge, Mass.: Harvard University Press.

———. 1996. *Aramis or the love of technology.* Cambridge, Mass.: Harvard University Press.

———. 1999. *Pandora's hope.* Cambridge, Mass.: Harvard University Press.

Latour, Bruno, and Steve Woolgar. 1986. *Laboratory life: The construction of scientific facts.* 2nd ed. Princeton, N.J.: Princeton University Press.

Levy, Steven. 1984. *Hackers: Heroes of the computer revolution.* New York: Doubleday.

Lewis, Phillip. 1963. *Recreation in Wisconsin.* Madison, Wis.: State of Wisconsin, Department of Resource Development.

———. 1964. Quality corridors for Wisconsin. *Landscape Architecture Quarterly* (January): 100–107.

Lill, Eduard. 1891. *Das Reisegesetz und seine Anwendung auf den Eisenbahnverkehr.* Wien: Commissions-verlag von Speilgelhagen und Schurich.

Lindgren, C. Ernesto S. 1969a. A minimum path problem reconsidered. *Harvard papers in theoretical geography 28.* Laboratory for Computer Graphics and Spatial Analysis, Harvard University.

———. 1969b. The use of geodesic curvature in the determination of geodesic lines. *Harvard papers in theoretical geography 29.* Laboratory for Computer Graphics and Spatial Analysis, Harvard University.

Lindgren, C. Ernesto S., and Carl Steinitz. 1969. Graphical representation of a matrix with application in spatial location. *Harvard papers in theoretical geography 33.* Laboratory for Computer Graphics and Spatial Analysis, Harvard University.

Little, James J., and Thomas K. Peucker. 1979. A recursive procedure for finding the intersection of two digital curves. *Computer Graphics and Image Processing* 10:159–171.

Lynch, Kevin. 1960. *The image of the city.* Cambridge, Mass.: MIT Press.

Mabbutt, J. A., and G. A. Stewart. 1963. The application of geomorphology in resources surveys in Australia and New Guinea. *Revue de Géomorphologie dynamique* 14 (7-8-9): 97–109.

Maklin, Charles. 1792. *Man of the world.* Abacus ebooks. www.abacci.com/msreader/ebook.aspx?bookID=11585

Mandelbrot, Benoit. 1967. How long is the coast of Britain? *Science* 156:636–638.

Manning, Warren. 1913. The Billerica town plan. *Landscape Architecture* 3:108–118.

Mation, Helvio. 1980. An application of computer graphics to network analysis. In *Harvard Library of Computer Graphics,* vol. 8, ed. Patricia A. Moore, 197–216. Cambridge, Mass.: Laboratory for Computer Graphics and Spatial Analysis, Harvard University.

Maxwell, J. Clerk. 1870. On hills and dales. *The London, Edinburgh and Dublin Philosphical Magazine and Journal of Science* 40:421–427.

McHaffie, Patrick. 2000. Surfaces: Tacit knowledge, formal language, and metaphor at the Harvard Lab for Computer Graphics and Spatial Analysis. *International Journal of Geographical Information Science* 14:755–773.

McHarg, Ian L. 1969. *Design with nature.* Garden City, N.Y.: Natural History Press.

Moore, Patricia, ed. 1978–1981. *Harvard Library of Computer Graphics.* Cambridge, Mass.: Laboratory for Computer Graphics and Spatial Analysis, Harvard University.

Morehouse, Scott, and Martin Broekhuysen. 1982. *ODYSSEY user manual.* Cambridge, Mass.: Laboratory for Computer Graphics and Spatial Analysis, Harvard University.

Morrill, Richard. 1984. Recollections of the 'quantitative revolution's' early years: The University of Washington 1955–65. In *Recollections of a revolution: Geography as spatial science,* eds. Mark Billinge, Derek Gregory, and Ron Martin, 55–72. London: Macmillan.

Murray, Timothy, Peter Rogers, David Sinton, Carl Steinitz, Richard Toth, and Douglas Way. 1971. Honey Hill: A systems analysis for planning the multiple use of controlled water areas. *Institute of Water Resources 71-9; NTIS AD 736 343 & 344.* Army Corps of Engineers.

Niemann, Bernard J., and Sondra S. Niemann. 1993. Lines of code and more: David F. Sinton. *Geo Info Systems* (November/December): 58–62.

Peucker, Thomas K. 1969. The law of travel and its application to rail traffic, translation of Eduard Lill 1891. *Harvard papers in theoretical geography 25.* Laboratory for Computer Graphics, Harvard University.

Peucker, Thomas K., Mark Tichenor, and Wolf-Keiter Rase. 1971. The computer version of three relief representations. In *Red Book,* VI.93–VI.94. Cambridge, Mass.: Laboratory for Computer Graphics and Spatial Analysis, Harvard University.

Peucker, Thomas K., and Nicholas R. Chrisman. 1975. Cartographic data structures. *The American Cartographer* 2:55–69.

Rhind, David. 1988. Personality as a factor in the development of a discipline: The example of computer-assisted cartography. *The American Cartographer* 15 (3):277–290.

Rosenfeld, Azriel, and A. Kak. 1976. *Digital picture processing.* New York: Academic Press.

Rubin, Jerrold. 1968. A Geospace mapping program. In *Proceedings, Sixth Annual URISA Conference,* 193–199. Clayton, Mo.: URISA.

Schmidt, Allan H. 1979. Future directions of computer graphics. *Context* 10:16.

Schmidt, Allan H., and Wayne A. Zafft. 1975. Progress of the Harvard University Laboratory for Computer Graphics and Spatial Analysis. In *Display and analysis of spatial data,* eds. John C. Davis and M. J. McCullagh, 231–243. London: John Wiley and Sons, Inc.

Selkowitz, Stephen E. 1968. Geography and an existence theorem: A cartographic computer solution in the localization on a sphere of sets of equally-valued antipodal points for two continuous distributions with practical applications to the real earth. *Harvard papers in theoretical Geography 21.* Laboratory for Computer Graphics and Spatial Analysis, Harvard University.

Shepherd, Donald. S. 1964. A SYMAP interpolation algorithm. In *Red Book*, 1.8–1.11. Cambridge, Mass.: Laboratory for Computer Graphics and Spatial Analysis, Harvard University.

———. 1968a. A two-dimensional interpolation function for irregularly spaced data. In *Proceedings, Twenty-third National Conference*, 517–524. Princeton, N.J.: Association for Computing Machinery and Brandon/Systems Press.

———. 1968b. A two-dimensional interpolation function for computer mapping of irregularly spaced data. *Harvard papers in theoretical geography 15.* Laboratory for Computer Graphics and Spatial Analysis, Harvard University.

———. 1969. A load-shifting model to reduce exposure to air pollution caused by electrical power generation. Honors thesis, Harvard College.

Simonett, David S. 1966. Future and present needs of remote sensing in geography. *CRES Report 61-12.* Center for Research, Engineering Science Division, University of Kansas.

Sinton, David F. 1978. The inherent structure of information as a constraint to analysis: Mapped thematic data as a case study. In *Harvard papers on geographic information systems,* vol. 6, ed. Geoffrey Dutton. Reading, Mass.: Addison Wesley.

———. 1991. Reflections on 25 years of GIS. *GIS World* special insert.

Smith, Neil. 1987. Academic war over the field of geography: The elimination of geography at Harvard, 1947–1951. *Annals of the Association of American Geographers* 77:155–172.

Steinhaus, Hugo. 1945. Sur la division des ensembles de l'éspace par les plans et des ensembles plans par des cercles. *Fundamenta Mathematica* 33:245–263.

———. 1960. *Mathematical snapshots.* New revised edition. Oxford: Oxford University Press.

Steinitz, Carl. 1967a. Computer mapping and the regional landscape. Unpublished manuscript. Laboratory for Computer Graphics, Harvard University.

———. 1967b. Congruence and meaning: The influence of consistency between urban form and activity upon environmental knowledge. PhD thesis, MIT.

———. 1993. Geographical information systems: A personal historical perspective, the framework for a recent project, and some questions for the future. In *European conference on geographic information systems.* Genoa, Italy: EGIS.

Steinitz, Carl, David Sinton, and Allan Schmidt. 1970. A general system for environmental resource analysis. Report to the public land law review commission, Washington, D.C. Cambridge, Mass.: Steinitz Rogers Associates, Inc.

Steinitz, Carl, H. James Brown, Peter Goodale, Peter Rogers, David Sinton, Frederick Smith, William Giezentanner, and Douglas Way. 1976. Managing Suburban Growth: A modeling approach. Landscape Architecture Research Office, Harvard University.

Steinitz, Carl, Paul Parker, and Lawrie Jordan. 1976. Hand-draw overlays: Their history and prospective uses. *Landscape Architecture* 66:444–455.

Steinitz, Carl, and Peter Rogers. 1970. *A systems analysis model of urbanization and change: An experiment in inter-disciplinary education.* Cambridge, Mass.: MIT Press.

Stewart, G. A., ed. 1968. *Land evaluation.* Melbourne: Macmillan.

Stewart, John Q. 1945. *Coasts, waves and weather.* Boston: Ginn and Company.

———. 1950. The development of social physics. *American Journal of Physics* 18: 239–253.

Stewart, John Q., and Newton L. Price. 1944. *Marine and air navigation.* Boston: Ginn and Company.

Stewart, John Q., and William Warntz. 1958. Macrogeography and social science. *Geographical Review* 48:167–184.

Sutherland, Ivan. 1964. Sketchpad: A man-machine graphical communication system. PhD diss., MIT.

Tanaka, K. 1950. The relief contour method of representing topography on maps. *Geographical Review* 40:444–456.

Teicholz, Eric, Denis White, and Nicholas Chrisman. 1976. The ODYSSEY mapping system: An introduction. Laboratory for Computer Graphics and Spatial Analysis, Harvard University.

Thomas, Adrian. 1970. OBLIX: A two and three dimensional mapping program for use with line plotters. In *Red Book,* v.50–v.52. Cambridge, Mass.: Laboratory for Computer Graphics and Spatial Analysis, Harvard University.

Thomas, D. N., and D. F. Marble. 1965. Use of remote sensors in urban information systems. *Technical Report 1 to Geography Branch, Office of Naval Research, Task NR 389-143 Contract 1228-37.* Northwestern University.

Tobler, Waldo. 1959. Automation and cartography. *Geographical Review* 49:526–534.

———. 1961. Map transformations of geographic space. PhD diss., University of Washington.

———. 1970. A computer movie simulating urban growth in the Detroit region. *Economic Geography* 26 (2): 234–240.

———. 1973. A continuous transformation useful in districting. *Annals, New York Academy of Sciences* 225:215–220.

———. 1974. Cartogram programs. University of Michigan, Department of Geography.

Tomlin, C. Dana. 1983a. A map algebra. In *Harvard Computer Graphics Conference,* vol. 2, 1–46. Cambridge, Mass.: Graduate School of Design, Harvard University.

———. 1983b. Digital cartographic modeling techniques in environmental planning. PhD thesis, Yale University.

———. 1986. The IBM-PC version of the Map Analysis Package. *Internal report LCGSA-85-16.* Laboratory for Computer Graphics and Spatial Analysis, Harvard University.

———. 1990. *Geographic information systems and cartographic modeling.* Englewood Cliffs, N.J.: Prentice Hall.

Tomlinson, Roger F. 1968. A geographic information system for regional planning. In *Land evaluation,* ed. G. A. Stewart, 200–210. Melbourne: Macmillan.

———, ed. 1972. *Geographical data handling.* Ottawa: IGU Commission on Geographical Data Sensing and Processing.

———. 1974. The application of electronic computing methods to the storage, compilation and assessment of mapped data. PhD thesis, University of London.

———. 1998. The Canada Geographic Information System. In *The history of geographic information systems: Perspectives from the pioneers,* ed. Timothy W. Foresman, 21–32. Upper Saddle River, N.J.: Prentice Hall.

Tomlinson, Roger F., and A. Raymond Boyle. 1981. The state of development of systems for handling natural resources inventory data. *Cartographica* 18 (4): 65–95.

Travis, M. R., G. H. Elsner, W. D. Iverson, and C. G. Johnson. 1975. VIEWIT: Computation of seen areas, slope and aspect for land-use planning. *Technical Report PSW-11/1975.* USDA Forest Service.

Tyrwhitt, Jacqueline. 1950. Surveys for planning. In *Town and country planning textbook,* ed. Association for Planning and Regional Reconstruction. London: Architectural Press.

Van Demark, Peter. 1976. Results of test runs for the Department of Administration portion of the NRIS project. University of Wisconsin Cartographic Laboratory.

Van Norman, Mark. 1985. Computer aided database management and performance prediction for schematic design. PhD thesis, University of California, Berkeley.

———. 1986. A digital modelshop: The role of metaphor in a CADD user interface. *Design Computing* 1:95–122.

Warntz, Chistopher W. 1968. The continent problem—geography and spatial variance. *Harvard papers in theoretical geography 9.* Laboratory for Computer Graphics and Spatial Analysis, Harvard University.

Warntz, William. 1957. Transportation, social physics and the law of refraction. *Professional Geographer* 9 (4): 2–7.

———. 1961. Transatlantic flights and pressure patterns. *Geographical Review* 51:187–212.

———. 1964. A new map of the surface of population potentials for the United States. *Geographical Review* 54:170–184.

———. 1965. A note on surfaces and paths: Applications to geographical problems. *Discussion paper 6.* Ann Arbor: Michigan Inter-University Community of Mathematical Geographers.

———. 1966. The topology of socio-economic terrain and spatial flows. *Papers, Regional Science Association* 17:47–61.

Warntz, William, and Allan Schmidt, eds. 1969–1974. *Red Book: Projects of the Laboratory for Computer Graphics and Spatial Analysis.* Cambridge, Mass.: Laboratory for Computer Graphics and Spatial Analysis, Harvard University.

Warntz, William, C. Ernesto Lindgren, Katherine Kiernan, Luisa Bonfiglioli, and Eduardo Lozano. 1971. The sandwich theorem: A basic one for geography. *Harvard papers in theoretical geography 44.* Laboratory for Computer Graphics and Spatial Analysis, Harvard University.

Warntz, William, and Michael Woldenberg. 1967. Concepts and applications: Spatial order. *Harvard papers in theoretical geography 1.* Laboratory for Computer Graphics and Spatial Analysis, Harvard University.

White, Marvin. 1978. The cost of topological file access. In *Harvard papers on geographic information systems,* vol. 6, ed. Geoffrey Dutton. Reading, Mass.: Addison Wesley.

White, R. Denis. 1976. CYCLOPS conventions and assumptions. *Internal report 76-5.* Laboratory for Computer Graphics and Spatial Analysis, Harvard University.

———. 1977. ODYSSEY file formats. *Internal report 77-1.* Laboratory for Computer Graphics and Spatial Analysis, Harvard University.

———. 1978. A design for polygon overlay. In *Harvard papers on geographic information systems,* vol. 6, ed. Geoffrey Dutton. Reading, Mass.: Addison Wesley.

———. 1982. A graphics system for instruction in computer graphics. In *Proceedings, Harvard Computer Graphics Week 1982.* Cambridge, Mass.: Graduate School of Design, Harvard University.

———. 1985a. Relief modulated thematic mapping by computer. *The American Cartographer* 12 (1): 62–68.

———. 1985b. Geographic information systems on microcomputers. *Internal report LCGSA-85-11.* Laboratory for Computer Graphics and Spatial Analysis, Harvard University.

White, R. Denis, and Allan Schmidt. 1975. A report on the conversion of twelve Urban Atlas files to extended DIME files and their use in the preparation of base-map files for computer mapping. *Internal report 75-6.* Laboratory for Computer Graphics and Spatial Analysis, Harvard University.

White, R. Denis, Jonathan Corson-Rikert, and Margaret Maizel. 1987. WYSIWYG digitizing: Real time geometric correction and topological encoding. In *Proceedings, AUTO-CARTO 8,* 739–743. Baltimore, Md.: American Congress on Surveying and Mapping.

Wiener, Nobert. 1948. *Cybernetics or control and communication in the animal and the machine.* New York: John Wiley and Sons, Inc.

Woldenberg, Michael. 1968. Spatial order in fluvial systems: Horton's laws derived from mixed hexagonal hierarchies of drainage basin areas. *Harvard papers in theoretical geography 13.* Laboratory for Computer Graphics and Spatial Analysis, Harvard University.

Woldenberg, Michael J., Gordon Cumming, Keith Harding, Keith Horsfield, Keith Prowse, and Shiam Singhal. 1970. Law and order in the human lung. *Harvard papers in theoretical geography 41.* Laboratory for Computer Graphics and Spatial Analysis, Harvard University.

Tomlinson, Roger   attends training course 1963—Northwestern, 13; designs CGIS, 42; convened symposium 1972, 118; at Endicott House symposium, 127; issues Saskatchewan RFP, 164; dissemination, 184; Saskatchewan report cited, 186

TOPAZ   174

topology   Corbett and DIME, 13; of surfaces, 59; of topography, 61; POLYVRT data structure, 105; of surfaces, 106; promotion, 108; USGS, 109; ODYSSEY, 115; Endicott House, 126; calculated on the fly, 180; data structures, 186

training course   Horwood 1963—Northwestern, 2; Fisher 1964 and 1965—Chicago, 2; Horwood 1963—University of Southern California, 5; Horwood 1962 and 1963, 8; quantitative geography 1961, 1962, and 1963—Northwestern, 9; Schmidt attends, 12; Fisher 1964 and 1965—Chicago, 13; Horwood—multiple sites, 13; Summer Institutes of Cartography 1962–1965—University of Washington, 13; Garrison 1963—Northwestern, 13; SYMAP 1967—Harvard, 13

transportation modeling   TOPAZ, 174

trend surface   SYMAP, 20

triangular irregular network   see TIN

tub on its own bottom   93

Tyrwhitt, Jacqueline   use of overlay, 43

Ullman, Edward   University of Washington, 8

University of Chicago   role in first SYMAP, 2; Berry, 3

University of Kansas   33

University of Washington   Horwood, 2; Horwood, 5; quantitative revolution in geography, 8

University of Wisconsin   Philip Lewis, 43; GRASP, 50; tests of NRIS, 118

UNIX   early versions, 119; ODYSSEY conversion, 179

Urban Atlas   project, 111

Urban Data Center   see University of Washington

Urban Studies Center   see University of Chicago

URISA   founded, 5

user interface   SYMAP, 29; consequences of interactive computing, 86; evolution, 120; ARTIST, 152; WYSIWYG in ROOTS, 180

USGS   plans for digital database, 109; response from Lab, 109; support for Endicott House, 126

Van Norman, Mark   hired, 174; designs SCHEMA, 177; photo, 188

vector   SYMAP, 20; combined with grid, 45; architectural drawings, 69; ODYSSEY graphics, 122; ARTIST, 152

Vector Product Format   110

video   training materials, 85; in Shafer committee recommendations, 99

viewshed   in IMGRID, 51

Warntz, William   presents to Computer Graphics Aficionados, 10; discussant at Computer Graphics Aficionados, 10; hired, 12; link to SYMAP interpolation, 32; barriers, 34; hired, 56; title, 57; plan to restore geography, 57; research on surfaces, 59; navigator, 62; Sandwich Theorem, 65; link to Steinhaus, 66; leaves Lab, 67; branching systems, 68; plans and research, 91; moves to Western Ontario, 92

Washington   see University of Washington

Waugh, Tom   programmer at Lab and Edinburgh, 91; stroked fonts, 122

Weiss, Carolyn   hired, 90

WHIRLPOOL   in original diagram, 117; absorbs other functions, 124; cross-band data structure, 128; polygon cycling, 129; planar enforcement, 131; benchmarks, 164

White, Anne Hunt   programs DIME interface, 135; works for Kate Rooney, 168; photo, 188

White, Denis   response to USGS, 109; Urban Atlas project, 111; conceives ODYSSEY, 116; designs CYCLOPS, 116; designs NUBS, 119; first design of globals, 123; not in commercialization team, 137; color spaces, 155; designs IMAGO, 173; collaborates with Chan, 174; develops ROOTS, 179; associate director, leaves Lab for EPA, 181; photo, 188

White, Marvin   at Endicott House symposium, 126

Wiener, Norbert   76

Winnick, Louis   discussions with Fisher, 3; observation on computer mapping, 9

Wirth, Niklaus   railroad track diagrams, 120

Woldenberg, Michael   discussant at Computer Graphics Aficionados, 11; hired, 12; from AGS to Harvard, 58; branching systems, 67; academic career, 91; philomorph, 152

World Data Bank   DIA contract, 97; addition of topological structure, 105; "unstructured as spaghetti," 109

Wyatt, Joseph   on Shafer committee, 98

WYSIWYG   ROOTS interface, 180

Yale   expels Census, 13; Horwood 1963 training course, 13

Yarbrough, Lynn   presents to Computer Graphics Aficionados, 10

Yet Another Compiler Compiler   comparison to LINGUIST, 121

Advanced Spatial Analysis: The CASA Book of GIS *1-58948-073-2*

ArcGIS and the Digital City: A Hands-on Approach for Local Government *1-58948-074-0*

ArcView GIS Means Business *1-879102-51-X*

A System for Survival: GIS and Sustainable Development *1-58948-052-X*

A to Z GIS: An Illustrated Dictionary of Geographic Information Systems *1-58948-140-2*

Beyond Maps: GIS and Decision Making in Local Government *1-879102-79-X*

Cartographica Extraordinaire: The Historical Map Transformed *1-58948-044-9*

Cartographies of Disease: Maps, Mapping, and Medicine *1-58948-120-8*

Charting the Unknown: How Computer Mapping at Harvard Became GIS *1-58948-118-6*

Children Map the World: Selections from the Barbara Petchenik Children's World Map Competition *1-58948-125-9*

Community Geography: GIS in Action *1-58948-023-6*

Community Geography: GIS in Action Teacher's Guide *1-58948-051-1*

Confronting Catastrophe: A GIS Handbook *1-58948-040-6*

Conservation Geography: Case Studies in GIS, Computer Mapping, and Activism *1-58948-024-4*

Designing Better Maps: A Guide for GIS Users *1-58948-089-9*

Designing Geodatabases: Case Studies in GIS Data Modeling *1-58948-021-X*

Disaster Response: GIS for Public Safety *1-879102-88-9*

Extending ArcView GIS (version 3.x edition) *1-879102-05-6*

Fun with GPS *1-58948-087-2*

Getting to Know ArcGIS Desktop, Second Edition Updated for ArcGIS 9 *1-58948-083-X*

Getting to Know ArcObjects: Programming ArcGIS with VBA *1-58948-018-X*

Getting to Know ArcView GIS (version 3.x edition) *1-879102-46-3*

GIS and Land Records: The ArcGIS Parcel Data Model *1-58948-077-5*

GIS for Environmental Management *1-58948-142-9*

GIS for Everyone, Third Edition *1-58948-056-2*

GIS for Health Organizations *1-879102-65-X*

GIS for Landscape Architects *1-879102-64-1*

GIS for the Urban Environment *1-58948-082-1*

GIS for Water Management in Europe *1-58948-076-7*

GIS in Public Policy: Using Geographic Information for More Effective Government *1-879102-66-8*

GIS in Telecommunications *1-879102-86-2*

GIS Means Business, Volume II *1-58948-033-3*

GIS, Spatial Analysis, and Modeling *1-58948-130-5*

GIS Tutorial for Health *1-58948-148-8*

GIS Tutorial: Workbook for ArcView 9 *1-58948-127-5*

GIS Worlds: Creating Spatial Data Infrastructures *1-58948-122-4*

Hydrologic and Hydraulic Modeling Support with Geographic Information Systems *1-879102-80-3*

Continued on next page

When ordering, please mention book title and ISBN (number that follows each title)

Books from ESRI Press (continued)

Ask for ESRI Press titles at your local bookstore or order by calling 1-800-447-9778. You can also shop online at www.esri.com/esripress. Outside the United States, contact your local ESRI distributor.

ESRI Press titles are distributed to the trade by the following:

In North America, South America, Asia, and Australia:
Independent Publishers Group (IPG)
Telephone (United States): 1-800-888-4741 • Telephone (international): 312-337-0747
E-mail: frontdesk@ipgbook.com

In the United Kingdom, Europe, and the Middle East:
Transatlantic Publishers Group Ltd.
Telephone: 44 20 7373 2515 • Fax: 44 20 7244 1018 • E-mail: richard@tpgltd.co.uk

ESRI Press • 380 New York Street • Redlands, California 92373-8100 • www.esri.com/esripress

On a PC with Windows, the CD should open automatically.

For Macintosh computer users, double-click the CD icon on your desktop. Find the "index.html" file and double-click it to play the CD.

SYSTEM REQUIREMENTS
- Apple QuickTime version 7 or greater
- Latest version of Adobe Reader
- 800 × 600 or higher-resolution monitor with at least 256 colors
- Modern Web browser such as Microsoft Internet Explorer, Apple Safari, or Mozilla Firefox

Microsoft Windows requirements
- Pentium processor-based PC or compatible computer
- At least 128 MB of RAM
- Microsoft Windows 98/Me/2000/XP

Apple Macintosh requirements
- 400 MHz G3 processor or faster
- At least 128 MB of RAM
- Mac OS X version 10.2 or later

TROUBLESHOOTING
- First make sure your computer meets the minimum system requirements above.
- Try updating and/or re-installing Apple QuickTime and Adobe Reader software. QuickTime version 7.0.4 has been known to cause issues. QuickTime 7.1 has been tested extensively and is known to work.
- Try updating and/or re-installing your Web browser software. Firefox has been tested for both Macintosh and Windows and is known to work.
- Windows systems should have the latest version of the Microsoft ActiveX plug-in.
- Make sure that JavaScript is enabled in your browser.